Defense Beat

Defense Beat

The Dilemmas of Defense Coverage

Edited by

Loren B. Thompson
Georgetown University

LEXINGTON BOOKS
An Imprint of Macmillan, Inc.
NEW YORK

Maxwell Macmillan Canada
TORONTO

Maxwell Macmillan International
NEW YORK   OXFORD   SINGAPORE   SYDNEY

Library of Congress Cataloging-in-Publication Data

Defense beat : the dilemmas of defense coverage / edited by Loren B.
  Thompson.
       p.   cm.
    Includes bibliographical references and index.
    ISBN 0-669-21842-1 (alk. paper)
    1. Television broadcasting of news—United States. 2. Government
and the press—United States. 3. Freedom of the press—United
States. 4. United States—Military policy. 5. War correspondents—
United States. 6. War photographers—United States. I. Thompson,
Loren B.
PN4888.T4D44   1991   91-11297
070.1′95—dc20   CIP

This book is published as part of the Georgetown International Security Studies Series,
Loren B. Thompson, consulting editor.

Lexington Books
An Imprint of Macmillan, Inc.
866 Third Avenue, New York, N. Y. 10022

Maxwell Macmillan Canada, Inc.
1200 Eglinton Avenue East
Suite 200
Don Mills, Ontario M3C 3N1

Macmillan, Inc. is part of the Maxwell Communication Group
of Companies

Printed in the United States of America

printing number
1   2   3   4   5   6   7   8   9   10

Contents

Introduction   vii

Part I   The History of U.S. War Coverage   1

1. The Media Versus the Military: A Brief History of War
   Coverage in the United States   3
   Loren B. Thompson

Part II   Perspectives on the Media-Military Relationship   57

2. The Washington Defense Journalist: An Eighteenth-Century
   View   59
   Paul Mann

3. The Military's War with the Media: Causes and
   Consequences   73
   Bernard E. Trainor

4. Covering the Pentagon for Television: A Reporter's
   Perspective   83
   David C. Martin

5. Covering the Pentagon for a Major Newspaper:
   A Reporter's Perspective   95
   Melissa Healy

6. Media Coverage of the Military: A Soldier's Critique   105
   Philip E. Soucy

7. A Culture of Incompetence: Why the Daily Press Covers
   Defense So Poorly   123
   Fred Reed

8. U.S. Defense Reporting: A British Perspective   135
   Lionel Barber

9. The Department of Defense Media Pool: Making the
   Media-Military Relationship Work   149
   Jeffrey J. Carnes

10. Constitutional Concerns in Denying the Press Access to
    Military Operations   165
    Marshall Silverberg

11. Afterword: The 1991 Middle East War   177
    Loren B. Thompson

Notes   183

About the Contributors   199

About the Editor   200

Introduction

The idea for this book was conceived in autumn 1989, at a time when many of the defining features of the postwar period were rapidly ebbing away. The failure of communism in the Soviet Union and Eastern Europe appeared to herald a relaxation of superpower tensions, and many observers were confidently predicting that the United States would soon earn a substantial peace dividend in the form of reduced defense spending. There were signs, however, that the decline of communism did not necessarily mean that the United States was entering a period of peace and tranquility; 1989 ended with the U.S. invasion of Panama, and within months after that operation was concluded, the United States had begun its biggest overseas deployment of military forces since the Vietnam War to counter Iraq's invasion of Kuwait.

The operations in Panama and the Persian Gulf were reported extensively in the national media, which raised numerous questions about the performance of U.S. forces, the wisdom of U.S. defense policies, and the nature of national interests. The controversy surrounding the operations was reflected in the persistent friction between the media and the military concerning the proper role of war coverage and the responsibilities of journalists when the lives of American soldiers are at risk. It was clear that many of the same problems that had emerged in coverage of past conflicts were still at work, undermining the relationship between journalists and soldiers.

Against this backdrop, it seemed an appropriate time to reexamine the perennial issue of media-military relations. Few books have been published on this subject in recent years, despite its obvious importance. Throughout the nation's history, the public has depended on journalists to report on the performance of U.S. forces in wartime and peacetime. Only rarely has the military been completely comfortable with what was reported. More often, soldiers have accused journalists of inaccuracy, insensitivity, emotionalism, irresponsibility, and other transgressions. Because of doubts about the trustworthiness of reporters, the armed forces traditionally have sought to limit their freedom to cover conflicts and have created an elaborate public relations bureaucracy designed to serve as a buffer between journalists and soldiers. This understandably provokes resentment among journalists, which contributes to the tension in media-military relations.

Some degree of tension is unavoidable and even desirable, but if the friction is not kept within manageable limits, it becomes a threat not only to those directly involved but also to the broader public whose interests both the press and the military serve. The purpose of this book is to provide some insight into and perspective on the media-military relationship that will help all concerned to work effectively together. The book consists of two parts. Part I presents a history of U.S. war coverage to provide a context for the current debate over media-military relations. This historical survey identifies the major themes in media coverage of past conflicts and explains how the media-military relationship has evolved. In part II, several of the nation's most distinguished defense journalists and commentators on media-military relations assess the status of the relationship and suggest ways in which it can be made to work better.

The book is aimed at three audiences. First, it is intended to serve as a source of insight and understanding for military personnel and journalists in sorting out their responsibilities to the public and to each other. Second, it is designed to serve as a text for students of journalism, political science, and military affairs who require a detailed introduction to the problems that surround coverage of national security issues. Third, it is aimed at the lay public interested in the quality of media-military relations and appreciative of the importance of adequate, accurate defense coverage.

The preparation of this book required considerable effort. I am grateful for the assistance provided by a number of people. The contributors to part II were remarkably prompt and responsive in completing their chapters. L.H. Malsawma, the publications officer of the Georgetown University National Security Studies Program, diligently reviewed and organized the various contributions so that they were ready for publication. Nora T. Kelley of the University Relations office conducted extensive research on press coverage of nineteenth-century conflicts, much of which was incorporated into part I of the book. Paul E. O'Connell, the editor at Lexington Books, was extraordinarily patient and supportive in encouraging the project's completion. Finally, Bill and Sally Seidman generously allowed me to use their homes in Washington, D.C., and Nantucket, Massachusetts, stimulating settings in which most of part I could be written. The support of all these people made this book possible, and they deserve much of the credit for whatever success it achieves.

I
The History of U.S. War Coverage

1

The Media Versus the Military: A Brief History of War Coverage in the United States

Loren B. Thompson

The framers of the U.S. Constitution envisioned a central role for the press in facilitating the functioning of democracy in the new nation. Writing in *Federalist* number 84, which first appeared in a New York newspaper in 1788, Alexander Hamilton emphasized the importance of a free press in protecting the nation against the intrigues of scoundrels and traitors. Hamilton observed that "the public papers will be expeditious messengers of intelligence to the most remote inhabitants of the Union."[1] The desire to ensure that the press could fulfill this role led the framers of the Constitution to include language in the First Amendment explicitly denying Congress the authority to make any law "abridging the freedom of speech, or of the press."

The unprecedented latitude granted to the press in the Constitution became one of the defining characteristics of the American republic. Half a century later, Alexis de Tocqueville remarked in his landmark analysis of American public life, *Democracy in America,* that "each individual American newspaper has little power, but after the people, the press is nonetheless the first of powers."[2] Describing the influence of the press as "immense," de Tocqueville confirmed that Hamilton's vision of its role had been realized: "It makes political life circulate in every corner of that vast land. Its eyes are never shut, and it lays bare the secret shifts of politics, forcing public figures in turn to appear before the tribunal of public opinion."[3] However, de Tocqueville acknowledged that an unfettered press was not without drawbacks: "I admit that I do not feel toward freedom of the press that complete and instantaneous love which one accords to things by their nature supremely good. I love it more from considering the evils it prevents than on account of the good it does."[4]

One problem with a free press that neither the framers nor de Tocqueville had given much thought to became readily apparent a generation after *Democracy in America* was published: the responsibilities of the press in wartime. The Civil War presented journalists with the biggest story in the young republic's history, a conflict in which the nation's survival was at stake. The danger of newspapers' acting as "expeditious messengers of intelligence" could not be ignored. Confederate generals regularly read northern newspapers to glean useful information about Union troop movements, military strength, and strategy. In addition, a number of northern newspapers espoused editorial positions hostile to the Union cause. In New York City, for example, nine of the city's seventeen newspapers favored slavery, while only five remained loyal to President Lincoln's administration throughout the war. These transgressions were compounded by a widespread tendency among war correspondents in the North and South alike to present partisan or distorted accounts of military actions. In some cases correspondents resorted to outright fabrication in order to present "eyewitness" accounts of major battles.[5]

The Lincoln administration eventually moved to impose censorship on journalists by seizing control of the telegraph lines that transmitted war news. Some Union generals went even further; William Sherman threatened to treat indiscreet journalists as spies. But other officers with political ambitions, including Generals George Meade and George McClellan, openly courted journalists in the hope of receiving favorable coverage. All too often, the behavior of both correspondents and officers was unethical and self-serving.

The experience of the Civil War demonstrated an inherent tension between the aims of journalists and the aims of soldiers in wartime. Soldiers wanted to avoid disclosure of sensitive information and objected to criticism of their performance. Journalists wanted unrestricted access to military information and the ability to use it in whatever manner they saw fit. Soldiers placed a premium on organization and discipline; war correspondents were so undisciplined and eccentric that one of their own characterized them as "bohemians."[6] Friction between these divergent priorities and styles was inevitable, as each new conflict after the Civil War illustrated. In the Spanish-American War, in World Wars I and II, in Korea and Vietnam, the tension continually reasserted itself, producing resentment and animosity between soldiers and representatives of the fourth estate.

This chapter explores how American journalists and soldiers have dealt with the tension between their respective roles in wartime since the founding of the republic. By tracing the evolution of media-military relations through the major conflicts in which the nation has engaged, I seek to identify the key issues and patterns of interaction that have shaped the relationship between American journalists and soldiers. Based on the evidence of past conflicts, I conclude with several suggestions concerning how the relationship can be managed in the future to minimize frictions and encourage cooperation between the media and the military.

It should be acknowledged at the outset, though, that some frictions will always be present in the relationship, and thus any cooperation will have its limits. Conflict between the media and the military is not merely unavoidable; it is essential. If journalists were to yield their right to criticize the military, they would relinquish one of their most important roles as protector of the public interest. Soldiers too have an important role to play in guarding the public interest, and their responsibilities will at times require placing restrictions on the prerogatives of the press.

It is perhaps somewhat ironic that two institutions so central to the preservation of democracy should frequently seem to be at war with each other. But that is hardly a novel state of affairs in American history. The founding documents of the republic assumed that a measure of conflict was inevitable and even desirable among the nation's public institutions. By establishing a series of adversarial relationships, it was argued, public institutions could be made to act as checks against ambitions detrimental to the national purpose. The challenge confronting journalists and soldiers is to make their fractious relationship work, so that both can serve the common good.

The Early Republic

The first war coverage in America predated the founding of the republic. During the Revolution, the various newspapers and journals published in the thirteen colonies attempted to keep their readers abreast of major developments in the rebellion against the crown. However, the three dozen papers being published in 1775, the year that hostilities began, lacked the means to provide regular, reliable war coverage. The parliamentary post was suspended in that year, and the constitutional post that replaced it was too inadequate to ensure timely conveyance of news. The flow of information was frequently interrupted by blockades and the operations of British military forces. In occupied cities such as Boston and New York, it was difficult to publish whatever news was received. Nearly half of the papers in existence at the beginning of the Revolution were forced to suspend publication at some point during the six-year conflict; other papers appeared to take their place, but many were short-lived, and some were suppressed.[7]

As a result of these problems, news of important battles did not reach some cities until weeks after they had occurred. The *Boston News-Letter* published the first brief account of the battles at Lexington and Concord on the same day that they took place—April 19, 1775. But accounts were not published in Philadelphia and New York until a week later, and the news took even longer to reach the southern colonies. The *Charleston Gazette* did not carry the story until May 9, and the *Savannah Gazette* published its first account on May 31.[8] Because of the delay in receiving news, many papers resorted to printing rumors and speculation as the rebellion continued. This tendency was encouraged by the intensely partisan character of many papers; most papers favored the patriot cause, but at least fifteen were loyal to the crown.

Even if adequate means for transmitting the news had existed, few papers had the resources to provide sustained and detailed coverage of the conflict. The entire population of the thirteen colonies numbered fewer than 3 million, and most people lived in isolated rural settlements. Nearly all of the newspapers in the colonies were local weeklies.[9] Some semiweeklies existed in the larger cities, but it was not until 1784, three years after General Charles Cornwallis's surrender at Yorktown, that the first daily paper began publishing in Philadelphia. For the most part, papers relied on the irregular arrival of private correspondence and official communiqués for war news, or they reprinted stories that had appeared in other papers.[10]

Despite the absence of an organized method for collecting and disseminating war news, papers in particular cities occasionally cooperated to improve the quality of local coverage. In New York, for example, several papers agreed to publish on different days of the week, so that fresh accounts of the conflict could appear daily.[11] Some papers also advanced their days of publication or published extra editions when important war news was received. In most cities, though, coverage of the Revolution was haphazard and unreliable throughout the conflict.

Similar conditions prevailed during the War of 1812. Although the number of newspapers and the frequency of their appearance had increased steadily during the intervening period, the same problems of insufficient resources, inadequate methods for transmitting news, and disruptions caused by military operations resulted in coverage that was tardy or unreliable. In the years following the war, however, the rapid growth of the nation and the emergence of new technologies greatly improved the ability of newspapers to provide timely and detailed coverage of distant events. Between 1800 and 1840, the population of the United States grew more than threefold, to over 17 million people. The rapid expansion of population was accompanied by a proliferation of newspapers, so that by 1840 most major cities had competing dailies. The larger papers now had both the resources and the space to provide extensive coverage of important news developments.

New technologies made it possible to transmit news much more quickly. In 1825 the first commercially successful railroad was opened in the United States, beginning a period of rapid improvement in the national transportation system that culminated with the completion of a transcontinental rail line in 1869. The telegraph was patented in 1837, and within a few years most of the major cities on the eastern seaboard had been linked together by telegraph lines. The telegraph revolutionized newspaper reporting by allowing nearly instantaneous transmission of information over great distances. A transatlantic telegraph cable was laid in 1866, bringing to an end the long delays that had previously typified American coverage of European news.

The Mexican-American War (1846–1848) occurred in the midst of this technological transformation, and war coverage benefited to a limited degree from the new means of transport and communication. However, because much of the military action during the war took place in remote locations where neither rail nor telegraph lines had been laid, the traditional method of transmitting war news by ship or horseback continued to be practiced. Nonetheless, the Mexican-American War witnessed two important innovations in coverage made possible by the increasing wealth of eastern metropolitan dailies: the creation of a dedicated overland express on horseback to hasten the delivery of war dispatches and the establishment of a network of field correspondents to provide more accurate and detailed accounts of military developments.

The overland express was created by James Gordon Bennett, publisher of the *New York Herald,* in December 1845. Recognizing that relations between Mexico and the United States were deteriorating rapidly, Bennett arranged with the *New Orleans Crescent City* to set up a two-way pony express that could carry news more quickly than the post office. When war with Mexico broke out in the spring of 1846, several other newspapers began participating in the project, making it possible to deliver news daily. War news was usually carried by horse from New Orleans to Philadelphia and then transmitted via telegraph to New York.[12]

The overland express continued throughout the war, greatly improving the timeliness of the war news that reached eastern cities. On April 10, 1847, the *New York Herald* announced that it had received four different war dispatches in the preceding twenty-four hours, a remarkable amount of news compared with the reporting of earlier conflicts. Nonetheless, there were still major delays in getting news from the war zone to newspaper readers. For instance, on October 21, 1847, the *Herald* contained the following announcement concerning military operations near Mexico City:

> Our readers will be pleased to see in this morning's *Herald* the long-looked-for intelligence from the city of Mexico. It reached New Orleans on the 13th inst., and was brought by the special overland express for the *New York Herald* and other papers. Owing to its importance, however, our special messenger was instructed to bring the intelligence to the government at Washington, and it will at once have general circulation throughout the country. This we thought due to the public.[13]

By the time the dispatch in question was printed, the news it reported was probably two weeks old. That fact notwithstanding, though, the willingness of newspapers to maintain a dedicated overland express for war news demonstrated that American journalism was entering a new age.

The second major journalistic innovation during the Mexican-American War, the creation of a system of field correspondents, was pioneered by George Kendall, editor and publisher of the *New Orleans Picayune*. In earlier conflicts, newspapers had generally relied on government communiqués and correspondence from persons who happened to be near the front rather than actually sending reporters to cover the action. Kendall not only went to the front himself but also assigned reporters to cover specific operations, so that his paper could provide a fuller picture of the war to readers. He assisted other papers to do the same, in the process helping to establish a tradition of professional, eyewitness war coverage that would become firmly rooted during the Civil War.[14]

The Mexican-American War was the last conflict in which the traditional, informal methods of covering war were still widely practiced by the American press. Increasing competition, improved technology, and other factors were creating new standards for war coverage, and newspapers that could not meet them were likely to see their circulation and reputation suffer. Similar standards were emerging in Europe, most notably as a result of the path-breaking coverage provided for *The Times of London* by William Howard Russell during the Crimean War (1853–1856). Russell's candid descriptions of the incompetence of the British high command and military bureaucracy so inflamed public opinion that they helped bring about the fall of the government.[15] Russell became famous, providing a role model for journalists on both sides of the Atlantic. Within a few years, the Civil War provided an opportunity for American correspondents to imitate him.

The Civil War

The Civil War was the most cataclysmic event the republic had faced since its birth. For four horrible years—from April 12, 1861, when the shelling of Fort Sumter began, until April 9, 1865, when General Robert E. Lee surrendered at Appomattox Courthouse—the United States was at war with itself. Over 800,000 soldiers were killed on both sides, a staggering loss in a nation of 31 million people. In the eleven states of the Confederacy, one in four white men of military age died. Millions more were maimed or injured or permanently traumatized. Vast tracts of the country were devastated by military operations. Virtually every citizen in the North and South was affected in some way by the war effort.

The scale of suffering and destruction caused by the American Civil War far exceeded that of other conflicts occurring in the mid-nineteenth century. European wars of the time tended to be limited struggles, confined to well-defined frontiers. In contrast, the conflict in America was largely a war of movement in which multiple fronts shifted back and forth across hundreds of miles of territory. As the fronts moved, millions of civilians were displaced, losing their possessions and in some cases their lives. The North increasingly waged a desperate war of attrition against the Confederacy, in which almost any type of civilian asset or property was treated as a legitimate military target. Communities were razed; homes were plundered; crops were burned. The plantation economy of the South was ruined. The struggle was conducted so indiscriminately that historians would later describe the period between 1861 and 1865 as the first example of "total war."[16]

The all-encompassing nature of the war was reflected in the nation's newspapers. Papers that seldom exceeded eight pages in length devoted a third or more of their space to dispatches and commentary about the war. Recognizing that many of their readers were personally affected by the war, the major newspapers of the North and South mounted unprecedented efforts to provide timely coverage of developments. This was particularly true of the New York City papers, which operated in the most competitive newspaper market in the country. There were seventeen newspapers in New York City at the outbreak of the war, and the wealthiest among them—the *Herald, Tribune,* and *Times*—expended huge resources on their war coverage. The *Herald* alone spent over half a million dollars on war correspondence and sent dozens of reporters to cover the action.[17]

Other papers could not afford such ambitious efforts but nevertheless spent large amounts on coverage. They were aided in providing extensive coverage by the newly created Associated Press (AP), which pooled the resources of many subscribing papers to field an army of correspondents. AP reporters were often more noteworthy for their telegraphic skills than their journalistic talents, but even so they ensured that most of the war's great battles produced eyewitness accounts, at least in the papers of the North. Newspapers also supplemented their accounts with those of other papers and printed correspondence received from soldiers at the front. The quality of coverage was uneven and sometimes misleading, but conscientious readers could still learn more about the war's progress, and in a more timely fashion, than had been possible in any previous conflict.[18]

The North sent 500 journalists to cover the war, about 150 of them special field correspondents representing specific papers.[19] Southern readers were less well served because the newspapers of the Confederacy generally had smaller circulations and far fewer resources than those of the Union. Nonetheless, the war was the dominant topic in southern papers, and many of them struggled valiantly to provide adequate information despite poor telegraph and mail service, paper shortages, and exclusion from Confederate encampments.[20]

Competitive pressures and the absence of relevant experience for covering so massive and desperate a conflict led journalists on both sides to engage in questionable practices. The *New York Herald,* one of the Union's leading papers, was accused of bribing government officials to obtain news. Many correspondents exaggerated their accounts of military operations and in some instances, such as the Battle of Shiloh in 1862, resorted to outright fabrication of so-called eyewitness reports. They wrote flattering stories about senior officers to win favor or support their papers' editorial positions. And despite an Article of War in the North proscribing trafficking in sensitive military information, newspapers on both sides routinely published facts helpful to the enemy. General Lee regularly studied Union newspapers for useful intelligence, and Generals Ulysses Grant and Sherman both considered resigning because of the propensity of journalists to ferret out and report their plans.[21]

The behavior of the press corps at the front earned them the derogatory sobriquet "bohemians" because of their "nomadic, careless, half-literary, half-vagabondish life."[22] Many journalists, however, demonstrated great enterprise and took serious risks to secure the news. A reporter for the *New York Herald* was taken prisoner and confined to a dungeon in Texas. Correspondents for the *New York Tribune* and *World* were captured running the blockade at Vicksburg and incarcerated for months before making an escape. Journalists for the *Herald* and *New York Times* were waylaid behind enemy lines by Confederate soldiers and robbed. A mob tried to hang a *Herald* reporter at Richmond, and a *Times* reporter barely escaped the same fate at Harper's Ferry.[23]

Correspondents understandably argued that they should be treated as noncombatants, but this was not a view widely shared by military officers on either side. The case for noncombatant status was undermined by the frequent publication of sensitive information in newspapers and compromised by the willingness of some correspondents at the front to take on military duties, such as acting as couriers and aides to senior officers. A *New York Herald* reporter dispatched to the Union army encampment at Cairo, Illinois, for example, was given the job of looking after military maps and plans. Some correspondents even took up guns, participating in the fighting.[24] In many cases, journalists had little choice but to carry out military tasks if they wanted to remain with the troops. Nonetheless, the blurring of lines between the military and journalistic professions contributed to a feeling among soldiers that correspondents were not really noncombatants.

The behavior of senior military officers toward correspondents varied considerably, often depending on the personality of the commanding general or the outcome of key battles. Confederate generals frequently denied southern journalists permission to travel with troops, a practice that some Union generals such as Sherman and Henry Halleck also tried to follow. General Meade had an offending reporter humiliated and expelled from his camp for writing that he had retreated after the Battle of the Wilderness. Other generals, including Grant, William Rosecrans, and Philip

Sheridan in the North, picked favorites who received preferential treatment. General McClellan, a lackluster commander with presidential ambitions, deliberately cultivated journalists in a position to advance his political career. The favoritism and disdain that many top officers showed toward journalists made it difficult for correspondents to write balanced, objective accounts of the war.[25]

Correspondents at the front were hampered by two other problems that persisted throughout the war: unreliable communications and uneven application of government policies concerning what could and what could not be reported. By the time the war began, 50,000 miles of telegraph lines had been strung in the eastern portion of the country, enabling newspapers to receive war news within hours of its occurrence. However, lines near the front were frequently cut, and military authorities routinely prevented the transmittal of news they considered detrimental to the war effort. The Union army's mail service was a poor alternative for correspondents operating under extreme competitive pressures because letters moved slowly and often were lost. The *New York Herald* claimed that half of the letters its field correspondents sent during the war were never received. In the South, the mails were even less efficient, sometimes taking a month to carry correspondence to its destination.[26]

The federal government seized control of telegraph lines leading to Washington, D.C., in April 1861, the same month the war began. General Winfield Scott, the commander in chief of Union forces, used this control to censor accounts of the North's defeat at the First Battle of Bull Run, so that it took weeks before many northerners realized the extent of the debacle. One month later, in August 1861, the War Department issued a sweeping general order pursuant to the fifty-seventh Article of War warning journalists that they were subject to court-martial if they disclosed sensitive military information. The general order defined such information so expansively that, had it been fully enforced, effective war coverage would have been nearly impossible. Editors and reporters alike ignored the order, and the Lincoln administration therefore decided to intervene more forcefully in the transmission of war news.[27]

On February 2, 1862, Congress authorized the president to place all telegraph lines within Union territory under military supervision. Thereafter, any war news being carried by telegraph lines in the North was subject to censorship, regardless of where it originated. However, because the Lincoln administration never promulgated a clear or consistent policy concerning what news was appropriate for publication, censorship was applied capriciously and unpredictably. Some censors were extraordinarily lax in their interpretation of what constituted sensitive news, while others prevented transmission of any dispatches that contained even a hint of criticism of the Union war effort. Correspondents could never be certain whether their dispatches would be transmitted or suppressed.[28]

With news from the front being frequently delayed or censored, many papers turned to their Washington bureaus for information on the progress of the war. However, the official communiqués of the War Department often contained a hodgepodge of disconnected facts and figures that did little to illuminate the larger issue of whether the Union was prevailing on the battlefield. Secretary of War Edwin M. Stanton, generally credited with inventing the wartime communiqué, deliberately distorted accounts of key battles and manipulated casualty figures to present a more positive account of the Union army's performance. When negative reports of the army's performance nonetheless were published, Stanton resorted to banning correspondents from the front, arresting editors, and suspending papers for violating censorship rules. In one case, he even ordered that a reporter for the *New York Tribune* be shot for refusing to hand over a sensitive dispatch.[29]

The uneven enforcement of censorship provoked much resentment among journalists but did not result in effective suppression of unfavorable news. The administration repeatedly attempted to strengthen its news policies by shifting responsibility for censorship between government departments and restating its standards of what could and could not be printed. It was unable, though, to establish a reliable mechanism for monitoring war news. This failure in part reflected disagreements within the administration concerning how stringent news controls should be. President Lincoln and his key advisers believed that positive press coverage was essential to the success of the war effort. Some advisers, such as Stanton, therefore favored draconian measures against newspapers that printed sensitive or critical material. Others argued that the administration should be careful not to alienate the press. The severity of press controls thus tended to vary, depending on which part of the government was administering censorship and the concerns of the moment.

The issue of limits on the freedom of the press in wartime arises in every conflict, but it was particularly pronounced in the Civil War. Because the nation was at war with itself, Lincoln and his advisers could not rely on the spontaneous patriotism that is often generated by wars against external threats to curb the excesses of the press. Northern newspapers were highly partisan and competitive, frequently shaping their news accounts to suit the political preferences of their owners or readers. The so-called copperhead press was openly sympathetic to the Confederate cause, sometimes to the point of deliberately undermining the war effort. Even newspapers that were supportive of both the Union cause and the Lincoln administration leveled a steady stream of criticism against the performance of the Union army and the administration of the War Department. For example on July 9, 1861, the *New York Times* printed the following scathing attack on the War Department:

It would seem as if some potent Spirit of Evil has cast its incurable curse upon the War Department of this country. During a period of eight long years, that office has been administered in the exclusive interests of treason and corruption. In it . . . high officers of the Army have been, one by one, suborned and corrupted, until, for a time at least, the very name of the Army conveyed with it the idea of possible infidelity and dishonor; in it financial frauds, wrongs, and robberies, have been concocted on a scale so gigantic that all the frauds and defalcations of the past have been forgotten or almost forgiven, in comparison with those which, during these eight years, have burst out of that hotbed of wickedness and corruption.[30]

The *Times's* allegations were accurate; Lincoln's first secretary of war, Simon Cameron, presided over such rampant corruption that the president was forced to replace him with Stanton in January 1862.[31] But the same month that the *Times* leveled its criticisms against the War Department, the Union army suffered its first major defeat at Bull Run. Valid though the *Times's* complaints might have been, they could not help but make some northerners question the Union's ability to prosecute the war successfully. Lincoln was loath to suppress newspapers that were doing no more than carrying out the role envisioned for them by the founders of the republic, but with the republic itself at risk, some members of his administration had fewer qualms. At least twenty papers were suspended in the North during the war.[32]

Whatever depredations may have been visited on the northern press during the war, they paled in comparison with the problems newspapers in the Confederate states faced. The South had fewer newspapers than the North, and they generally had much smaller circulations. With fewer resources, the southern papers were able to field fewer correspondents, and the treatment southern journalists experienced at the front was, if anything, worse than that suffered by their northern counterparts. In May 1862, General Braxton Bragg expelled reporters from his headquarters in Mississippi, and Bragg's example was soon imitated by most other Confederate commanders. The result, as Joseph J. Mathews has observed, was that southern newspaper readers often were deprived of war news: "For a great battle or campaign to occur without the presence of representatives of the Northern newspapers was exceptional; for the Southern press to be inadequately represented was commonplace."[33]

Many southern war correspondents adopted pseudonyms to protect themselves, a practice that raised questions as to the credibility of accounts appearing in the Confederate press. The southern states also imposed heavy censorship on newspapers throughout the war.[34] For editors already struggling with depleted staffs, poor communications, and a shortage of newsprint, censorship was an added burden that compromised their ability to provide adequate war coverage. The quality of coverage was further eroded by the tendency of southern papers to avoid criticizing the Confederate cause, a trait that encouraged self-censorship when bad news arrived.

Reporting of the Civil War in both the North and South thus left much to be desired. For all the failings of the press, though, and all the obstacles placed in its path by hostile or indifferent authorities, correspondents nonetheless managed to provide coverage that was unparalleled in any previous conflict in its scope, detail, and timeliness. Although no correspondent emerged from the American Civil War to rival Britain's William Howard Russell, dozens of correspondents carried out their journalistic responsibilities competently and bravely. By the time the war ended in the spring of 1865, a tradition of extensive and reasonably professional war coverage had been established that would endure in all the future conflicts in which the nation became engaged.

The Spanish-American War

Once Confederate forces were disarmed, the Union army rapidly demobilized. Within eighteen months after Lee's surrender, the army had been reduced from one million officers and enlisted men to a mere 57,000. It fell to about 25,000 men in 1869, the level at which it remained until the outbreak of the Spanish-American War in 1898.[35] This was a remarkably small military force for a country that had nearly forty million inhabitants in 1870, particularly in view of the recently defeated South. The minimal size of the U.S. military establishment during the thirty years following the Civil War reflected the absence of significant external threats and a belief among the nation's leaders that the South was too exhausted to rise again. The War Department's budget was slashed from $1 billion in the last year of the Civil War to $58 million in 1870; naval expenditures declined from $123 million to $22 million.[36]

Despite the absence of U.S. involvement in major conflicts during the 1870s and 1880s, American journalists still found wars to cover. In 1870 the Franco-Prussian War began in Europe, and the New York newspapers hastened to dispatch correspondents to the front. The Franco-Prussian conflict witnessed an important innovation in war coverage when veteran correspondent George W. Smalley of the *New York Tribune* arranged a press pool with the *London Daily News* to share dispatches from the front. Smalley's information-sharing scheme made it possible for the *Tribune* to carry a lengthy description of the Battle of Gravelotte only two days after the engagement occurred. The telegram describing the battle cost $5,000 to transmit, but it enabled the *Tribune* to carry a remarkably detailed and timely account of a key event in European history.[37]

A longer-running story with more domestic appeal during the 1870s and 1880s was the Indian wars that periodically broke out on the western frontier. During the two decades following the end of the Civil War, the federal government adopted a policy of forcing the Indians west of the Mississippi to give up most of their ancestral lands and remain on reservations. When tribes such as the Apache and Sioux resisted the incursions of settlers into their lands, the army was sent to suppress them. The War Department's strategy for dealing with Indians who refused to enter reservations was to annihilate them. This approach was summarized in characteristically blunt terms by General Sherman, who had assumed command of the Military Division of Missouri that included most of the Indian country; Sherman stated that the federal government should "act with vindictive earnestness against the Sioux, even to their extermination, men, women, and children."[38]

Sherman's view was widely supported not only in the army but also in Congress and by major newspapers. Although there was never much doubt as to their outcome, the campaigns against the western Indians generated much interest among newspaper readers. The most sensational development during the Indian wars was the massacre of General George Armstrong Custer's regiment at Little Big Horn in the Montana Territory in 1876. Custer, a Civil War hero who was much admired for his bravery, led a poorly planned attack against a superior force of Sioux Indians that resulted in his entire unit's being wiped out. The loss of 261 men was the biggest defeat suffered by the U.S. Army since the Civil War, and it quickly became front-page news across the country.

Accounts of the battle were slow in reaching eastern newspapers because of the remote location where the engagement occurred. The only correspondent who had accompanied Custer, an AP correspondent named Mark Kellogg, was killed in the fighting. The *New York Times* printed its first sketchy account of the massacre on July 6, eleven days after the battle took place. As more information became available, the *Times* and other newspapers devoted most of their front pages to describing the debacle and assessing its implications. Although there was little sympathy for the Indians, many papers were highly critical of Custer's tactical performance. The *Times* offered these observations on its front page on July 7:

> So far as an expression in regard to the wisdom of Gen. Custer's attack could be obtained at head-quarters, it was to the effect that Custer had been imprudent, to say the least. . . . Custer dropped squarely into the midst of no less than ten thousand red devils and was literally torn to pieces. The movement made by Custer is censured to some extent at military head-quarters. . . . The older officers say that it was brought about by that foolish pride which so often results in the defeat of men.[39]

The defeat at Little Big Horn was a major embarrassment for the army, but Custer's superiors quickly attributed it to his disobedience of orders and continued to prosecute the war against the Indians. In 1886 the Apache chief Geronimo surrendered, and four years later Sitting Bull, the Sioux leader, was killed at Wounded Knee. Both events were extensively covered in the nation's newspapers, some of which erroneously reported that Sitting Bull had led the Sioux who defeated Custer's force at Little Big Horn. Sitting Bull's death effectively marked the end of the Indian wars. By 1890 the western Indian tribes had been either destroyed or subdued, and the settlement of the West proceeded without further major incidents. The pacification of the western Indians coincided with the gradual closing of the American frontier. The United States was now settled from coast to coast and would never again fight a war within its borders.

The final decade of the nineteenth century saw a surge in nationalism that led some to advocate the creation of an overseas American empire comparable to those of the European powers. This imperial impulse was short-lived and controversial, but it was sufficiently strong to bring about a war with Spain in 1898.

For years the American press had railed against Spain's misrule of the remnants of its empire in the Caribbean and the Pacific. Spain was accused of maintaining a despotic rule, particularly in Cuba and the Philippines, that regularly committed atrocities against native peoples. In 1895 a rebellion broke out in Cuba, and U.S. newspapers began to report that Spanish military forces were carryng out atrocities not only against the Cubans but also against resident Americans. The reports were wildly exaggerated and in some cases clearly intended to provoke a U.S. military response. The following inflammatory dispatch from Cuba, for example, appeared in the *New York World* on May 17, 1896: "No man's life, no man's property is safe. American citizens are imprisoned or slain without cause. American property is destroyed on all sides. . . . A new Armenia lies within 80 miles of the American coast. Not a word from Washington! Not a sign from the President!"[40]

Emotional reporting such as the *World's* dispatch was far from rare in nineteenth-century American journalism; however, there was so much distorted, untrue reporting about the situation in Cuba in the late 1890s that W.A. Swanberg has characterized the performance of the press during the period as "the most disgraceful example of journalistic falsehood ever seen."[41] The routine publication of fabricated and inflammatory stories came about as a result of competition between two New York newspapers, Joseph Pulitzer's *World* and William Randolph Hearst's *Journal*. Both papers were representative of a new phenomenon in journalism, the mass circulation daily. Newspapers traditionally had appealed to an educated elite, but with the spread of literacy and the emergence of an urban working class during the late nineteenth century, a new breed of newspapers began to appear that emphasized crime and scandals.

This trend was most pronounced in New York, the nation's largest city and most competitive newspaper market. In 1883 Joseph Pulitzer purchased the struggling *New York World* and began transforming it into a crusading newspaper aimed at the city's working-class neighborhoods. The *World* achieved steady circulation gains and became highly profitable by offering a daily diet of lurid crime stories, sex scandals, and accounts of official malfeasance. In 1895, the same year the rebellion in Cuba began, William Randolph Hearst bought the *New York Journal* and began competing with the *World* for the mass circulation market. The two newspapers featured a sensational brand of eye-catching reporting that came to be known as yellow journalism (a term apparently referring to the popular "Yellow Kid" comic strip that was printed in monochrome yellow in the daily *World*).[42]

The circulation war between the *World* and the *Journal* fostered a competitive spirit that rationalized publishing any story, no matter how vulgar or misleading, if it was likely to attract readers. The Cuban rebellion, with its reports of struggling revolutionaries, vicious colonial rulers, violated women, and the like, was well suited to the style of the yellow journalists. The hysterical tenor of the Cuban coverage was reflected in a description of General Valeriano Weyler, the Spanish military commander on the island, which was printed in the *Journal* on February 3, 1896: "Weyler the brute, the devastator of haciendas, the destroyer of families, and the outrager of women . . . there is nothing to prevent his carnal, animal brain from running riot with itself in inventing tortures and infamies of bloody debauchery."[43] Considering the fact that Weyler had barely assumed his command when this passage was printed, the *Journal*'s characterization was somewhat overdrawn. The truth of the matter was that neither the *Journal* nor the *World* knew much about what was happening in Cuba in 1896 and 1897 because Spanish authorities were limiting the movements of their correspondents and censoring their dispatches. The rebellion was largely confined to the island's jungle interior where few journalists could reach it, much less report it. Nonetheless, the *Journal* and *World* continued their agitation for U.S. intervention, and by early 1898 the McKinley administration was under heavy pressure from Congress and the public to act more decisively. On January 25, 1898, the battleship *Maine* was dispatched to Havana to protect U.S. citizens from pro-Spanish rioters. Three weeks later, on February 15, the *Maine* was destroyed by an explosion that killed 260 U.S. sailors.

The cause of the *Maine* disaster was never clearly established, but the yellow press immediately seized on it as a pretext for declaring war against Spain. On February 18 a bold headline in the *Journal* declared that "the warship Maine was split in two by an enemy's secret infernal machine." Two days later the *Journal*'s front page contained a fanciful drawing of the *Maine* sitting on the bottom of Havana's harbor beneath a headline ascribing the wreck to "Spanish treachery." Following the lead of the New York papers, newspapers across the country whipped up a war fever that forced the reluctant President McKinley to put the question of war before Congress. Despite the fact that Spain had met most U.S. demands for resolving the crisis in Cuba, Congress voted to declare war.[44]

The brief conflict that followed Congress's declaration of war was a very mismatched affair. On May 1 Commodore George Dewey's fleet demolished the Spanish naval force in the Philippines and blockaded Manila harbor. Two months later, on July 3, the Spanish fleet in Cuba suffered a similar fate. On July 17, Spanish army units surrendered the city of Santiago de Cuba after two weeks of resisting a U.S. force of 15,000 soldiers that had landed in Cuba in June. U.S. forces occupied Puerto Rico a week later and in mid-August marched into Manila. By late August the war was over; in December Spain signed a treaty granting Cuba independence and ceding its other possessions in the Pacific and Caribbean to the United States.

The New York newspapers covered the Spanish-American War as vigorously as they had promoted it. At least 200 correspondents turned up in Cuba to report on the progress of U.S. forces, with the largest contingents representing the *Journal* and the *World*. According to some estimates, the total number of reporters, artists, and photographers sent by U.S. papers to cover the war in the Caribbean and Pacific was 500, as many journalists as had covered the Civil War. Coverage of the action in Cuba was especially heavy because of its proximity to the United States. Spanish authorities had cut the Havana cable line to the United States shortly after the sinking of the *Maine,* so the AP and several newspapers hired boats to carry dispatches to the cable office at Key West, Florida. The *New York Journal* had a fleet of ten boats in and around Cuba, including the personal yacht of William Randolph Hearst, from which the publisher directed his correspondents' coverage.[45]

The *Journal* spent $3,000 per day on its coverage, or about $500,000 during the course of the conflict, a huge expenditure for so brief a conflict, but it brought the *Journal* handsome gains in circulation. The combined circulation of the morning and evening *Journal* had surpassed 1 million for the first time during the coverage of the *Maine* disaster, and at the height of the fighting in Cuba it regularly reached 1.5 million. The *World's* circulation was not far behind. Neither paper made money on its war coverage; the high cost of coverage, the need to print extra editions, and a decline in advertising revenues resulted in big losses. But Hearst was convinced that his expanded circulation base would bring benefits in the future, and the *World* could not afford to let the *Journal* outperform it on the most important story of the decade. The papers therefore continued to produce a staggering quantity of war coverage throughout the conflict.[46]

The quality of coverage was another matter. Although newspapers such as the *New York Times* attempted to provide balanced accounts of the war, many of the nation's newspapers imitated the example of the *Journal* and the *World* in purveying emotional, misleading, and occasionally fabricated coverage. Correspondents made little effort to maintain the status of disinterested observers, frequently taking on military chores and participating in the fighting. James Creelman, for instance, whom Hearst had hired away from the *World,* led a bayonet charge against Spanish forces in Cuba.[47] Even among the correspondents who refused to participate in military activities, there was a pervasive tendency to exaggerate and romanticize the performance of U.S. soldiers. This produced interesting copy, as in the accounts of Teddy Roosevelt and the Rough Riders charging up San Juan Hill (actually they charged up Kettle Hill), but it arguably did little to give the average newspaper reader a clear picture of the war's progress.

Military censorship of the correspondents' dispatches was quite lax, in part because of the highly positive tone of most of the coverage. Newspapers regularly carried detailed reports about military maneuvers, troop strength, and so on without suffering official criticism. The McKinley administration made a feeble attempt to control the publication of sensitive information by designating a former *New York Tribune* reporter as military censor in New York, but his efforts were bitterly resisted by journalists and had little impact on what was reported.[48] The war ended so quickly that there was no opportunity to impose more effective controls.

Historians often refer to the Spanish-American War as a key event in the emergence of the United States as a world power. This may well be true, but the war also marked a moral low point in the coverage of conflicts by the American press. The war was unquestionably avoidable and occurred largely to satisfy the promotional goals of competing New York newspapers. Once the war was underway, the yellow press exploited the action shamelessly to sell papers while doing little to illuminate the large implications of a U.S. victory. The tragic U.S. suppression of the Filipino independence movement after the war and the need for U.S. forces to return periodically to Cuba during the early twentieth century demonstrated that neither the American public nor its leaders fully understood some of those implications. The yellow press, which had agitated so persistently for the war, bore much of the blame for the conflict's unfortunate aftermath.

The Filipino Insurrection

The peace treaty that the United States and Spain signed on December 10, 1898, ceded control of the Philippines to America in return for a payment of $20 million. The terms of the treaty were greeted with dismay by Filipino nationalists, who had hoped that Spain's defeat would be quickly followed by the establishment of an independent republic. President McKinley, however, had embraced the view of Republican expansionists that the United States should retain control of the Philippines in order to ensure U.S. access to the markets of Asia. McKinley also endorsed the opinion of prominent imperialists such as Whitelaw Reid, the publisher of the *New York Tribune,* that the Filipinos were incapable of sustaining a stable government.[49]

Filipino nationalists understandably disagreed. After several months of uneasy truce, fighting between U.S. troops and nationalist forces broke out in February 1899. Under the leadership of Emilio Aguinaldo, the nationalists soon adopted guerrilla tactics to counter the superior organization and weaponry of U.S. forces. The U.S. Army commander in the Philippines, General Elwell S. Otis, responded by waging a brutal counterinsurgency campaign against the nationalists. By the time the insurrection collapsed in 1902, at least 200,000 Filipinos had died. U.S. losses numbered 5,000, more than had been killed fighting the Spanish in Cuba.[50] At the height of the insurrection, 70,000 U.S. troops, most of the U.S. Army, were deployed in the Philippines.

The war in the Philippines was controversial in the United States. Anti-imperialist newspapers such as the *Boston Transcript,* the *Springfield Republican,* and the *New York Post* regularly carried accounts of atrocities committed against Filipinos by U.S. troops. Some of these accounts were exaggerated, but many were true. As part of the counterinsurgency campaign, U.S. troops razed villages, destroyed crops, forcibly detained noncombatants in concentration camps, and tortured suspected nationalist sympathizers. Several officers were subsequently tried for war crimes, including a general who ordered his troops to shoot any males they encountered over the age of ten.[51] The excesses of the army were seized upon by Democrats and other anti-imperialists in bitter criticism of the expansionist policies of the McKinley administration.

Recognizing that they were engaged in a controversial enterprise, General Otis and his successors imposed rigid censorship on the telegraph messages of all newspaper correspondents. The application of censorship was facilitated by the fact that the Philippines were 6,000 miles from the United States and prompt transmission of news required use of the Manila cable office. Uncensored dispatches could still be sent through the mail, but the distances meant that these would take weeks to reach their destinations. Military authorities justified the censorship by arguing that much of what appeared in the American press about the war was untrue or potentially helpful to the insurgents. This view was shared by others sympathetic to the American presence, such as federal judge William Howard Taft, who returned from a fact-finding mission to warn the president that stories of atrocities were ruining the morale of U.S. soldiers.[52]

In July 1899 the Philippines correspondents of several leading newspapers and press associations issued a joint statement alleging that General Otis was using censorship to present "an ultraoptimistic view that is not shared by the general officers in the field." They charged that Otis had exaggerated the extent of dissension within the nationalist movement, underestimated the number of troops needed to quell the insurrection, and concealed widespread illness among his soldiers. General Otis responded by accusing the correspondents of "conspiracy against the government." He threatened to court-martial the journalists and expel them from the Philippines.[53]

The correspondents' allegations created a sensation in Washington. Only weeks earlier, the War Department had cabled Otis that he must treat all correspondents equally, following a complaint by the AP correspondent in Manila that military authorities were discriminating against him. Another cable sent to Otis on September 9 advised him to accord correspondents the "most liberal treatment" and recommended that he relax censorship restrictions. Otis replied that he would do so, and shortly after the War Department announced that censorship in Manila had been abolished. In reality, though, censorship continued to be imposed, and the official censor in Manila professed ignorance of any orders concerning a relaxation of controls on what could be transmitted.[54]

According to James A. LeRoy, who wrote a retrospective assessment of U.S. military performance in the Philippines in 1914, the continued enforcement of censorship had an unforeseen, and undesired, effect on coverage of the insurrection in the United States: "The very fact that the censorship of news dispatches existed, and that the official outgivings at Manila and Washington had been impeached, made it the more easy for all kinds of distorted tales to be circulated in the United States and to obtain there more or less credence."[55]

General Otis eventually requested reassignment, but the war in the Philippines remained controversial. In March 1901 the rebel leader Aguinaldo was captured and under duress acknowledged U.S. sovereignty. Faced with the prospect of continued death and destruction at the hands of the U.S. Army, other rebel leaders began surrendering. The last nationalist leaders gave up in June 1902, and on July 4 President Roosevelt announced the "successful conclusion" of the conflict. However, the accounts of atrocities and indiscriminate brutality perpetrated by U.S. troops were not forgotten. In the words of one historian, these stories "left a dark cloud hanging over the Army's service in the Philippines."[56] By the time the army next went to war, many of the officers who had served in the Philippines had ascended to senior commands, and they were determined to prevent a repetition of the kind of coverage that had discredited their service during the Filipino insurrection.

World War I

Although the United States had imitated the great powers of Europe by acquiring an overseas empire in the late nineteenth century, the traditional American aversion to involvement in European politics remained intact. During the early years of the twentieth century, U.S. foreign policy was largely preoccupied with consolidating American influence in the Western Hemisphere. The United States competed with European countries for influence in Asia, but it avoided the entangling alliances with Old World regimes that Washington, Jefferson, and other leaders had warned against. When war broke out in Europe in 1914, President Woodrow Wilson expressed the preference of the vast majority of Americans in proclaiming neutrality. Two years later Wilson won reelection with the slogan "He kept us out of war."

Even as Wilson was expounding his support for continued neutrality, however, events were gradually drawing the United States closer to war. The British navy's mastery of the seas ensured that even if the United States maintained a policy of neutrality, most of the war goods it was willing to sell to the combatants would flow to the Allied powers. Recognizing this fact, Germany launched a submarine campaign against transatlantic shipping that reached its peak in 1917. As American lives were lost, the nation gradually turned against Germany. This trend was accelerated by an effective British propaganda effort in the United States and the clumsy attempts of German agents to sabotage munitions shipments to the Allied powers. On April 6, 1917, Congress declared war on Germany. Russia's exit from the war in late 1917 solidified U.S. support for the Allied cause by allowing Western leaders to portray the war as a battle between the forces of democracy and autocracy.

The war that the United States entered in the spring of 1917 was unlike any other the world had witnessed. Both the geographical scope of the conflict and the scale of the carnage were unprecedented. By the time the United States declared war, France had suffered 3.5 million casualties, Germany had lost 2.5 million, and Britain had lost over 1 million. In one day during the Battle of the Somme, July 1, 1916, the British army suffered 60,000 casualties, more than a third of whom died.[57] This exceeded the worst losses of the American Civil War, the earlier conflict that seemed most similar in character to the European war. Technology had transformed war; the failure of strategy to keep pace with the means of waging war resulted in engagements where thousands of soldiers lost their lives to make gains on the battlefield measured in yards. As in the American Civil War, the increasing desperation of the combatants led to the mobilization of entire societies to feed the war effort. But the Civil War had been a war of movement in which the intrinsic advantages of the more populous, industrialized North made the final outcome likely from the start. In contrast, the European war by late 1914 had bogged down in static trench warfare, which continued for years because of the lack of clear advantage on either side.

Even before the United States entered the war, Americans sent to cover the war realized they were facing an extraordinary journalistic challenge. The scale of the conflict dwarfed the resources of most newspapers for covering it, and the stringent censorship regulations imposed by both sides often prevented the transmission of whatever news was gathered. News had become, in the words of historian William M. Hammond, a "strategic commodity" that the battling nations were intent on controlling to serve their respective war efforts.[58] The British and French military establishments pursued this goal initially by excluding reporters completely from the war zone. When the less restrictive policies of the Germans resulted in favorable coverage of their military performance, the Allies loosened their own restrictions somewhat. But both sides insisted on strict censorship of all cable and mail dispatches by war correspondents, and this largely obscured the nature and implications of what was occurring at the front.[59]

Since the United States remained neutral during the first two and a half years of the war, few limits were placed on what American newspapers could print about it until 1917. American coverage of the war during these early years tended to favor the Allied powers' version of events because Britain had severed the transatlantic cables between Germany and the United States. This made the war communiqués of the British and French governments considerably more accessible to American newspapers than those of the Central Powers. Nonetheless, the war coverage in U.S. newspapers was more balanced and in some ways more detailed than that in the media of any of the warring nations because no official attempt was being made to control it.

The absence of formal restraints on U.S. coverage began to change as soon as the United States entered the war. Ten days after war was declared against Germany, President Wilson asserted that any publication providing "aid or comfort" to the enemy would be subject to prosecution for treason. Two months later, in June 1917, Congress passed an espionage act imposing stiff fines and imprisonment on publishers deemed to be promoting disloyalty. This was followed in October 1917 by passage of the Trading-with-the-Enemy Act, which authorized censorship of all overseas messages. On May 16, 1918, Congress approved further controls on the press through the Sedition Act, which made a legal offense of printing any material that contained "disloyal, profane, scurrilous or abusive language about the form of government of the United States."[60] By the time large numbers of U.S. troops began arriving in Europe in spring 1918, the legal framework for censorship of war coverage was well established.

A bureaucratic apparatus had also been created to regulate war coverage and encourage support for the war effort. The Trading-with-the-Enemy Act created a Censorship Board that worked closely with the attorney general and postmaster general to prevent transmission or dissemination of information injurious to the war effort. In addition, a propaganda agency, the Committee on Public Information, was established to release official information about the war and promote public support for it. The committee's news division issued 6,000 releases about the war, most of them dutifully published by the nation's newspapers. Its advertising division placed advertisements in newspapers and magazines appealing to citizens' patriotism and sense of national purpose. With the exception of a few news organizations such as the Anglophobic Hearst chain, most of the major papers accepted the need to back the war effort and maintain public morale.[61]

The restrictions on American journalists at the front, while less onerous than those imposed on the correspondents of other countries, were much more demanding than in past wars. In order to be accredited as a correspondent with the American Expeditionary Force (AEF) in France, a reporter was required to swear an oath of loyalty before a representative of the secretary of war, pay a $1,000 fee for equipment and maintenance, and post a $10,000 bond as guarantee of his good behavior. If the reporter failed to conduct himself as a "gentleman of the press," the bond was forfeited. Once at the front, the reporter was required to wear a green armband identifying him as a correspondent and submit all of his dispatches to official censorship.[62]

Censorship at the front was managed by the Military Intelligence Service, commonly known as G-2, which reported to the commander of the AEF. The person responsible for monitoring reporters' activities was Frederick Palmer, an experienced war correspondent who earlier in the war had been the only American journalist accredited to cover the British army on the western front. When the United States entered the war, Palmer had accepted a major's commission in the army in order to head the military censorship effort. He attempted to adapt the British army's method of managing correspondents, which included a detailed description of what could not be printed and specific punishments for infractions of censorship regulations, to the job of managing American war coverage. He did not insist, as the British and French did, that American correspondents be accompanied by military escorts; reporters were free to accompany troops as they saw fit and even go "over the top" during battles. But all correspondents were required to return to headquarters to have their dispatches censored, and any attempt to circumvent censorship was grounds for expulsion from the front.[63]

The army initially sought to limit the number of accredited correspondents with the AEF to a mere thirty-one reporters; however, it also allowed nonaccredited journalists to cover the action as visiting reporters. Accredited correspondents were accorded privileges not available to visitors, but so many visiting journalists showed up—over 400 at one point—that the system for monitoring them broke down.[64] The large number of visitors permitted to visit the front increased the resentment of accredited reporters about the restrictions placed on their activities. Censorship was so thorough that it sometimes extended to the deletion of seemingly innocuous information, such as reporters' expense accounts. Moreover, the official war releases issued by Palmer's office tended to contain little useful information and to exaggerate the successes of the AEF.[65] Editors and reporters regularly complained about the strictness of censorship, but to no avail. As a result, much of the coverage from the western front concerned human interest stories and minor events with little bearing on the progress of the war.

The most ambitious reporting effort mounted by any other American or European newspaper during the war was that of the *New York Times.* Under the leadership of managing editor Carr Van Anda, the *Times* repeatedly beat its rivals in the speed and detail of its coverage. During the twenty months that the United States was at war, the *Times*'s weekly cable costs averaged $15,000—about $780,000 per year. The cost of cables was increased by Van Anda's insistence that important news be transmitted at the "full double urgent" rate. On some days, the *Times* omitted sixty to seventy columns of advertising to make room for its extensive war coverage.[66] This resulted in large revenue losses, but circulation increased substantially, and the *Times* solidified its reputation as one of the most respected newspapers in the country. Its war coverage was all the more impressive in view of the fact that 189 of its staffers and pressmen had left their jobs to join the military when the United States entered the war.

The *New York Herald, Chicago Tribune,* and other newspapers also mounted major efforts to cover the war. Smaller papers were able to draw on the coverage of the big metropolitan dailies and had access to the reports of numerous news and feature services. The tenor of coverage tended to be heavily patriotic and supportive of the war effort. There was little inclination to question the performance of the nation's political and military leaders because most papers had embraced the notion that America was fighting to make the world safe for democracy. Even the stringent censorship restrictions were accepted as disagreeable but necessary, and few papers sought to circumvent them.[67]

Despite the patriotic tone of war coverage, one negative theme emerged during the war that blossomed into a full scandal after the conflict was over: the incompetence of the army's supply bureaucracy. Shortly after the United States declared war, journalists, including Floyd Gibbons of the *Chicago Tribune,* began reporting that U.S. troops seemed poorly equipped for the rigors of battle. The seeming inability of the army to support the AEF adequately proved to be a problem throughout the war. The army took more than a year to deploy a large ground force on the western front, and even after it did so, it had to rely on supplies provided by its allies to wage war. Of the thousands of aircraft and tanks ordered by the army from American industry during mobilization, not a single one reached France before the armistice in November 1918.[68] Reporting of the army's supply scandals was somewhat muted while the war was still in progress, but it became a big story once victory was secured. Allegations of ineptitude and conflicts of interest resulted in a congressional investigation, which found that the mobilization had been largely botched.[69] Coverage of the scandal, reminiscent of similar problems in earlier wars, undercut the positive image of the army created by accounts of its successes on the battlefield.

World War I ended within months after the AEF was fully deployed in Europe. Once Germany's spring offensive of 1918 on the western front failed, the German government recognized that the war was lost. On November 11, 1918, an armistice was declared ending the war. Because of the short duration of America's active involvement in the fighting, U.S. casualties were relatively light compared with those of the other major combatants. Of 4 million troops mobilized to fight the war, the U.S. army suffered 106,378 deaths, of which fewer than half were battle deaths. The total number of U.S. dead and wounded for all of the services during World War I was 320,518, fewer than the losses incurred by some of the European countries in key battles such as Verdun and Passchendaele. Germany suffered over 7 million casualties in the war and France over 6 million.

Europe had lost a generation of young men; in the United States, the much lighter losses produced a less profound impact on the national psyche. American newspapers had described the war as a crusade to make the world safe for democracy, and with that crusade now successfully concluded, the inclination of many Americans was to return to domestic concerns. The idealistic tenor of much of the war coverage reinforced the popular feeling that America was above the petty politics of Europe and should continue to distance itself from the intrigues of Old World diplomacy. While it is an exaggeration to say that the United States retreated into isolation after World War I, it is clear that the public and many of its leaders had not learned the lesson that the United States must remain involved in European politics to prevent future wars. A quarter of a century later, the United States once again found itself at war in Europe.

World War II

The uneasy peace that followed World War I in Europe lasted for barely a generation before collapsing. The Treaty of Versailles that formally ended the war had transformed the map of Europe, but it had done little to relieve the underlying tensions that caused the conflict. In some ways, it made them worse; the draconian terms imposed on Germany by the victorious Allied powers slowed its recovery from the war and inflamed resentments that found their expression in support for fascism. Particularly after the onset of the Great Depression in the 1930s, the hopes for a more just and democratic world order rapidly evaporated. In 1934 Adolf Hitler came to power in Germany, and the following year he repudiated the Treaty of Versailles. He then set about remilitarizing Germany and re-claiming territories that had been lost in the war. Meanwhile, in Asia, Japan's increasingly militaristic government mounted an aggressive cam-paign to become the dominant power in the western Pacific. In 1937 Japan invaded China, bringing it into direct conflict with U.S. policies toward the region.

As the world descended into turmoil during the 1930s, the U.S. gov-ernment was preoccupied with trying to ameliorate the domestic conse-quences of the depression. The rise of fascism in Europe and Asia was widely deplored, but there was little desire to take a leading role in challenging its spread. Many Americans had come to believe that U.S. involvement in World War I was a tragic mistake encouraged by venal arms merchants and a pro-British president; they were determined that the United States would not again be drawn into the decadent politics of Europe. The wish to insulate the United States from the problems of Europe resulted in the passage of a series of neutrality acts between 1935 and 1937 that prevented the United States from taking sides in foreign conflicts. President Franklin Roosevelt opposed the acts as infringements on his constitutional prerogatives, but he was not wholly unsympathetic to the isolationist viewpoint. During the 1938 Czech crisis, he sent a message to Hitler stating that the United States had "no political involve-ments in Europe and will assume no obligations in the conduct of the present negotiations."[70]

Roosevelt's views on foreign commitments changed rapidly after the outbreak of war in Europe in 1939, but those of most other Americans did not. In September 1941, after the fall of France and the blitz of London, nearly 80 percent of Americans still opposed participation in the war.[71] Roosevelt tried to prepare the nation for war by winning partial repeal of the neutrality acts, introducing conscription, increasing military budgets, and aiding Britain, but he was limited in his actions by the depth of antiwar sentiment. A substantial segment of the press was bitterly opposed to U.S. involvement in the war and vigorously criticized any administration policies that appeared to make such involvement more likely. The most influential isolationist paper was the *Chicago Tribune,* which was so determined to keep America out of the war that on Decem-ber 4, 1941, it published the contents of a sensitive War Department document purportedly revealing "F.D.R.'s War Plans." The *Tribune's* story, printed under a banner headline on page 1, described a massive war effort that would embroil the United States in global conflict:

> WASHINGTON, D.C., DEC. 3—A confidential report prepared by the joint army and navy high command by direction of President Roosevelt calls for American expeditionary forces aggregating 5,000,000 men for a final land offensive against Germany and her satellites. It contemplates total armed forces of 10,045,658 men.
>
> One of the few existing copies of this astounding document, which represents decisions and commitments affecting the destinies of peoples throughout the civilized world, became available to the *Tribune* today.
>
> It is a blueprint for war on a total scale unprecedented in at least two oceans and three continents, Europe, Africa, and Asia.[72]

The *Tribune* report was an embarrassment for the Roosevelt administration and created an uproar among antiwar forces in Congress; however, only three days after the report appeared, Japan attacked Pearl Harbor, and further resistance to involvement in the war ceased. On December 8, 1941, Congress voted overwhelmingly to declare war against Japan. Germany and Italy then joined with Japan in declaring war on the United States, and Congress responded by declaring war on them. In less than a week, the United States had gone from being a nonbelligerent to being at war in both Europe and Asia.

By December 1941 the American media had been covering the war for more than two years. The war had been a big story even before the United States entered it, but it now became a story that eclipsed all others. The volume of war coverage generated by American newspapers, magazines, and radio from December 1941 to August 1945 was so huge that it exceeded the capacity of even the most diligent readers and listeners to absorb. When war had broken out in Europe in 1939, nearly all American coverage was generated by eight sources: the nation's three news services—AP, United Press, and International News Service; four major newspapers—the *New York Times, New York Herald-Tribune, Chicago Tribune,* and *Chicago Daily News;* and a single feature service operated jointly by several metropolitan papers, the North American Newspaper Alliance. According to one estimate, 99 percent of U.S. spot war coverage during 1939 came from one of these sources.[73] Once America entered the war, though, sources of war coverage proliferated until hundreds of separate dispatches were being filed daily.

The number of correspondents covering the war reflected the scale of conflict. During the four years the United States was at war, the War Department accredited 1,800 reporters to cover the army, and the Navy Department accredited 800. The 2,600 correspondents were not all active simultaneously, but it has been estimated that at any time between late 1941 and mid-1945, about 800 American journalists were covering the war at various locations around the world. The largest concentration of correspondents was in Europe, where Allied headquarters accredited 1,338 American, British, French, and neutral correspondents, of which the American contingent was by far the largest.[74]

The character of American coverage during World War II reflected changes in both the nature of warfare and types of communications media. In terms of the latter, World War II was the first conflict extensively covered by radio. The United States had three commercial radio networks at the beginning of the war, and each competed in providing the most timely and detailed coverage. The immediacy of radio had a profound impact on how the war was covered, for it was now possible to report events as they occurred. This was usually precluded by censorship restrictions, but radio nonetheless consistently beat the print media in reporting important breaking news.

Another new set of media participants in war coverage were the mass circulation newsweeklies and feature magazines such as *Time, Newsweek, Life,* and the *Saturday Evening Post,* most of which had begun publication during the 1920s and 1930s. The demand generated by these publications for dramatic war pictures resulted in a vast increase in the number of so-called photojournalists at the fronts during World War II. In World War I, most of the photos from the front had been provided by military photographers, but in World War II photojournalists produced far more of the pictorial coverage. By late 1944 Allied headquarters in Paris was reviewing 35,000 photographs every week.[75]

Still another new group of journalists at the front were the representatives of newsreel companies like Pathe and Movietone. During the 1920s and 1930s newsreels had become standard fare at the nation's movie theaters, and a number of companies had sprung up to satisfy the public's appetite for exciting footage of major events. The advent of lightweight, hand-held movie cameras—like the development of compact cameras for photojournalists and wire recorders for radio reporters—enabled the newsreel companies to send their personnel into the thick of battle to capture the pathos of war as never before. The newsreels, which tended to be emotional and simplistic, provided a new dimension to war coverage. During the final months of fighting in Europe, newsreel companies from the Allied countries produced 100,000 feet of film per week.[76]

More than merely the means of war coverage changed in World War II. The attitude of governments toward war coverage changed too. When World War I began in 1914, the governments of both the Allied and Central Powers regarded war correspondents as at best a nuisance and at worst a threat to the war effort. Once the fighting bogged down on the western front, however, the increasingly desperate leaders of each country enlisted the press in the campaign to maintain public morale. By the time World War II commenced in 1939, the notion that the media would play a critical role in building support for the war effort was widely accepted, and governments made provisions for accommodating correspondents who were willing to provide the kind of coverage desired. Even among military officers, the need to have the war covered, and covered correctly, was generally recognized.[77]

In one way, the new attitude made correspondents' jobs easier. The armed forces of Britain and the United States made an effort to facilitate coverage of military action and released copious amounts of information about how the war was proceeding. However, there was a quid pro quo: reporters were expected to write positive, supportive stories that would reflect well on the performance of the military and the policies of the government. The understanding among senior officers that journalists should contribute to the war effort was epitomized by General Dwight Eisenhower's remark to a group of editors that "I have always considered as quasi-staff officers, correspondents accredited to my headquarters."[78] Such status brought important privileges, but it also implied a duty not to question military practices and policies.

Most correspondents understood and accepted the limits on what they could say or write. The concept of the war correspondent as a participant in the effort to secure victory combined with the formal and informal restrictions on the kinds of information that could be disseminated to produce coverage that heavily emphasized the human dimensions of conflict. Much of the coverage during World War II was concerned with the experiences of individual soldiers and small units at the front. Reporters were drawn to such material not only because of the constraints on what they would cover but also because of the need to make the vast and complex struggle in which the country was engaged meaningful to an audience that was overwhelmed by information about the war. The most widely read American correspondent of the war was Ernie Pyle, a journalist who specialized in describing the war from the perspective of the common soldier.[79] The most popular editorial cartoonist was Bill Mauldin, who depicted the travails of two infantrymen named Willie and Joe. Pyle, Mauldin, and others sometimes poked fun at the military, but the underlying message of their work was that the war was a disagreeable enterprise that nonetheless had to be won.

As in World War I responsibility for censorship of war coverage in World War II was divided between civilian authorities on the home front and military authorities in the war zones. Censorship within the United States was carried out by the Office of Censorship, established on December 19, 1941, pursuant to the First War Powers Act. President Roosevelt designated Byron Price, the AP executive editor, as the director of the censorship office and gave him "absolute discretion" to review all cables, mail, and radio copy entering or leaving the United States. Depending on the content, communications could be passed without changes, passed with deletions, delayed, or completely suppressed.[80] The Office of Censorship quickly became a sprawling bureaucracy, employing at its peak 11,500 personnel across the country and with an annual budget in 1943 of $26.5 million.[81]

One of Price's first acts as director of domestic censorship was to prepare a voluntary code of restraint for editors and publishers. The first edition of the *Code of Wartime Practices for the American Press* was published on January 15, 1942. A similar code was issued at the same time for radio broadcasters. The codes described in detail the kinds of war information considered inappropriate for publication or broadcast, including the location of ground and naval deployments, the size and nature of war contracts, the capacity and output of war plants, casualty reports, and ship sinkings. Radio weather reports were also limited out of fear that they would be monitored and used by the enemy. Journalists were allowed to make exceptions to the list of proscribed subjects if they received prior approval from the Office of Censorship.[82]

A civilian Office of War Information was also created to foster support for the war effort and develop propaganda to be directed at Axis and neutral countries. The Office of War Information was headed by Elmer Davis, a radio broadcaster generally credited with having taken an enlightened position on the sorts of information that should be available to the public. Although Davis was not directly responsible for censorship, he devoted much time to prodding military authorities to permit a freer flow of information out of the war zones, arguing that it would be easier to maintain public support for the war effort if citizens believed they were being told the truth.[83]

Military censorship in the war zones tended to be more restrictive than that of civilian authorities on the home front. Particularly in the Pacific theater, both the army and navy were strict in limiting the release of information. General Douglas MacArthur, the senior army commander in the theater, encouraged favorable coverage of his own exploits but dealt harshly with reporters who attempted to circumvent censorship. Admiral Ernest King, the commander in chief of the U.S. fleet, withheld information about naval losses in the Pacific long after any military justification for doing so remained.

The different standards of military and civilian censors became apparent in June 1942 when the *Chicago Tribune* disclosed that the navy had possessed advanced warning of Japanese strategy in the Battle of Midway. Although the *Tribune* had received its information from sources at sea, it erroneously submitted the story to civilian censors, who passed it. Upon seeing the story, Admiral King immediately suspected a major breach of security, since the navy's insight into Japanese plans had been made possible by the breaking of the Japanese military code. The *Tribune* was apparently unaware of this fact but still came very close to being prosecuted. Fortunately, the Japanese did not change their code.[84]

One of the remarkable aspects of U.S. wartime censorship was that it was a voluntary effort that nonetheless managed to work quite well. The code of practices drafted by the Office of Censorship was not backed by legal enforcement authority but rather relied on a gentlemen's agreement with the press for its effectiveness. Editors and reporters frequently complained about the way in which the code was applied, but there were surprisingly few infractions of the basic guidelines.[85] A particularly striking example of how well the voluntary restraint system worked was the nearly complete secrecy surrounding work on the atomic bomb. Many journalists were aware of the large facilities built to refine uranium and fabricate the bomb at places like Oak Ridge, Tennessee, and Los Alamos, New Mexico, but very little appeared in print about the program, code-named the Manhattan Project, until August 6, 1945, when Hiroshima was bombed. William Laurence, the science reporter of the New York Times, had been invited to prepare a secret history of the Manhattan Project by its military administrators, and he managed to do so without ever disclosing the nature of the project to his editors. As a reward for his discretion, Laurence was allowed to accompany the second atomic bomb mission against Nagasaki on August 9, 1945, and prepare an exclusive story.[86]

The New York Times led the American press in providing extensive, timely coverage of World War II, just as it had during World War I. However, the reporting of the later war was such a massive undertaking that no single news organization could hope to cover all the important events. It became accepted practice to create press pools to ensure full coverage of military operations, an approach to news gathering that broadened access to vital information but reduced the likelihood of exclusive reports. In 1942, for example, the nation's three biggest picture agencies—Acme, AP, and International News Service—joined with Life magazine to pool their resources for covering the war. This allowed the participating organizations to station photographers in every location around the world where military action was likely to occur, but it also meant that they would have to share the resulting coverage.[87]

Radio and print journalists made similar provisions to cover major military actions, such as the Normandy invasion in 1944. This was necessary not only because of the scale of operations but also because it was impractical for the military to accommodate all the journalists who wished to cover a particular action. A total of 558 writers, photographers, cameramen, and radio reporters were accredited to cover the Normandy invasion, but less than a tenth of this number participated in the initial press pool. As it was, the journalists who actually reached the French coast on D day generated 400,000 words of copy that first day. Three weeks after the invasion had begun, military censors in France had already reviewed 6 million words of copy, 32,242 photographs, and 284,900 feet of film.[88]

Coverage on so vast a scale is difficult to characterize accurately, just as the war itself was difficult for reporters to describe in terms meaningful to their audiences. Aggregate statistics—numbers of reporters, words of copy, and so on—provide an indication of the size of the journalistic effort, but they cannot capture the hardships and danger correspondents at the front experienced. Noting that 37 correspondents were killed and 112 wounded while covering the war, Frank Luther Mott has calculated that the casualty rate for journalists was four times higher than that of the fighting forces.[89] Reporters continued to compete vigorously for news in World War II as they had in earlier conflicts, but like their military counterparts, individual journalists increasingly became bit players in an enterprise that was beyond the capacity of any of the participants to grasp fully. The romance of being a war correspondent, like the romance of war, was largely gone.

World War II formally ended on September 2, 1945, when representatives of the Japanese government signed surrender terms aboard the battleship *Missouri* in Tokyo Bay. During the preceding six years, 55 million military personnel and civilians had died in the most destructive conflict the world had ever seen. The U.S. armed forces alone had suffered over 1 million casualties: 405,399 deaths and 670,846 wounded. In characteristic fashion, America had waged the war as a crusade for justice and democracy, just as it had waged earlier wars. But after World War II, there would be no return to "normalcy." The war had obliterated the old international system, and the new order that was emerging would draw the nation onto the world stage as never before. Most Americans were proud of their increased stature in the world, but they were also ambivalent at the prospect of being continually involved in the political affairs of Europe and Asia. Their ambivalence would be reflected in the coverage of future conflicts.

The Korean War

World War II destroyed fascism, but it did not eliminate all the threats to Western democracy. Despite suffering massive losses, the Soviet Union emerged from the war with its strategic position greatly improved. The two traditional obstacles to its eastward and westward expansion, Japan and Germany, were devastated. Great Britain, long its competitor for influence in southwest Asia, was exhausted. It soon became apparent that Joseph Stalin would seek to exploit the weakness of Russia's historic rivals to expand Soviet influence in both Europe and Asia. In response to this threat, the Truman administration in 1947 enunciated a policy of containment aimed at countering the spread of communism. Containment required the United States to provide political, economic, and military aid to nation's threatened by communist subversion or aggression.

In 1949 communist revolutionaries in China led by Mao Zedong succeeded in driving pro-Western nationalist forces from the mainland and consolidating their control over the world's most populous nation. That same year, the Soviet Union conducted its first successful test of a fission device, ending the American monopoly of atomic weapons technology. These two events created a crisis atmosphere in Washington, where the Truman administration was under heavy pressure to do more to halt the growth of communist power and influence. When the communist government of North Korea invaded South Korea on June 25, 1950, the administration seized the opportunity to make a stand.

Although Truman's secretary of state, Dean Acheson, had recently declared Korea to be outside the U.S. defense perimeter in Asia, the administration believed that the North Korean invasion had been encouraged by Stalin and was part of a larger pattern of communist aggression at various points on the Sino-Soviet periphery. The United States urged the United Nations to take action, and on June 27, during the absence of the Soviet representative, the Security Council called on U.N. member states to come to the assistance of South Korea. President Truman responded by ordering U.S. troops into Korea. General Douglas MacArthur, the head of the U.S. Far East Command, was appointed the commander of the U.N. force in Korea, which, aside from the South Korean army, consisted largely of U.S. military units. Thus began the Korean War, a bitter conflict that would continue for three years and result in the deaths of 54,26 American servicemen.

The Korean War was one of the most controversial conflicts in American history, and the relations between the military and the media representatives covering it reflected that controversy. Within weeks after the initial North Korean attack, over 200 correspondents had been accredited to cover the war in Korea or at MacArthur's headquarters in Tokyo. The majority of the correspondents were Americans, and it was the American journalists who suffered the heaviest losses. During July and August, as North Korean forces rapidly advanced southward, twelve correspondents were reported killed, wounded, or missing; ten of them were American.[90]

The first U.S. troops went into action on July 5, 1950, and were badly defeated. As U.N. forces fell back, American correspondents reported the debacle in detail, including interviews with wounded and traumatized soldiers. Although no formal censorship had been imposed on media reporting, military representatives began assailing the coverage as irresponsible, excessively critical, or helpful to the enemy. MacArthur nonetheless resisted instituting censorship, preferring to rely on the voluntary restraint of journalists.[91] Media-military relations improved markedly in September when U.N. forces successfully counterattacked, launching a daring amphibious landing far behind North Korean lines at Inchon. The North Korean advance collapsed, and during October U.N. forces drove deep into North Korea. By late October the North Korean capital of Pyongyang had been captured, and U.N. military units had reached the Yalu River on the border between North Korea and China.

It appeared that victory was near until October 26, 1950, when a huge force of Chinese troops attacked across the Yalu. U.N. forces retreated before the Chinese onslaught until late December, when lines stabilized around the thirty-ninth parallel at the Korean peninsula's midsection. A two-year stalemate ensued, during which domestic criticism of the war in the United States grew steadily stronger. The loudest criticism came from Republicans, who complained that the Truman administration was limiting General MacArthur's ability to achieve victory. Rejecting the notion that the war should be a limited conflict fought for limited objectives, some critics advocated using atomic bombs against the Chinese. When MacArthur himself threatened the Chinese with atomic attack in April 1951, President Truman replaced him with General Matthew B. Ridgway. MacArthur's removal provoked a firestorm of criticism in Washington from those favoring a more aggressive military strategy. The continuing stalemate in Korea was a key factor in the Republican election victory of 1952, when Dwight D. Eisenhower was elected president on a pledge to end the war.

While domestic criticism of the war mounted, American correspondents were having a difficult time reporting the conflict. In addition to the dangers associated with covering a rapidly changing military situation and the problems caused by primitive communications—only one telephone line out of Korea was available to reporters in the early months of the war—correspondents had to contend with the growing resentment of U.S. military officers over the content and tenor of war coverage. During the retreat of U.N. forces in November and December 1950, many correspondents had written stories critical of the high command's performance. Because no formal censorship was in effect and correspondents could not obtain consistent guidance concerning information that was too sensitive to report, there were repeated disagreements between the military and journalists about whether the press was acting responsibly. Two reporters representing the AP and United Press were expelled from Korea for writing dispatches deemed helpful to the enemy.[92]

The frequent disclosure of information about troop movements, military strategy, and the like convinced many senior officers that the voluntary restraint system was not working. There was also a widespread perception within the military that media criticism was negatively influencing public opinion in the United States, undermining the war effort. Military officers were not alone in believing that the voluntary restraint approach to war coverage was a failure; the Overseas Press Club petitioned the Defense Department to institute censorship so that journalists could receive clear guidelines concerning what was inappropriate for publication.[93]

On December 18, 1950, Secretary of Defense George C. Marshall summoned a dozen media representatives to his office to discuss problems surrounding coverage of the war. The meeting resulted in a resolution stating that the military should assume responsibility for reviewing media reports from the combat area. On December 23 8th Army headquarters in Korea began requiring that all press reports, radio broadcasts, and photographs be submitted for clearance before transmission. A week later MacArthur's headquarters in Tokyo issued an official censorship code to war correspondents. The code stated that stories would not be cleared for transmission unless

(1) they are accurate in statement and implication,
(2) they do not supply military information to the enemy,
(3) they will not injure the morale of our forces or our Allies, and
(4) they will not embarrass the United States, its Allies, or neutral countries.[94]

The cumulative effect of these changes was to abolish voluntary restraint and establish a stringent system of censorship at both the front and in Tokyo. Since nearly all the dispatches originating at the front were transmitted though Tokyo, this amounted to double censorship: dispatches were reviewed first by 8th Army censors in Korea and then again at Far East Command headquarters in Tokyo. This system caused significant delays in the transmission of stories, but at least correspondents at the front could no longer be accused of disclosing sensitive information. Military censors were empowered to delete all sensitive material from dispatches, although they were not permitted to alter the wording of stories. They were allowed to make suggestions to journalists on how stories might be revised to satisfy censorship requirements. The same basic criteria were applied to all newspaper stories, magazine articles, motion picture films, and photographs, except that in the case of photographs, pictures that might be recaptioned by the enemy for propaganda purposes were also suppressed.[95]

The imposition of censorship reduced but did not eliminate frictions between the military and the media. Military officers continued to resent criticisms of their performance that appeared regularly in the media, and sensitive information still managed to make its way into print from sources outside the war zone. On June 18, 1951, for instance, *Newsweek* published a map identifying troop strengths and deployment areas for all 8th Army units in Korea.[96] Correspondents were dissatisfied too because censorship was often applied unevenly or arbitrarily. Not only did the army, navy, and air force each have somewhat different standards for determining what was sensitive, but there was also disagreement between the censors in Korea and those at Far East Command headquarters in Tokyo.[97]

In June 1951, after MacArthur's removal, the censorship system was simplified so that dispatches would be reviewed only once before transmission. Most censorship thereafter occurred at military headquarters in Korea and was carried out by censors who had been trained by the Far East Command's Press Advisory Division in Tokyo. The system was improved in late 1952 when the Defense Department shifted responsibility for reviewing dispatches from intelligence to public information personnel and brought all three military services under a uniform code of censorship.[98]

Problems with war coverage nonetheless persisted. Peace negotiations began in July 1951 and continued sporadically until an armistice was signed on June 26, 1953. During the time the talks were in progress, several stories appeared in the media that were based on communications with communist sources. These were criticized as undercutting the U.S. negotiating position and thereby providing support to the enemy. Military officers continued to criticize the perceived propensity of correspondents to emphasize bad news from the front, while correspondents objected to the seemingly self-serving way in which the military tried to manage the news. Relations between the media and the military remained tense.

The character of American war coverage during the Korean conflict, like the character of the relationship between those who fought the war and those who reported it, was decidedly different from World War II. The belief that correspondents should support the war effort and avoid overt criticism of the military, so widely held among journalists during World War II, was largely missing in Korea. The resentment among military officers over the media's failure to "get on the team" produced an adversarial relationship marked by distrust and irritation on both sides. This fractious relationship reflected many factors, including the limited nature of the conflict, the widespread domestic opposition to the way in which it was fought, and the serious reversals that U.S. troops suffered on the battlefield. Above all, the breakdown in military-media relations reflected a growing disagreement between soldiers and journalists about the proper role of war coverage. A generation later in Vietnam, this disagreement reappeared with a vengeance.

The Vietnam War

The controversy surrounding the Korean War did not lead the Eisenhower administration to abandon Truman's policy of containment, but it did lead to a rethinking of how that policy should be operationalized. The widespread domestic opposition to the way in which the war was conducted seemed to indicate that it would be difficult to maintain public support for protracted conventional conflicts aimed at the limited goal of containing communist aggression. The public, or at least key elements within the Republican party, wanted a more decisive approach to dealing with the communist menace. In addition, President Eisenhower was disturbed by the cost of the conventional buildup needed to prosecute the Korean conflict, and he doubted the nation's ability to afford the kind of defense posture required to counter communist aggression using purely conventional means.

In 1953 Eisenhower proposed a different approach to organizing U.S. military forces designed to address both of these problems. Called the New Look, it involved substituting nuclear weapons for conventional capabilities in a wide range of possible military contingencies. By relying on its superior nuclear weapons technology to deal with communist aggression, Eisenhower argued, the United States could acquire tremendous firepower relatively cheaply, and that firepower would have a decisive impact on the outcome of most foreseeable conflicts. The strategy formulated to support the New Look came to be known as massive retaliation, a vaguely stated doctrine that implied the United States might launch a nuclear attack against the Soviet Union if it believed Soviet leaders were fomenting aggression in Europe or Asia.[99]

Eisenhower and his advisers had good reason to believe such a strategy would work because the implicit threat to use nuclear weapons in Korea in 1953 seemed to play a role in convincing Chinese and North Korean leaders to agree to armistice terms.[100] Nonetheless, as Soviet nuclear capabilities grew in the mid- to late 1950s, massive retaliation was increasingly assailed by domestic critics as dangerous and unbelievable. How likely was it, critics asked, that the United States would use nuclear weapons to counter conventional aggression if this might result in the Soviets' using their own nuclear weapons in retaliation? In the 1960 presidential campaign, Democratic nominee John F. Kennedy pledged to rebuild U.S. conventional capabilities so that the nation would not be overly dependent on the threat of nuclear war to deter communist aggression.

On his election, Kennedy immediately initiated a review of U.S. defense policies, which concluded in replacing the doctrine of massive retaliation with a new concept, flexible response. Flexible response required the development of highly capable conventional forces that could respond in kind to any level of aggression, including guerrilla warfare. This led, among other things, to the creation of the Special Forces (better known as the Green Berets), a dedicated counterinsurgency force. Kennedy also advocated more vigorous U.S. involvement in the political affairs of developing countries believed to be threatened by communist subversion. One such country was South Vietnam.

Like Korea, Vietnam had been partitioned into a communist north and a noncommunist south after indigenous revolutionaries defeated

French colonial forces in 1954. By the time Kennedy became president in 1961, the pro-Western government of South Vietnam was fighting a communist guerrilla movement, the Vietcong, whose aim was to unite the two parts of Vietnam under a single communist regime. The roots of the conflict were complex and little understood by U.S. leaders, who were mainly concerned with stopping the spread of communism. When the position of the South Vietnamese government began to deteriorate, Kennedy and his advisers decided the United States should expand its economic and military assistance to the embattled regime in Saigon. This decision set in motion a gradual escalation of U.S. involvement in Vietnam that eventually led the United States to assume much of the responsibility for fighting the war there. U.S. combat troops were not introduced until after Lyndon Johnson became president in 1963, but during the Kennedy years the number of U.S. advisers in the country increased from 2,000 to 15,000.[101]

There were few American journalists in South Vietnam to cover the buildup of U.S. advisory personnel during the early 1960s. Only one U.S. newspaper, the *New York Times*, had a full-time correspondent in the country. Most of the news about Vietnam that appeared in the American media came from four news agency reporters representing the AP, United Press International, Reuters, and Agence France Presse. *Time* and *Newsweek* also had part-time stringers in Saigon, but other major U.S. media outlets showed little interest in the growing American presence in South Vietnam.[102] There were three basic reasons for the lack of interest. First, Southeast Asia historically had not been a region where the United States had important political or economic ties; most reporters and editors knew little about Vietnam or the factors that had given rise to its civil war. Second, although the U.S. military role in South Vietnam had begun to expand rapidly, few Americans were dying in the war. Third, the Kennedy administration had adopted a deliberate policy of concealing the extent of U.S. military involvement in the war.

The U.S. policy of deception was driven by a desire to portray the government of South Vietnamese president Ngo Dinh Diem as politically and militarily competent. It was not. Kennedy and his advisers feared that if the deficiencies of Diem's government—pervasive corruption, harsh treatment of dissidents, lackluster military performance—were widely known, public support for U.S. involvement would wane. Thus, even as U.S. military involvement increased, particularly in carrying out the air war against the Vietcong, U.S. government representatives in Saigon and Washington pursued a policy of highlighting South Vietnamese military successes and downplaying the American presence. This practice was formalized in a February 1962 directive to the U.S. mission in Saigon, known as cable 1006, which stated that "it is not . . . in our interest . . . to have stories indicating that Americans are leading and directing combat missions against the Vietcong."[103] Pursuant to cable 1006, the U.S. mission classified most documents concerning the U.S. military role in South Vietnam and excluded reporters from military operations where the full extent of that role would be apparent.

Denied access to information by senior U.S. diplomatic and military representatives, some of the American correspondents in Saigon turned to junior officers and Vietnamese sources for insights into the progress of the war. The evidence they uncovered painted an unflattering picture of the Diem government's performance. U.S. military personnel were participating regularly in counterinsurgency operations because of the apparent inability of the South Vietnamese army to prosecute such operations successfully on its own. Most of the air strikes against Vietcong targets were being flown by American pilots, and they were frequently using napalm, a fact that the U.S. mission had not disclosed. Furthermore, the campaign to strengthen popular support for the Diem regime in the countryside, a vital part of the counterinsurgency effort, was having little impact.[104]

As these facts became known to U.S. reporters, the tone of their dispatches grew increasingly pessimistic about the prospects for defeating the Vietcong. The stories written by *New York Times* correspondent David Halberstam were so negative that the Kennedy administration sought to have him replaced as the paper's Saigon representative. The *Times* refused, and Halberstam continued to write critical accounts of the war. Other reporters, such as Malcolm Browne and Neil Sheehan of the AP, did the same. Convinced that negative coverage would undercut the war effort, the U.S. mission and Military Assistance Advisory Group persisted in concealing bad news. This led the correspondents to doubt the veracity of information released by government representatives, a perception that came to be known in Saigon and Washington as the credibility gap.

The Kennedy administration responded to the negative coverage by questioning the accuracy of stories and the ability of reporters. Correspondents were accused of being naive and inexperienced, a charge that may have had some validity; Halberstam, Browne, and Sheehan were only in their late twenties. The administration's vigorous defense of its policies created a problem for editors in the United States. The pessimistic dispatches coming out of Saigon were contradicted by the generally positive reports about the war being written by their Washington bureaus. Which accounts should they believe? The editors' uncertainty was compounded by the fact that by no means were all of the reports from Vietnam negative; some supported the administration's interpretation of events. Most editors chose to downplay the negative coverage from Saigon, assuming, at least for a time, that government officials probably had a better idea of the war's progress than correspondents did.[105]

President Kennedy was assassinated in November 1963. His successor,

Lyndon Johnson, continued the U.S. military buildup in Vietnam but not the policy of attempting to conceal the extent of U.S. involvement in the war. Johnson was convinced that the United States would have to take a far more active role in the fighting if the Vietcong were to be defeated, and this meant the use of U.S. combat troops. Aside from the impossibility of concealing a major U.S. role in fighting the war, Johnson believed it was important to gain the support of the media for an expanded U.S. presence in Vietnam. He encouraged a more open discussion of the war that would allow reporters to understand better the reasoning behind U.S. policies. In June 1964 General Maxwell D. Taylor became the U.S. ambassador to South Vietnam. Two months later General William Westmoreland assumed command of U.S. military forces in the country. Taylor and Westmoreland began adjusting policies for dealing with the media so that there would be a freer flow of information to correspondents. They met frequently with reporters and improved the transportation and communications facilities available to them.

The same month that Westmoreland took command, August 1964, Congress passed the Gulf of Tonkin resolution giving the president broad discretion to use U.S. military forces to "maintain peace" in South Vietnam. The resolution provided the legal basis for what was to be a massive buildup of U.S. military forces in Southeast Asia, which began in earnest after Johnson was reelected president in November 1964. Early in 1965 U.S. tactical aircraft began flying regular combat missions in South Vietnam. In June 23,000 U.S. troops were committed to ground combat. The U.S. military presence throughout the country grew rapidly; by the end of 1965 184,000 U.S. military personnel were deployed in South Vietnam.

The buildup of U.S. ground forces was accompanied by a surge in the number of correspondents covering the war. By mid-1964 the number of accredited U.S. and foreign correspondents in South Vietnam had grown from a handful to about 40. A year later the number had leaped to 400. The ranks of journalists continued to swell until 1968, when over 600 accredited correspondents and dozens of nonaccredited ones were covering the war.[106] Not all of these people were actually visiting the front or writing dispatches. Accreditation procedures were notoriously lax; many of those given press credentials were actually secretaries, technicians, interpreters, and the like. Furthermore, among those who were journalists, many represented relatively obscure outlets.[107] Nonetheless, by the summer of 1965, scores of U.S. reporters were attending the Military Assistance Command's daily briefings, and a few dozen were in the field with U.S. troops.[108]

As the American role in the fighting expanded during 1964 and early 1965, U.S. military officers became concerned that the growing number of journalists in South Vietnam might report information militarily useful to the Vietcong. To minimize the likelihood of this happening, Barry

Zorthian, the senior press officer at the U.S. mission, negotiated a code of voluntary restraint with correspondents. Some reporters were initially suspicious because of their earlier dealings with the mission, but Zorthian's reputation for openness and candor eventually won them over.[109] The correspondents were also aware that if they developed a reputation for reporting sensitive information, they could be excluded from briefings, be denied access to transportation, and might lose key sources.

The voluntary restraint system worked well, but military officers remained worried about the disclosure of sensitive information. In February 1965 General Westmoreland proposed that censorship be instituted to protect military security. A three-day conference was held the following month in Honolulu by the Defense and State departments to consider whether more stringent procedures for managing war coverage were desirable. The conference concluded that censorship would probably be unworkable. In the absence of a formal declaration of war, U.S. military commanders in Vietnam lacked the legal authority to impose comprehensive censorship. They also lacked the control over communications and transportation that would be necessary to enforce censorship. Even if an administrative apparatus to establish such control was created, it would be difficult to censor the dispatches of foreign journalists covering the war. Furthermore, while some reporters might welcome the imposition of censorship, many would interpret it as a return to the policy of concealment that prevailed in the early 1960s.[110]

For all of these reasons, it was decided that the system of voluntary restraint should be continued. The Vietnam War thus became the first conflict the United States had been involved in since the nineteenth century where formal censorship of media coverage did not occur. From the standpoint of military security, the voluntary restraint approach worked. During the entire period of U.S. involvement in the fighting, less than a half-dozen serious breaches of security took place, remarkable in the light of the size and diversity of the press corps in Saigon and the opposition to the war that some correspondents openly expressed.[111] The threat that journalistic privileges might be withdrawn undoubtedly encouraged reporters to practice self-censorship.

The price of preserving the system of voluntary restraint was that reporters were free to write and say whatever they wished about the war so long as they did not disclose sensitive information. As U.S. participation in the war continued to escalate during 1966 and 1967, many correspondents wrote highly critical stories questioning the most fundamental assumptions of U.S. policy in Vietnam. They repeatedly criticized the corruption and ineptitude of the South Vietnamese government, which had been run by a series of military juntas after the assassination of President Diem in a coup in late 1963. The criticism barely abated when Nguyen Van Thieu was elected president of South Vietnam in 1967 because Thieu was elected with only 35 percent of the vote in circumstances suggesting widespread electoral fraud.[112]

Lacking a system for suppressing negative war coverage, the Johnson administration mounted a massive public relations campaign to try to maintain public support for the war. In Saigon this meant an endless series of press releases, briefings, and background interviews for the media stressing purported progress in winning the war. In Washington senior members of the Johnson administration constantly reiterated the theme that the Vietcong were gradually being defeated. Secretary of Defense Robert S. McNamara frequently conducted detailed statistical briefings on enemy body counts, munitions expended, hamlets pacified, and so on to demonstrate that the Vietcong were losing the capacity to sustain their aggression. The public relations campaign succeeded in temporarily bolstering public support for the war effort, but it did so by engendering expectations that could not be met. When developments in Vietnam contradicted the administration's optimistic projections, the officials who had presented them were discredited.

One of the eventual casualties of the mismatch between projections and reality was General Westmoreland, the commander of U.S. forces in South Vietnam. Traditionally U.S. military officers had confined their wartime remarks to the media to assessments of tactical developments, leaving the discussion of broader political issues to the nation's elected officials. However, President Johnson had pressured Westmoreland to become actively involved in selling the war to the public, a move that drew the general into partisan debates about the conduct of the war. Johnson's desire to downplay bad news led Westmoreland to present highly positive assessments of the military situation—assessments that to some degree were contradicted by the intelligence he was receiving. When the Vietcong launched coordinated attacks against dozens of South Vietnamese cities and villages during the Tet New Year holiday in January 1968, the strength of the communist offensive led many to conclude that Westmoreland was out of touch with military realities or, worse, had been misleading the public. Westmoreland's credibility never recovered.[113]

The Tet offensive proved to be a turning point in the war. Although the Vietcong suffered a major defeat, the Johnson administration's optimistic assessments had led many observers to assume the Vietcong were incapable of mounting such an ambitious operation. The American media interpreted the offensive as a major setback in the U.S. military effort that belied claims of progress in winning the war. Public opinion turned decisively against the war, and President Johnson was forced to seek a negotiated settlement of the conflict.[114]

Coverage of the Tet offensive engendered much resentment among military officers, who believed that the media had presented unduly alarming interpretations of the offensive. Television reporters in particular were singled out for criticism because of the supposedly inflammatory tone of their coverage and their failure to correct initial reports that U.S. forces had suffered a major defeat. The widespread anger among officers exacerbated a deterioration in military-media relations that was already well underway before the Tet offensive. The causes of the deterioration were similar to those that had engendered tension between the media and the military in the Korean War: reporters felt that they were not receiving straightforward assessments of the war effort and therefore sought out alternative sources of information that offered more critical analyses. Military officers interpreted this as an attempt to challenge their judgment and regarded much of the resulting coverage as irresponsible and inaccurate.

Two episodes in the reporting of the war, one before Tet and one after, reflected the growing distrust between soldiers and journalists. The first episode took place in late 1966 and early 1967 when the *New York Times* published a series of articles by assistant managing editor Harrison Salisbury about the U.S. bombing campaign against North Vietnam. In 1966, the U.S. Air Force had initiated a B-52 bombing effort code-named Rolling Thunder that was aimed at military targets near the North Vietnamese capital of Hanoi. The government of North Vietnam alleged that Rolling Thunder involved deliberate attacks against civilian centers, a charge vigorously denied by the Johnson administration. Salisbury's dispatches supported the North Vietnamese charges and reported extensive damage to civilian areas. The series provoked a controversy in the United States about whether the Johnson administration was truthfully describing the nature of the air war. It subsequently emerged that many of Salisbury's key points were in error and that he had used information from North Vietnamese propaganda pamphlets without attribution.[115] Despite Salisbury's mistakes, his series contributed to the widespread belief of a credibility gap in the administration's statements about the war. Many military officers drew a different conclusion: some journalists seemed more interested in making a point than in getting the story straight.

A second episode underscoring the deterioration of media-military relations occurred in 1969. On March 16, 1968, a company of U.S. soldiers under the command of Lieutenant William L. Calley had massacred over a hundred unarmed Vietnamese civilians in the village of My Lai. A year later the army began an investigation that resulted in Calley's being charged with mass murder. The investigation initially drew little attention, but in November 1969 several major newspapers ran stories about the massacre by freelance reporter Seymour Hersh. Hersh's stories raised questions concerning whether the atrocities committed at My Lai were an isolated incident or represented a broader pattern in the U.S. conduct of the war. When reports of other atrocities began to appear, the My Lai massacre became a big story.[116]

There was no question that a massacre had taken place, but much of the coverage in the national media seemed to suggest that atrocities committed by U.S. soldiers were a commonplace occurrence in Vietnam. A number of commentators claimed that the massacre reflected the "racist" nature of U.S. war policies. The controversy was reminiscent of similar atrocity charges that had been printed in the press during the Filipino insurrection at the beginning of the century, and the army responded in a similar fashion: it acknowledged that some war crimes might have been committed but rejected the notion that such crimes were commonplace or a product of U.S. policies. However, the belief that the army was covering up additional atrocities persisted in some quarters and contributed to the general decline of military morale. Many members of the military were embittered by charges in the media that war crimes had occurred frequently, regarding such charges as yet another example of irresponsible reporting.

The growing animosity of military officers toward the media was not a uniform trend. As in past conflicts, the friction between soldiers and journalists tended to ebb and flow with the fortunes of war. When the war was going well, as it often seemed to be in the mid-1960s, there was a greater willingness to tolerate the presence of journalists and assist them in doing their jobs. When the military suffered reverses, as during the Tet offensive in 1968, resentment toward the media increased, and journalists were blamed for the declining public support of the war effort. Complaints about war coverage within the officer corps also tended to differentiate between print journalists and television reporters, with the latter receiving the greater criticism.

Vietnam was the first major conflict covered extensively by television. Although some television coverage of the Korean War had occurred, camera technology in the early 1950s was too unwieldy to permit daily coverage of events at the front. Moreover, there were only 10 million television sets in use in the United States in the early 1950s, so most Americans were not exposed to television coverage of Korea. By the time U.S. combat troops began fighting in Vietnam, there were over 100 million television sets in American homes, and television had become the preferred source of news for much of the public. Camera technology was constantly improving, so that television crews were increasingly mobile; by the late 1960s, a typical camera crew carried less than twenty pounds of equipment (versus thirty-five pounds in the early 1960s). Transmission facilities improved too; beginning in 1970 satellite transmission technology made it possible to air film from Vietnam the same day it was shot.[117]

All three American television networks made a major commitment of resources to covering the war. By the time of the Tet offensive, each network had dozens of personnel in its Saigon bureau, and collectively the networks were spending $4 million to $5 million annually on war coverage. There was much debate during and after the war about the impact of this coverage on public opinion. Many observers believed that it played an important role in turning the public against the war, particularly in 1968 when coverage of the Tet offensive suggested that U.S. forces had suffered a big setback. However, survey analysis of viewer sentiment indicated that television played a more passive role; viewers who supported the war thought television coverage supported their position, while those opposing the war thought it validated their views.[118]

Whatever impact television may have had on public sentiment about the war, there is widespread agreement that much of the coverage was "banal and stylized."[119] Both for competitive reasons and because of the nature of the medium, television correspondents tended to favor combat footage that was full of action but lacked explanatory or contextual detail. The resulting coverage often provoked strong emotions among viewers without significantly contributing to their understanding of the larger issues at stake in the war. This problem was noted by many of the senior officers who served in Vietnam. A survey of 100 of them after the war found only 4 percent thought the public had benefited from television coverage, while 91 percent felt that television coverage was "not a good thing" because it was either too sensational or "out of context."[120]

The negative perception of television coverage among senior officers was undoubtedly related in some degree to the outcome of the war. By the time Richard M. Nixon was elected president in November 1968, over a half-million U.S. military personnel were deployed in South Vietnam, prosecuting a massive war effort against the Vietcong and North Vietnam. However, public opinion had turned against the war, and the U.S. government had begun seeking a negotiated settlement of the conflict. During his first term of office, President Nixon began the process of Vietnamization—turning over responsibility for conducting the war to the South Vietnamese military—and gradually withdrawing U.S combat troops. As the pace of withdrawals accelerated in 1970 and 1971, the focus of media coverage shifted to peace talks that had been initiated with North Vietnam and the Vietcong in Paris.

The winding down of the U.S. war effort was accompanied by a decrease in the number of correspondents covering the war. In 1969 the number of accredited reporters in South Vietnam fell to 467 from 637 the previous year. The decline continued in 1970 and 1971, so that by 1972 only 295 correspondents remained, the smallest number since 1965. In 1973 representatives of the United States, North and South Vietnam, and the Vietcong signed an armistice agreement in Paris largely ending U.S. involvement in the war. Although numerous violations of the cease-fire accord took place, by the summer of 1974 the number of correspondents in Vietnam had fallen to 35.[121]

In retrospect, the willingness of communist representatives to agree to a cease-fire was clearly part of a strategy to secure diplomatically what they had failed to achieve on the battlefield: the defeat of South Vietnam. The depth of antiwar sentiment in the United States made it unlikely that once American forces were extricated from the conflict they would ever return. When full-scale war broke out again between North and South Vietnam in early 1975, the United States did not intervene. Within a few weeks, North Vietnamese forces had advanced far southward, overwhelming all resistance. In April the last U.S. personnel in Saigon were evacuated as North Vietnamese troops entered the outskirts of the capital. A few brave journalists remained to cover the final communist victory, which was achieved on May Day 1975.[122]

The outcome of the Vietnam War unquestionably represented the worst defeat suffered by the U.S. military in its history. Over 58,000 American servicemen died in Southeast Asia between 1961 and 1975, and 153,000 were wounded. Hundreds of billions of dollars had been spent prosecuting the war, and the domestic tranquility of the United States had been deeply disrupted. In the end, it had all been for nothing: the enemy had won, achieving the unification of Vietnam under communist rule that it had been seeking since the late 1940s.

Vietnam was a severe trauma for the U.S. military, one from which it would not recover for many years. The causes of the American defeat were complex, and the most important ones probably had little to do with the quality of U.S. military performance. In the search for explanations, many military officers concluded that the frequently critical coverage of the war effort had been an important factor in bringing about the U.S. defeat. By questioning government policies in Vietnam and highlighting the worst aspects of American involvement, it was argued, the media made it impossible to maintain public support for the war. Once the North Vietnamese appreciated the extent of antiwar sentiment in the United States and the constraints it imposed on the nation's political leaders, they could craft a diplomatic strategy that would remove America from the war and leave South Vietnam vulnerable to defeat.

There is much truth in this interpretation of events. It is not clear, however, that the government of South Vietnam ever had the popular support necessary to sustain an adequate defense of its sovereignty, and it was unreasonable to expect that the United States would maintain a massive military presence in Southeast Asia forever. Whatever their transgressions may have been, the main objective of most U.S. correspondents in Vietnam was simply to report the war as accurately as possible, and many of them did this well. As the U.S. Army's own official history of media coverage in Vietnam concluded, "It is undeniable . . . that press reports were . . . often more accurate than the public statements of the administration in portraying the situation in Vietnam."[123] Nonetheless, the belief among military officers that the media contributed to America's defeat in Vietnam has persisted to this day and is the principal reason for the continuing animosity between the media and the military.

After Vietnam

In the late 1970s it became fashionable within the U.S. Department of Defense to refer to guerrilla insurgencies such as the Vietnam War as low-intensity conflicts. The term was coined to describe an increasingly common type of warfare in which front lines and rear areas were ill defined, political objectives outweighed military ones, and the principal goal was to win over the "hearts and minds" of populations in contested regions. "Low-intensity conflict" hardly seemed an adequate description for what had transpired in Vietnam—hundreds of thousands of people had died and millions of tons of munitions had been expended—but the term did highlight the growing prevalence of conflicts that were fundamentally different in character from the conventional encounters in World Wars I and II and the Korean War.[124]

The concept of low-intensity conflict was gradually refined to encompass peacekeeping, guerrilla warfare, terrorism and counterterrorism, and so-called peacetime strike contingencies such as the 1986 bombing of Libya. Although this was a diverse category of activities, they all had in common the idea of military operations in which there was no formal declaration of war and the United States was not fully mobilized for the conduct of hostilities. Low-intensity conflicts thus posed special challenges for both the military and the media, challenges that the Vietnam experience seemed to suggest they were ill prepared to meet.

One of the problems that the media encountered in reporting low-intensity operations was that they were often over before journalists arrived on the scene or even were aware of them. This happened in the 1975 *Mayaguez* incident, the abortive 1980 effort to rescue U.S. hostages in Iran, and the 1986 bombing attacks on Libya. Additionally, in the aftermath of Vietnam, the U.S. military was exceedingly cautious about permitting reporters near hostilities for fear of being criticized. The military's caution was reinforced by the politically charged atmosphere in which many low-intensity operations took place. Counterterrorism strikes, hostage rescues, and the like may not have involved the same high stakes as major conventional battles, but they generally occurred against a backdrop of political controversy in which failure could discredit political leaders and destroy military careers. They also required complete secrecy to succeed, a quality that did not encourage media participation.

Additional dilemmas were posed by the rapid advances in news gathering technologies. Lightweight videotaping equipment, satellite communications, and a host of other innovations made it possible to report hostilities in remote locations very quickly—so quickly, in fact, that the reports might influence the outcome of the hostilities. The danger that military security might be compromised by premature disclosure of sensitive information was greater than ever. The competitive spirit that prevailed in television news departments intensified this danger because reporters were under constant pressure to beat rival networks. This sometimes led reporters to become part of the story by participating in hostage negotiations, interviewing key players in crisis situations, and so on. It was becoming increasingly difficult to separate the media from the message.

Journalists understandably resented the efforts of military officers to limit their coverage and frequently accused the military of attempting to conceal key aspects of their activities. These charges confirmed many officers in their belief that the media were irresponsible and could not be trusted. The friction between soldiers and journalists came to a head in 1983 when the United States invaded the Caribbean island nation of Grenada. On October 25, 1983, elements of all four U.S. military services began a hastily planned operation to suppress a Marxist revolution on the island. One facet of the operation involved rescuing several hundred U.S. medical students believed to be threatened by the new revolutionary regime. In order to preserve the element of surprise and minimize casualties, the operation was planned and executed in complete secrecy, with no media participation. Journalists attempting to reach the island were excluded until two days after the fighting began, and then only small groups under military escort were allowed in for three more days. Reporters already on the island were initially prevented from filing stories. Restrictions on coverage were not fully relaxed until October 30, by which time the fighting had ceased.[125]

The exclusion of journalists from Grenada during the fighting provoked widespread criticism in the media. Reporters and editors complained that the restraints on them had deprived the public of vital information and had been imposed at least in part to hide such deficiencies in military performance as inadequate intelligence and poor tactical communications. The Defense Department generally rejected these complaints, contending that early media participation in the operation might have compromised its success and increased casualties. An article in a Defense Department publication subsequently stated, "No one in a position of responsibility in the military sufficiently trusted the press to keep a secret that could cost the lives of American servicemen."[126] The tone of coverage also tended to support the military's concern that reporters would be excessively critical of the operation. Secretary of Defense Caspar W. Weinberger later noted in his memoirs that "much of the media initially treated our Grenada operation as an unprovoked aggression against a peaceful Caribbean island of no strategic importance. The impression given was that the ordinary people of Grenada resented and resisted the intervention. In reality, an astonishing 97 percent of Grenadians polled later believed that they had truly been rescued by 'Papa Reagan.' "[127]

The challenge of managing news coverage of military operations in the modern environment was demonstrated by the size of the press contingent that sought to report the Grenada invasion. Although the intervention was a relatively minor operation that was concluded within a few days, hundreds of journalists tried to cover it. By October 27, 1983, two days after the invasion began, 369 American and foreign journalists had congregated on the neighboring island of Barbados, awaiting transit to Grenada. As Peter Braestrup has observed, this was roughly equal to the number of journalists accredited to General Eisenhower's headquarters in 1944 on the eve of the Normandy invasion. The ABC television network alone had twenty-five personnel in Barbados, a group bigger than the entire U.S. press pool that went ashore in Normandy on D day.[128]

It was clear that hundreds of journalists could not be allowed to roam about Grenada while fighting was still in progress; however, the Defense Department was sensitive to the criticism that it had made inadequate preparations to accommodate media coverage. In November 1983 the chairman of the Joint Chiefs of Staff established a commission to investigate how media relations could be better handled in future operations. The commission consisted of fourteen journalists and press relations officials and was headed by Major General Winant Sidle, who had served as senior information officer with the Military Assistance Command in Vietnam between 1967 and 1969. On August 23, 1984, the Sidle panel released its final report. It offered eight recommendations for facilitating future coverage of military operations:[129]

1. Public affairs planning for military operations should be conducted concurrently with operational planning.

2. If media pools appear to be the only feasible means of affording access to an operation, the pools should be as large as possible and should be used only so long as is absolutely necessary.

3. The Defense Department should study how to create "a preestablished and constantly updated accreditation or notification list of correspondents" that can be used to assemble a media pool on short notice.

4. The "basic tenet governing media access to military operations" should be the principle of voluntary compliance with security guidelines; "violations would mean exclusion of the correspondents concerned from further coverage of the operation."

5. Public affairs planning for military operations should include sufficient equipment and qualified military personnel to allow adequate coverage.

6. Planners should carefully consider the communications requirements necessary for media coverage so long as these do not interfere with military operations.

7. Planners should make provisions for the transportation needs of media representatives.
8. The Defense Department should take steps to improve communication and mutual understanding between the media and the military.

The most important aspect of the Sidle panel's recommendations was the proposal that a national media pool be created to cover operations in which full media access was not feasible. The media representatives on the panel made it clear that while they did not like the idea of restricting access to operations, a pool was preferable to complete exclusion. Secretary Weinberger accepted the commission's findings and directed the assistant secretary of defense for public affairs, Michael Burch, to begin implementing the recommendations. After discussions with members of the media, Burch formulated a pool concept that would include the following representation:

One news agency correspondent.

One news agency photographer.

One network television correspondent.

Two television technicians.

One network radio correspondent.

One national newsmagazine correspondent.

One national newsmagazine photographer.

Three newspaper correspondents.[130]

Procedures for designating a rotating group of pool reporters were established, and in April 1985 the national media pool had its first trial run, an exercise in which pool members were deployed to Honduras. The exercise did not go well; secrecy was compromised before it even began. In five additional exercises during 1985, 1986, and 1987, procedures were refined to the point where the system seemed to be functioning reasonably well. In July 1987 the first operational deployment of the national media pool took place when journalists were sent to the Persian Gulf to cover operation Earnest Will, the navy's escorting of oil tankers. Despite some minor problems, the pool did an acceptable job of reporting the escort operation. It thus appeared that a workable arrangement had been established for reconciling military security concerns with the needs of the media.[131]

In December 1989 the national media pool was activated for its first true combat deployment. Early on the morning of December 20, U.S. military forces launched a series of airborne attacks and landings in Panama aimed at deposing the country's anti-American dictator, Manuel Noriega. The military operation was a success; within days, most key tactical objectives had been achieved, and Noriega was reduced to the status of a fugitive. The pool deployment proved to be a fiasco. The sixteen-person pool that arrived in Panama hours after the invasion had begun was kept far from the fighting because of the security concerns of the U.S. commander on the scene. When reporters were finally given permission to venture forth into the combat area, helicopters to transport them were not available and communications for transmitting their stories frequently malfunctioned. The military's arrangements for facilitating coverage were so poorly conceived and executed that the assistant secretary of defense of public affairs accused U.S. officers in Panama of "incompetence," and pool members joked that the pool's motto should be *semper tardis* ("always late").[132]

Not all of the mistakes were committed by the military. *Time* magazine compromised the operation's security in the course of deciding which of its correspondents should accompany the pool. Several pool members did not bring valid passports or appropriate gear. Most of the reporters in the pool had no experience in covering combat.[133] But even if the journalists had been fully prepared, the way in which the Pentagon handled the deployment made effective coverage of the early action impossible. A Defense Department report on what went wrong later concluded that "excessive concern for secrecy prevented the Defense Department's media pool from reporting the critical opening battles of the U.S. invasion of Panama."[134] Noting the many logistical problems and delays the pool encountered, the report questioned whether its deployment was necessary:

> The decision to send a news pool from Washington was highly questionable. The story could have . . . been covered by a pool formed from U.S. news personnel already in Panama. . . . The Pentagon pool was established to enable U.S. news personnel to report the earliest possible action in a U.S. military operation in a remote area where there was no other American press presence. Panama did not fit that description.[135]

Even after Panama was opened up for coverage by other correspondents, problems continued to occur. The U.S. Southern Command in Panama had been expecting twenty-five or thirty journalists to cover the operation. When over three hundred reporters, photographers, cameramen, and sound technicians poured into the country, military press relations personnel and facilities were overwhelmed. The *Boston Globe* summarized the results:

> The U.S. government, after acquiescing to demands that it open Panama to coverage, has made it all but impossible for journalists to do their jobs during much of the last week. Indeed, more than 100 members of the

news media opted to take a military flight home on Saturday [December 24], many of them without filing a story. . . .

Until Saturday, armed guards had prevented reporters from leaving the U.S. military installations where they had been confined since Thursday, in many cases without a place to sleep other than on concrete or linoleum floors.

There were few telephones, just two at the principal facility at Howard Air Force Base where 350 members of the news media were kept. Those who could get to phones found themselves waiting for hours to get calls through the strained Panamanian central telephone facility. . . .

Then too, Murphy's Law—if something can go wrong, it will—seems to have taken hold in the army's overburdened public relations apparatus here.

The result, in many cases, has been a lack of information that has been reflected in the coverage of the U.S. intervention.[136]

Problems arose again in August 1990 when the United States began a major deployment of forces to Saudi Arabia to counter Iraq's invasion of Kuwait. The Pentagon initially decided not to activate the pool, reversed itself several days after the deployment had begun, and then reversed itself again two weeks later and allowed hundreds of journalists to visit the troops. Journalists complained that the guidelines for reporting the Saudi operation were too restrictive and that they were being denied access to important information. Pentagon concerns that media coverage might compromise security were increased when the air force chief of staff, General Michael J. Dugan, gave a candid interview to several correspondents, revealing sensitive information about U.S. war plans. Dugan was dismissed for his indiscretion.[137]

The American media and military thus began the final decade of the twentieth century still bedeviled by many of the same difficulties that had hampered the conduct and coverage of past conflicts. Although relations between the media and the military seemed to be improving, the relationship remained distinctly adversarial in character. Soldiers continued to worry that reporters would compromise security and distort the facts, while journalists continued to resent efforts to limit their ability to cover military operations. The viability of the media pool concept was being questioned by soldiers and journalists alike, but no clear alternative had emerged. After 200 years of war coverage, the problems causing friction between the media and the military were still at work and unlikely to be resolved to the satisfaction of either side any time soon.

Conclusions

Alexander Hamilton's prediction in *Federalist* 84 that "the public papers will be expeditious messengers of intelligence to the most remote inhabitants of the Union" has come true to a degree far greater than he probably could have imagined. In his day, it often took weeks for important information to reach the small number of people who read the papers. News of the battle at Lexington and Concord in 1775 did not appear in some southern papers until more than a month after they occurred. News from Europe took much longer to arrive, and news from the rest of the world seldom arrived at all.

Today the mass media—the successors to the "public papers" of the eighteenth century—make it possible for vast segments of the public to observe important developments as they happen. Citizens throughout the nation routinely watch live coverage of the deliberations of Congress, and have access to many different accounts of the government's performance on key issues. The public has come to expect that historical events in distant places, such as the brutal suppression of demonstrators in Tiananmen Square and the opening of the Berlin Wall, will be available for viewing on the same day that they occur.

The advent of nearly instantaneous global news coverage in the late twentieth century is unquestionably a major achievement, comparable in importance to the emergence of mass circulation newspapers made possible by the spread of literacy in the late nineteenth century. In the special case of war, the new means of gathering and presenting the news create dilemmas that the founders of the republic never had to consider. The same media that provide citizens with access to distant battlefields can be used to transmit information that influences the outcome of military operations. They can also be exploited by adversaries to undermine public support for those operations, a danger made greater by the prevailing fealty of journalists to the principle of objectivity; news gatherers are expected to act as neutral conveyors of information, a role definition that increases their vulnerability to manipulation by enemies.

In order to avoid the possibility that the tremendous power of the news media will be used to subvert national interests, it is essential that journalists and soldiers share a common understanding of the proper role of war coverage. Unfortunately, history demonstrates that such understanding is difficult to achieve and seldom endures from one conflict to the next. Occasionally a conflict such as World War II occurs in which the necessity of victory is so widely accepted that the media and the military can work effectively together to achieve a shared goal. More often, though, wars are controversial, and the correspondents sent to cover them become caught up in the controversy. Edward R. Murrow, the famous radio correspondent whose reports from London during the blitz helped make the case for American entry into World War II, was blacked out by his own network a decade later for criticizing U.S. involvement in Korea.[138]

When wars are controversial, as most are, it is inevitable that some of the coverage of them will be critical or negative. Even if reporters are careful not to disclose sensitive information, soldiers will object to the tenor of coverage as detrimental to the war effort, disloyal, and so on. To a large degree, this simply reflects divergent views among soldiers and journalists as to the proper role of war coverage. But it may also reflect a belief among solders that negative coverage is endangering their lives or making defeat more likely. When this belief becomes widespread within the military, as it did in both the Korean and Vietnam wars, it is very difficult for soldiers and journalists to work together. And yet they must work together. Finding ways to reduce the friction in media-military relations is important. This can be achieved, even during intensely controversial wars, if some basic principles are recognized.

First, soldiers and journalists need to understand that there is no ideal solution to the dilemmas posed by war coverage. Heavy censorship of war dispatches may reduce the danger of unnecessary casualties, but it may also deprive the public of information critical to the preservation of democratic institutions. Unbridled freedom to report whatever takes place on the battlefield may guarantee that such information reaches the public, but it could also result in needless deaths or military defeat. The constraints imposed on the media in wartime will always be a trade-off between the undesirable consequences of these two extremes. Whatever arrangements are established for managing war coverage, they can operate effectively only if the media and the military cooperate to make them work. In the absence of cooperation, the likelihood of coverage that is inaccurate, dangerous, or irresponsible increases. Neither soldiers nor journalists should expect to be totally comfortable with the guidelines governing war coverage, but they should be able to recognize that it is in their own interests to make those guidelines work so that excesses can be avoided.

If the recent pattern of limited wars fought for limited purposes persists, the preferred approach to managing war coverage probably will emphasize some form of voluntary restraint on the part of journalists rather than extensive censorship. Heavy censorship makes much sense in total wars where national survival is at stake, such as World War II, but it is difficult to justify to journalists and the public in less intense conflicts. The virtue of voluntary restraint, when it works, is that it reduces the resentment of journalists about limits placed on their coverage while giving soldiers some confidence that the media can be trusted. But voluntary restraint cannot work spontaneously. The military must provide correspondents with detailed guidelines as to what should not be reported and to assist them in those cases where the guidelines may be ambiguous. The media must police themselves, so that reporters who go too far suffer some type of peer group sanction. If both sides do their jobs correctly, voluntary restraint can function well; if they do not, the system rapidly breaks down.

A second principle that needs to be recognized is the obligation of journalists to be adequately prepared for the challenge of reporting conflicts. Responsible war coverage is a demanding undertaking, and it requires correspondents who are conversant with military affairs. Prior to the Vietnam War, most journalists who covered wars could draw on personal experiences in the military services to help them place events in a meaningful context. Today many journalists who cover conflicts have never been in the military and have little appreciation of why the armed forces function the way they do. The result is that their coverage frequently betrays a fundamental ignorance of military realities. Reporters often lack the most basic understanding of how weapons work, how the armed forces are organized, why certain tactics are used, and so on. This reflects a failure to train journalists adequately for their job, and it needs to be remedied. It is not essential to have served in the military to be a competent war correspondent—although it certainly helps—but surely reporters should know what a battalion is or how a tank works before they begin sending dispatches from the front.

Third, military personnel need to recognize that the press plays a central role in the functioning of democracy, and reporting wars is one part of that role. Many soldiers have come to regard media representatives as enemies who can be neither trusted nor dealt with honestly—an attitude detrimental to the public interest that should not be tolerated. The entire journalistic profession should not be made to bear the burden of enmity fostered by a military mythology about who lost the Vietnam War. Perhaps some journalists deserve to be mistrusted and criticized; most do not. To their credit, the military services have recently demonstrated awareness that they have a problem in their attitude toward the media and have taken steps to encourage a more positive relationship. These efforts are in the military's own interest and should be continued.

Observance of these three principles will help mitigate the tensions between journalists and soldiers; however, there is no way those tensions can be eliminated entirely. Even if the dilemmas of war coverage are fully appreciated on both sides and journalists and soldiers develop a sympathetic view of each others' needs and responsibilities, frictions will persist. Tension between major public institutions is inherent in the functioning of democracy, and it is not surprising that such tension is most pronounced in a setting where lives are being lost and national interests are at stake. The friction that often permeates media-military relations should not be seen as a completely undesirable phenomenon. To some extent, it simply reflects the fact that democracy is working as planned. Viewed in this light, the conflict between journalists and soldiers is not only unavoidable; it is part of what wars are fought to defend.

II
Perspectives on the Media-Military Relationship

2

The Washington Defense Journalist: An Eighteenth-Century View

Paul Mann

> A journalist is an historian, not indeed of the highest class, nor of the number of those whose works bestow immortality upon others or themselves; yet, like other historians, he distributes for a time reputation or infamy, regulates the opinion of the week, raises hopes and terrors, inflames or allays the violence of the people. He ought therefore to consider himself as subject at least to the first law of history, the obligation to tell truth.
> —Samuel Johnson, "Of the Duty of a Journalist" (1758)

Samuel Johnson, the eighteenth-century literary genius, won fame for compiling the first historical dictionary of the English language. For much of his life, however, he eked out a living as a miscellaneous journalist in London. He was thoroughly versed in journalism's practices and pitfalls when the trade was in its infancy.

I will use his "Of the Duty of a Journalist" to examine a few of the traps that snare Washington journalists, including defense reporters. I will argue that we report too much for each other and our government sources; that this phenomenon isolates us from our readers and audiences; that our remoteness is evident in a lack of imaginative understanding of what the public finds relevant and accessible; that our insularity adds to the public's feeling that national affairs, including defense, are alien. In addition, the complexity of most of today's issues isolates reporters from the public, just as it divides government and the citizen.

The national beat resembles the local one; in some ways, the federal government is just the village board writ large. Moreover, the pressures to "go local" on a given beat thrust reporters into the role of Washington insider, which tends to divorce them from their audiences. This is particularly true of military affairs. The subject remains largely foreign to the popular mind despite the expanded media coverage prompted by the Reagan buildup and recent U.S.-Soviet arms control initiatives. The reason seems to be traceable to both the nature of military affairs and to the ways in which journalists cover them. At least three characteristics of the military make it hard for the public to understand: its huge mass, its enormous diversity and specialization, and its arcane vocabulary. The pressures on Washington defense reporters to be an insider are fused with the difficult nature of the beat in a manner that thwarts public understanding of the subject.

Escaping this dilemma would be difficult; substantial, if not revolutionary, changes in journalism would be required. At least as much time and space would have to be devoted to basic instruction in military issues as to the reporting of them. At the same time, major improvements in public and civic education would have to be achieved to spur popular interest in national security affairs.

In about a thousand words, "Of the Duty of a Journalist" provides both the layperson and the practitioner with keen insights into what reporters must contend with in their daily round and why they are likely to fall down. If, after the exercise, the layperson has a better understanding of the journalist and the journalist a renewed appreciation of the infirmities of the profession, then perhaps some small step will have been taken toward closing the gulf that exists between the two.

The gulf is deep. The public holds reporters in low esteem, perceiving them as arrogant, pushy, self-righteous, churlish, and biased. Like the sports industry, the news industry is replete with vicious elbowing and knees to the groin. Journalists are besotted with the craze to get the story first. They worship at the feet of the false god competition, smug in the notion that rivalry will spontaneously fulfill journalism's obligations as a public trust. The public is not deceived; it does not care a brass farthing who gets a scoop. Samuel Johnson wrote 230 ago:

> The present state of many of our papers is such that it may be doubted not only whether the compilers know their duty, but whether they have endeavored or wished to know it. . . . [Journalists] know, by experience, however destitute of reason, that what is desired will be credited without nice examination; they do not therefore always limit their narratives by possibility, but slaughter armies without battles, and conquer countries without invasions. There are other violations of truth admitted only to gratify idle curiosity which yet are mischievous in their consequences and hateful in their contrivance.[1]

It has been said that in reporting the news, journalists write history's first draft. There is some truth to this, but it is an undiscriminating remark. It comes close to suggesting that a journalist is a historian by definition, which is not true, and it ignores that not all news is history and not all facts are historical facts.

Still, when journalists assume a historian's perspective, they may be better equipped, in Johnson's words, to judge what will be plain and what will be obscure to the public. As historian Paul Gagnon wrote recently, history teaches judgment and farsightedness. The journalist's daily business is the immediate, which causes nearsightedness.

Good journalism requires judgment of a high order. Edward Hallett Carr, the British historian, noted thirty years ago: "Every journalist knows today that the most effective way to influence opinion is by the selection and arrangement of the appropriate facts. It used to be said that facts speak for themselves. This is, of course, untrue. The facts speak when the historian [or journalist] calls on them. It is he who decides which facts to give the floor, and in what order and context."[2] It is in these everyday decisions that journalists exercise judgment in haste. Most would agree that a historical perspective can assist in that exercise.

But journalists are students of human nature as well as history. They know something about judgment that Paul Gagnon did not acknowledge. An ancient Roman essayist put it succinctly: "Every man prefers belief to the exercise of judgment." It is the temptation to believe that journalists are asked, professionally, to resist. Being mortal, they sometimes exercise disciplined judgment and at other times succumb to belief. They are prone to mischief in either instance. "We're a race of spies," wrote the popular journalist of the French Revolution, Nicolas Edme Restif de la Bretonne. "We don't participate or form bonds, yet we describe, classify and sometimes confuse everything. That's why we're a curious lot."

Johnson's vision is an ideal. Ideals are important, but they are not often effective as techniques, in either journalism or other professions.

"What would happen if men remained faithful to the ideals of their youth?" Don Paolo asks in Ignazio Silone's novel, *Bread and Wine.*[3] In response, Don Luigi raises his arms to heaven as if to say, "It would be the end of the world!"

The Local Character of the National Beat

More than twenty years have passed since my cub days chasing local news, but the Washington beat still reminds me of the local one. During the past ten years, my reporting assignments have included the Defense Department, the State Department, Congress, and the White House. Each of these institutions has seemed somewhat like a small-town community, with its own distinct subculture and folkways. Each has in common some of the parochialism and insularity prevalent in villages and towns.

Each has its own "mayor"—cabinet secretary, House Speaker, or president. Each has its own "aldermen" or "board of supervisors." In the State and Defense departments, these include counselors, under secretaries, assistant secretaries, and deputy assistant secretaries; in the White House, they comprise the cabinet and National Security Council; in Congress, they are committee heads, caucus leaders, and floor whips, who in certain roles function as in-house ward heelers.

Each of these institutions has its own administrative and bureaucratic legions. These are arrayed in countless "precincts," led by "bosses" who, somewhat reminiscent of old-time political machines, maintain communal traditions while the elected officials come and go.

Top federal agencies mimic each other. The Defense Department contains within it a miniature State Department, the branch for international security policy. The State Department houses a tiny Defense Department, the politico-military affairs division. The president has an Office of Management and Budget and the legislature the Congressional Budget Office. The White House also has a composite State and defense Department, the National Security Council.

There are other features that convey the feeling of localness. The Defense Department has its own shopping "mall," bus depot, cafeteria, kiosk, and metro stop. The State Department has its own bookstore and "campus" auditorium, the Loy Henderson. Congress has its own barber and shoeshine shops, "Inside Mail" service, and a miniature subway system between the Capitol and the House and Senate office buildings. The buzzers summoning droves of lawmakers to floor votes evoke memories of the change of classes in high school. The White House is the pristine little haven set apart as the village estate or local museum.

For a reporter, the most obvious similarity is in the press facilities. Reporters permanently assigned to the White House, the Defense Department, the State Department, and Congress have their own desks, cubicles, filing booths, or galleries. These resemble the little bullpens of local newspapers.

The Hazards of Being an Insider

Good reporters immerse themselves in the subculture that constitutes their beat. Gaining knowledge of a beat, learning to speak its common tongue: these oblige journalists to take on some of the coloration of the local community to which they are assigned. To succeed, they must become insiders.

Certain occupational hazards attend this role. I have said (based on the admittedly soft ground of personal impression) that journalists report too much for each other. This impression is not new. In 1981 the Brookings Institution, a liberal public policy think tank in Washington, D.C., published an insightful book by Stephen Hess, *The Washington Reporters.*[4] From a succession of interviews, surveys, and questionnaires in the late 1970s, involving hundreds of reporters, Hess found that Washington reporters regarded themselves as "increasingly out of touch with the nation." He quoted a former reporter, who recounted his days at the *New York Times,* as saying, "We really wrote for one another. Our primary reference group was spread around us in the newsroom." Tellingly, Hess discovered a relationship between reporters who felt out of touch with the rest of the country and the degree to which they fraternized with their brethren in Washington. Nearly half those surveyed said their closest friends in Washington were other journalists. And among their nonjournalist friends, at least 55 percent were in government or government-related fields, such as lobbying or political party work. Reporters who said that none of their closest friends were journalists believed the press corps was more isolated than those who said their three closest friends were reporters.

The question arises: are journalists out of touch, or do they just feel out of touch? Journalists are no better qualified than anyone else at self-diagnosis, so skepticism is in order. Rather than isolation, they may be suffering from paranoia, another occupational hazard. Hess quoted a wire service man. "Reporters anywhere are out of touch. Even when I was in North Carolina, I didn't focus on roads and schools, which people really care about. I wrote about ERA [equal rights amendment], which is what I cared about."

If it is true that reporters everywhere are out of touch, then Washington reporters may be doubly so. They not only write too much for themselves and each other; they also write too much for their government sources.

The national press corps provides invaluable information to the federal government. It performs the same indispensable task for the government community that local reporters do in cities, towns, and villages across the country. They are essential interlocutors for those who inhabit federal agencies. Defense and other officials like to grumble about their treatment in the press but admit that some part of what they know about the goings on in their own agencies, to say nothing of those in others, comes from reporters. Indeed, government officials constantly use the media as the cockpit in which to fight through policy disputes and turf battles. That is the principal reason so much is leaked to the press. It is a major arena for thrashing out public policy.

This has generated a thriving export-import business among reporters and their government news sources. These transactions are vital to the functions of press and government. But it is reasonable to suppose that this insider trading in information compounds the reporter's isolation from the public. The Washington reporter's insularity is interlocked with the government bureaucrat's. The reporter is moving stories from the beat back to the beat. The loop is closed. The public is put in the position of eavesdropper.

It was Samuel Johnson's opinion that the journalist,

> above most other men, ought to be acquainted with the lower orders of mankind, that he may be able to judge what will be plain and what will be obscure; what will require a comment and what will be apprehended without explanation. He is to consider himself not as writing to students and statesmen alone, but to shopkeepers and artisans, who have little time to bestow upon mental attainments, but desire, upon easy terms, to know how the world goes.[5]

This will always be good advice, no matter what period of history a journalist is living in. Reporters surveyed in the Brookings study said that travel, getting out among the people, was the answer to their isolation. That is a solution but one insufficient to the times.

Political commentators have suggested in recent years that the sheer complexity of today's issues (defense is a prime example) has driven a dangerous wedge between the American people and their government. They have argued that the health of the republic may be at some risk because voters believe that great matters of state are largely inaccessible to them. Complexity is said to heighten citizens' perceptions of the great distance between themselves and the levers of power. In consequence, the argument goes, they are robbed of incentives to be well informed and to participate in the electoral process.

This sounds rather like pop psychologizing, yet it also has the ring of plausibility. By one account, the nation's founders anticipated it. The *Philadelphia National Gazette* quoted James Madison in 1791 as saying, "The larger a country, the less easy for its real opinion to be ascertained, and the less difficult to be counterfeited . . . the more extensive a country, the more insignificant is each individual in his own eyes. This may be unfavorable to liberty." My guess is that the public's feelings of remoteness from great issues are as varied and complicated as the issues themselves and will not submit to generalization. But to the extent the public does feel that affairs of state are remote, surely Washington reporters risk accentuating the feeling by writing too much for themselves, for each other, and for their sources.

Proximity to Power

Perhaps the greatest hazard to Washington reporters is their proximity to great power—to those who wield it and broker it. As relative insiders, they experience power and privilege vicariously. They bask in the glamour of entrée to the Oval Office or the well of the Senate. From one end of

Pennsylvania Avenue to the other, they have ringside seats to history in the making. They are at pains to say that the White House is the most boring beat in Washington and joke that they bear witness more often to soporifics than to history. Much of this is attitudinizing. They are in love with being at the center of things—or at least the illusion that they are.

In this proximity to power, in their vicarious experience of it, journalists risk believing they know more than they do. Their access to top sources, however limited, is still beguiling. Especially when stripping away a little bit of military secrecy, a reporter can begin to feel quite worldly.

This is a wonderful irony because Washington journalists know next to nothing independently. They are very much at the mercy of their sources. This is truer today than ever before because, as the Brookings study showed, they use no documents in nearly 75 percent of their stories. This is a dreadful waste of often valuable, even crucial, information, which could be used to authenticate the credibility of oral sources.

Hess pointed out that the news is skewed by those sources most willing to talk. And "reliance on oral research makes a reporter risk becoming 'the prisoner of the source.'"

No other journalist has more determination than the Washington reporter determined not to be deceived. The stakes are highest on the national beat. Yet they would have a greater claim to realism and credibility if they acknowledged how often they are likely to be misled. "The journalist, however honest, will frequently deceive, because he will frequently be deceived himself," Samuel Johnson wrote. "He is obliged to transmit the earliest intelligence before he knows how far it may be credited; he relates transactions yet fluctuating in uncertainty; he delivers reports of which he knows not the authors. It cannot be expected that he should know more than he is told, or that he should not sometimes be hurried down the current of a popular clamor. All that he can do is to consider attentively, and determine impartially, to admit no falsehoods by design, and to retract those which he shall have adopted by mistake."[6]

Apart from events—presidential vetoes, congressional votes, Supreme Court decisions—much of Washington news, especially that about the brokering of power, is second-hand news, collected from senior officials, deputies, aides, staff, and "sources." Reporters are not candid with the public about the impact of this filtering process. They do not attend, to name only a few, meetings of the president and his chief of staff, the Cabinet, the National Security Council, the Joint Chiefs of Staff, or the closed sessions of congressional committees. I suspect that the authoritative tones in which journalists report the news convey the misimpression that they are writing or speaking from firsthand knowledge, however numerous the attributions provided. They do not often go about admitting to readers and audiences that they are the prisoners of their sources, frequently secondary and tertiary sources at that.

Cynicism also inclines journalists to believe they know more than they actually do. They employ cynicism as a kind of badge of honor for protection from deception. On occasion, however, they are too cynical by half, and this can be as self-deceiving as proximity to power. An excess of cynicism and suspicion precipitates rushing to judgment and imputing dark motives to politicians and government officials when such motives do not always exist.

Something about the profession—perhaps overexposure to the nether side of human nature or the radical unhappiness of life—tempts journalists to believe that the practice of cynicism makes one appear more credible. Tacitus caught the truth of this in Book One of the *Histories*: People listen with ready ears to spite, "for flattery is subject to the shameful charge of servility, but malignity makes a false show of independence."[7]

This is why they do not ever want to write a puff piece, especially about a politician. It involves "the shameful charge of servility." To protect their credibility, reporters almost always try to point out what a leader's ulterior motives or self-interests may have been—I emphasize "may have been"—in making a decision or taking action. This makes them look savvy and tough, attributes they value highly. They also ascribe political motives because they believe privately that the voters are too ignorant to do so.

To be sure, there is room for cynicism, or at least enlightened skepticism, on this score. As Garry Wills put it in *Nixon Agonistes*, "Politicians are very deft at persuading themselves that the world's best interests just happen to coincide with the advancement of their own careers."[8] Cicero sent a letter to his friend Atticus in 49 B.C. asking, "Are men to rule provinces and direct affairs, not one of whom could steer his own fortunes for two months?"

It does not follow, however, that a leader is never disinterested, never acts on the merits, never puts the national interest ahead of his or her own. To be sure, government leaders do not set aside self-aggrandizement nearly as often as they should—it is bound to figure as at least one component in most of their calculations—but it is a fairly safe bet that they do so more often than reporters give them credit for, which is to say almost never.

After a press conference with, say, the president, the secretary of defense, or some other official, reporters talk shop, discussing the ambiguities of what was said and speculating on what was left unsaid. Was there a hidden agenda? they ask. Any political significance to the timing of the press briefing? Was the president sending a signal to the Congress on some issue or testing public opinion before introducing a policy initiative? Did the official go public to resolve some internal policy dispute between agencies or between cabinet secretaries? Did the give-and-take of the press conference suggest that the president or the secretary might have been "taken prisoner" by his advisers on an issue?

They are trying to deduce the story behind the story—a laudable objective if there is one. They suffer from no inability to formulate plausible interpretations, which they seek to buttress with views from "informed sources." But plausibility is not accuracy, and sources have their own purposes. Even if they did not, they naturally proffer varying, sometimes conflicting, accounts of their superiors' thinking.

What is striking about all this is journalists' confidence that they can rapidly divine what is going on backstage, let alone apprehend events at stage center that have not yet matured. Confidently they engage in instant analysis on television and confidently write the news analysis column for the next edition. Not infrequently, these are done with impressive flair, fluency, intelligence, shrewdness—and apparent credibility. And yet, how quickly their opinions and understanding might change were they placed suddenly inside the White House or the defense secretary's office.

"Infinite are the secrets of a prince; infinite the things to which he must attend," wrote the sixteenth-century Italian diplomat and historian Francesco Guicciardini. "It is therefore rash to judge their actions hastily. Very often what you think he has done for one reason, he has done for another; what you think done by chance or imprudently, is in fact done with great skill and profound wisdom."[9]

The Defense Beat

Retired Republican Senator Barry Goldwater lamented the military establishment's huge mass some years ago when he was chairman of the Senate Armed Services Committee. "We're the only country that I know of in the world that has four Air Forces, a Navy with an Air Force and an Army, an Army with a Navy and an Air Force that doesn't have any boats yet, they haven't been around long enough."[10]

As others have remarked countless times before, the scope and scale of the U.S. military establishment are beyond the capacity of the human mind to visualize. So too is its $300 billion annual budget. Even to the well versed, the dimensions of the military virtually defy imagination, as Goldwater knew.

A reporter could have a lifetime career covering a single one of the thousand facets of the military: any one of the four services (and some of their constituent agencies); the Office of the Secretary of Defense; strategy, tactics, doctrine, operations and maintenance, research and development, planning and budgeting, management, technology, weapons, contracting, procurement law, training, personnel, intelligence, counterintelligence, war-gaming, strategic, theater and battlefield nuclear weapons; conventional forces, the North Atlantic Treaty Organization, communications, command and intelligence, logistics, recruiting, the guard and reserves.

Each of these and countless other elements is characterized by mammoth sprawl and excruciating intricacy.

Goldwater's Democratic successor as committee chairman, Senator Sam Nunn, (D–Georgia), spoke the definitive word on the military's diversity and specialization, illustrating how they trap lawmakers in an avalanche of minutiae. Nunn recalled that one fiscal year, Congress had altered the army's budget request for smoke grenade launchers and muzzle boresights, pared the navy's request for parachute flares and practice bombs, and directed the air force to cut funding for garbage trucks, street cleaners, and scoop loaders. "This is ridiculous!" Nunn exclaimed. "The current Congressional review of the defense program would make a fitting version of the popular game Trivial Pursuit."[11]

As if the military's trackless size and complexity were not enough, journalists must negotiate them engulfed by military parlance. This impels them to become bilingual lest they be shut out. The Pentagon speaks in the awful tongues of jargon and acronyms, those archenemies of cogent thought, clear exposition and comprehensible reporting. Journalists communicate in Mil-speak—ATAs, ATFs, ASATs, SICBMs, SINCGARs, JSTARs, SALT, START, INF, CFE, ABM, MIRV, AWACS, WWMCCS, ALCM, GLCM and SLCM, CV, CVA, and CVAN—to engage military sources and persuade them of their credibility. Sooner or later, even the most disciplined reporters will discover themselves lapsing into this argot in their stories.

In too many instances, they cannot avoid it. Stories about arms control, for example, would be impossible to write without references to ICBMs (intercontinental ballistic missiles), SLBMs (submarine-launched ballistic missiles), MIRVs (multiple independently retargetable reentry vehicles), ALCMs (air-launched cruise missiles), and SLCMs (sea-launched cruise missiles). Acronyms can be spelled out, and frequently they are. But when they litter the page, they disfigure it, guaranteeing the reader's eyes will glaze over. Spelling them out begs the question of whether readers know what *ballistic* means or what a reentry vehicle is. If readers had the time and patience to learn these basics, they would then face the arduous task of figuring out nuclear theology's mathematical formulas for computing such inscrutable equations as warhead-to-target ratios. The relevance of this, even to the most well-informed reader, is on par with Albertus Magnus and medieval Scholasticism. It is surprising, therefore, with what frequency jargon-laden defense stories make the front page of the nation's leading newspapers or the inside of popular newsweekly magazines. How many harried readers will plough through them?

To bring the matter into sharper focus, consider these questions. How many readers or viewers nationwide could identify the secretary of defense? How many would recognize the name of the chairman of the Joint Chiefs of Staff, the nation's supreme military body? How many would know the elemental distinction between strategic (long-range) and tactical (short-range) weapons? How many would know (or care) that Congress deliberates two defense budgets in each fiscal year? Why was it that during Senate ratification of the intermediate-range nuclear forces treaty, public opinion polls showed that a majority of the American people favored the treaty but did not know what INF meant?

This journalistic problem is not new either. Samuel Johnson criticized the military coverage in the eighteenth-century London press for its inaccessibility to the public. "Terms of war and navigation are inserted which are utterly unintelligible to all who are not engaged in military or naval business," he complained. Surely he would be aghast at the appalling plague the military-industrial complex has visited upon the language in the twentieth century. If that plague were lifted tomorrow, defense reporters would find it easier to relay news of the subject to the nation and the nation would find it easier to understand. But as a whole, the subject probably would remain alien to the public.

It is a pity that military affairs are so foreign to the popular mind because so much of the nation's treasure is sacrificed to national security and too much of that treasure is wasted. Moreover, the subject can be fascinating and intellectually compelling.

If some critical proportion of the voting public were truly well informed about defense, greater pressures for accountability might be brought to bear on elected officials. Congressional and press oversight is now scattershot and unfocused. Only public indignation could turn this situation around.

That does not appear to be in the cards. In recent times, no politician of national stature has been able to tap a pool of public resentment against military waste. By official Defense Department admissions, waste in the form of rework, scrap, and poor quality control has cost the taxpayers tens of billions of dollars annually over the past ten years. Extrapolating from these estimates, perhaps hundreds of billions of dollars have been lost since the end of World War II. Yet this does not play in Peoria. Here again it may be the magnitude of the problem that blunts popular understanding of it and thence demands for reform.

Despite the increased resources the national media devoted to defense in the 1980s, public ignorance of the subject has remained widespread, according to various opinion polls. One could argue from this evidence that the public deserves some credit for cleaving to the axiom that ignorance is bliss.

Imagine a group of men and women from around the country coming to Washington for ninety days to participate in the Pentagon's planning and budgeting process and attend some defense budget hearings on Capitol Hill. It would not be long before they joined Senator Nunn in pronouncing the system ridiculous. They might find it difficult to decide, however, which is worse: the absurdity or the tedium.

Accordingly, the bulk of defense coverage in the popular media will continue to be driven by events. Reporters, editors, and producers are well aware that public interest is confined largely to the outbreak of war, job losses associated with reductions in military spending, or the occasional scandal. Otherwise the subject will go unremarked in the public forum. In the mid-1980s polls indicated the loss of public interest in the Reagan buildup before it had really begun. Notably this occurred before the outcry over $600 toilet seats and the spareparts price scandal. Reaction to that was predictable. It was one of those rare instances in which the public could identify with a defense issue because they had firsthand experience with which to compare the price of a screwdriver at the local hardware store with that paid by the Pentagon. Unfortunately the media failed to instruct the public adequately or evenhandedly about the nature of the purchasing system that makes such pricing inevitable. Moreover, it should be remembered that the media did not ferret out the story, a sobering commentary on journalistic initiative. Secretary of Defense Caspar W. Weinberger lighted the fuse. It produced a firestorm because of its timing. It coincided with a nearly $2.5 trillion peacetime buildup.

With defense spending now in decline, it is unlikely the media will unleash a swarm of investigative reporters in search of waste and scandalous prices. The subject is not trendy anymore. The drug war and the savings and loan crisis have supplanted it.

The point is that the press probably could unearth such stories at any time, not only because of the chronic nature of abuse but also because of the built-in nature of waste and inefficiency in military procurement. To a journalist's consternation, however, a serious treatment of the problems of procurement collides head on with the endlessly complicated and stultifying character of the subject.

Conclusion

Is it up to defense reporters to persuade the public of the relevance of military affairs to them as taxpayers and citizens? Should they confine coverage only to those issues with which citizens can personally identify?

Samuel Johnson appeared to think so. He said the reporter is to consider that he writes for artisans and shopkeepers as well as statesmen and that therefore he is to write "upon easy terms." He said the journalist could hope that his labors would not be overlooked if he strove to inquire after truth, diligently imparted it, resolutely refused to admit into his paper whatever is injurious to private reputation, related transactions with greater clearness than others, and sold more instruction at a cheaper rate.

Today matters seem even more difficult (though the search for truth has never been easy). The grievous need for instruction, in military affairs and many others, appears larger than journalists can fill. Yet, paradoxically, the demand to fill it is at an ebb. If opinion polls are to be believed, the public is not interested.

Few weeks go by without some report in the press about public ignorance of current affairs, high politics, history, geography, mathematics, and science; about the lamentable state of public education; about growing illiteracy and the shriveling of fundamental skills in reading and writing. Regrettably, there are few signs that citizens are being trained in what Franklin Roosevelt called the high Athenian sense, which compels a person "to live his life unceasingly aware that its civic significance is its most abiding."[12]

Presumably the deficiencies of public and civic education place enlarged tutorial burdens on journalists. Clearly when national education is in decline, journalists are put at a further disadvantage.

To function properly, national reporters must be able to assume some irreducible level of public interest in matters of state. Otherwise they are consigned to an unworthy choice: their reporting must sink to an egregiously low common denominator that is without pertinence to the nation's discourse, or they must be content with reporting inside the cocoon that already has grown up around them, their colleagues, their sources, and statesmen.

Washington journalists have much to answer for in regard to walling themselves off from the public. They are long overdue for a protracted bout of professional introspection in that regard. It is in their own interest to dismantle the cocoon—and in the interests of the republic as well.

But it is very difficult to see how reporters can reawaken popular interest in serious affairs, military or otherwise, in the absence of singular improvements in public education. They have an undeniable role in public education but cannot remedy its defects, having so many of their own.

Samuel Johnson admonished journalists to tell truth. "This is not much to be required," he said. "Yet this is more than the writers of news seem to exact from themselves." Perhaps he was being disingenuous. Surely this poetic genius, who understood profoundly the treacheries of human motive, recognized that inquiring after truth—note that he said "truth," not "the" truth—is, to say the least, problematical. Or perhaps by "truth" he meant accuracy. Whichever he meant and however easy he believed telling truth was, Johnson also knew the task was easy to evade. Why this is so was made plain by Josh Billings, the nineteenth-century land agent who published almanacs and collections of witticisms: "As scarce as truth is, the supply has always been in excess of demand."

3
The Military's War with the Media: Causes and Consequences

Bernard E. Trainor

At first they are polite, respectfully prefacing each question with "sir." But when faced with their own prejudices, the veneer of civility evaporates, hostility surfaces, and the questions give way to a feeding frenzy of accusations. I have experienced this phenomenon repeatedly when discussing relations between the military and the media with young officers and cadets at service academies and professional military schools. It is clear that today's officer corps carries as part of its cultural baggage a loathing for the press.

Indeed relations with the press—a term applied to both print and television media—are probably worse now than at any other period in the history of the republic. I say this recognizing that Vietnam is usually cited as the nadir in military-media relations. At least during the Vietnam War, military men actually experienced what they judged to be unfair treatment at the hands of the fourth estate, and the issue was out in the open.

The majority of today's career officers, however, have had no association with the press. Most of them were children during the war. But all of them suffer this institutional form of posttraumatic syndrome. It is a legacy of the war, and it takes root soon after they enter service. Like racism, anti-Semitism, and all other forms of bigotry, it is irrational but nonetheless real. The credo of the military seems to be "duty, honor, country, and hate the media."

Although most officers no longer say the media stabbed them in the back in Vietnam, the military still smarts over the nation's humiliation in Indochina and subconsciously still blames television and the press for loss of public support for the war. Today the hostility manifests itself in complaints that the press will not keep a secret and that it endangers lives by revealing details of sensitive operations. The myth of the media as an unpatriotic, left-wing antimilitary establishment is thus perpetuated.

Having spent most of my adult life in the military and very little of it as a journalist, I am more qualified to comment on military culture than that of the media, and I must admit that in the post-Vietnam years, I too was biased against the media. But having feet in both camps now gives me a unique perspective, which I try to share with each, particularly the military.

Did the press stab the military in the back during Vietnam? Hardly. The press initially supported the war, but as casualties mounted and the Johnson administration failed to develop a coherent strategy to bring it to a satisfactory conclusion, the press became critical. Whether it influenced public opinion or simply reflected it will be argued for years to come. But it was a misguided policy that was primarily at fault for the debacle, not the media.

The media, however, were guilty of instances of unfair and sensational reporting that veterans of that war still resent. This was particularly true in the latter stages when the nation was weary of nightly war news and cub newspaper and television journalists tried to make headlines out of thin gruel. More supervision over them should have been exercised by editors, but it was not, and many in the military, already frustrated by the war, felt that the press was deliberately trying to humiliate them.

The legacy of the war sharpened the tension that exists between the media and the military, but it is not its cause. The roots of tension are in the very nature of the institutions. The military is hierarchical, with great inner pride and loyalties. It is the antithesis of a democracy and must be so if it is to be effective. It is action oriented and impatient with outside interference. Many things it legitimately does make little sense to civilians, who have little knowledge of military matters. The military wants only to be left alone to carry out its assigned mission. A free press, on the other hand, is one of the great virtues of a democracy, wherein the concentration of power is viewed as a danger.

The press is a watchdog over institutions of power—military, political, economic, and social. Its job is to inform the people about the doings of its institutions. By its very nature, it is skeptical and intrusive. As a result, there will always be a divergence of interests between the two. That both are essential to the well-being of the nation is beyond question, but the problem of minimizing the natural friction between the two is a daunting one.

I have found striking similarities between my colleagues in both camps. Both are idealistic, bright, totally dedicated to their professions, and technically proficient. They willingly work long hours under arduous conditions, crave recognition, and feel that they are underpaid. The strain on family life is equally severe in both professions. But there are notable differences. A journalist tends to be creative; a soldier is more practical. Reporters are independent; military men are team players. The former tend to be liberal and skeptical; the latter are conservative and obedient.

The all-volunteer force in a subtle way has contributed to this friction. At the height of the cold war and throughout the Vietnam War, the military was at the forefront of American consciousness. Scarcely a family had no son or other loved one liable to the draft. As a result, the shadow of national service cast itself over the family dinner table and generated a personal interest in the armed forces in all Americans. The experience of fathers and older brothers who had fought in World War II and Korea maintained a lively interest in soldiering. With the end of the draft and the advent of a professional army, this awareness disappeared along with the pertinence of the older generation of warriors. Only the families of those who volunteered for the service kept touch with the modern army.

The military, which for so long was part of society, drifted away from it. Military bases are now few and far between and located in remote areas, unseen by most Americans. A large percentage of volunteer servicemen marry early and settle down to a life where their base and service friends are the focal point of their lives. No longer do uniformed soldiers rush home on three-day passes whenever they can get them. When servicemen do go home, they do so wearing civilian clothes. They are no longer given the tolerant attitude of the public toward the military in eccentricity of dress and hair style; they are no longer marked by short haircuts and shiny shoes. Off post, they are indistinguishable in appearance from the civilian cohort.

To the average civilian, the term *military* has came to be equated with the Pentagon, intercontinental missiles, $600 toilet seats, and other manifestations of waste, fraud, and abuse. The flesh-and-blood association the public formerly had with the armed forces has atrophied; the military has become just another bureaucracy in the public's mind. For its part, the military, in the relative isolation of self-contained ghettos, has lost touch with a changing America. It focuses on warlike things and implicitly rejects the amorality of the outside world it has sworn to defend. In an age of selfishness, the professional soldier takes pride in selflessness. A sense of moral elitism has emerged within the armed forces, which is apparent today to any civilian who deals with the military. The all-volunteer force not only has created a highly competent military force; it has also created a version of Cromwell's Ironside Army, contemptuous of those with less noble visions. It is no wonder that those who choose the profession of arms look with suspicion upon those of the press who pry into their sacred rituals.

There is another big difference that bears directly on the relationship between the media and the military; the military is hostile toward journalists, while journalists are indifferent toward the military. To journalists, the military is just another huge bureaucracy to report on, no different from Exxon or Congress. But whereas businesspeople and politicians try to enlist journalists for their own purposes, those in the military try to avoid journalists and when they cannot face the prospect defensively with a mixture of fear, dread, and contempt.

Most of my military brethren would be surprised to know that when asked for an opinion about the military, professional young journalists with no association with the military rate career officers highly. They view officers as bright, well educated, dedicated, and competent, although they wonder why anyone would make the service a career. Their prejudgment of enlisted personnel is far less flattering. Most journalists view enlisted men and women as disadvantaged, not-too-bright, high school dropouts who come from broken homes and cannot fit into civilian society.

But after journalists have first reported on the military, their views are radically different. They will lavishly praise the enlisted personnel they met and relate how enthusiastic they were, how well they knew their jobs, how proud they were of what they were doing, and how eager they were to explain their duties. Genuine admiration and enthusiasm come through in the reporter's retelling of experiences. "But what of the officers?" "The officers? . . . Oh, they're a bunch of horses' asses."

To know why such a critical assessment of officers is made, one has only to take a hypothetical, though typical, walk in the journalist's shoes on his or her first interview with a senior officer. In this interview, it happens to be a general.

After an endless round of telephone calls to set up the interview, the well-disposed journalist, notebook and tape recorder in hand, arrives at headquarters and is met by a smiling public affairs officer who signs the journalist in and provides a pass. The officer walks the visitor through a series of offices under the baleful stare of staff factotums; the escort confirms the legitimacy of the stranger's presence. At last the journalist arrives at a well-appointed anteroom where everyone speaks in hushed tones.

After a wait, the door to a better-appointed office opens, and the journalist is ushered in with the announcement, "THE general will see you now." Not knowing whether to genuflect, our visitor enters the sanctum sanctorum vaguely aware of others entering also. Graciously received by the general, this outsider is invited to sit down THERE, while the general resumes his place behind his imposing desk backed by flags and military memorabilia. Besides the general and the public affairs officer, several other officers of varied ranks are present; they are not introduced. All take seats at the nod of the general; one places himself facing the general but slightly to the rear at the outer edge of the reporter's peripheral vision.

Following introductory pleasantries, the interview gets underway with the journalist setting the tape recorder on the coffee table and opening a notebook. This triggers a similar action on the part of the others. The visitor's tape recorder is immediately trumped by at least two others, and the general's entourage poises with pencils and yellow legal pads to take note of the proceedings. Throughout the interview, marked by elliptical responses to questions, the journalist is aware of knowing looks, nods, and shrugs being exchanged among the others. More disconcerting is the series of hand and arm signals being given to the general by the officer sitting to the rear and acting like an operatic prompter. The journalist is given his or her allotted time to the second and then escorted out of the office as the general busies himself with the papers on his desk.

After turning in the badge and being wished "Good day!" the journalist is back out on the street wondering what it was all about. Why all the lackeys? Were they hiding something? Why the signals? Didn't the general know enough about the subject to discuss it without a prompter? Puzzled, the representative of the press walks away wondering whether the host was a charlatan or a fool.

Obviously this illustration is an exaggeration, but those who have been through the process know that it is barely an exaggeration. Military officers raise suspicions because they appear defensive and protective.

The attitude of the military when meeting with the press is bound to affect that of the press, and vice versa. If it is one of mutual suspicion and antagonism, the relationship will never improve, and, in the end, it is the American public who will be the loser.

There is nothing more refreshing than an open relationship. Senior officers know their business and can talk about it sensibly without a bunch of flacks around, and they should do so. Journalists know that there are some topics that are off-limits in any meeting with the press and respect the obligation of a military officer not to disclose information he or she should not. It is a poor journalist indeed who tries to trap an officer into a disclosure that is legitimately classified. In many cases, the tape recorders and legions of witnesses are protective devices in case a journalist does a hatchet job on the person being interviewed. This is useless protection because a reporter who is out to paint a deliberately unfair picture of a person or institution will do it regardless of recorded safeguards of accuracy. The best protection against the unscrupulous is not to deal with them.

Each of the services has expended great effort at improving military-media relations. Public affairs officers are trained at Fort Benjamin Harrison, and all major commands have graduates of the school to act as a bridge between the warrior and the scribe. Installations and war colleges sponsor symposia, seminars, and workshops to improve relations with the media. Special tours of military installations and activities are conducted for the press by the Defense Department and the services, and some components of the fourth estate even reciprocate. But these efforts have little effect on military attitudes and make few military converts because most of them end up on focusing on the mechanics of the relationship rather than its nature.

What is frequently overlooked by the military is that journalism is as professional as the military, with pride in its integrity and strict norms of conduct for its members. For example, it is absolutely forbidden on the *New York Times* to tape an interview secretly by telephone or in person or to mislead as to the identity of the reporter. Most other newspapers have similar restrictions. As a result, there are few instances of yellow journalism today. The journalistic world knows who the unscrupulous are within its ranks and gives them short shrift. An unscrupulous journalist will never last on a reputable paper, and advertisers upon which a newspaper depends for its existence are not inclined to place ads in papers with a reputation for unfair reporting.

This is not to say that journalists will not use every legitimate means to dig out a story. The reputation of government agencies, including the military, for overclassifying, withholding the truth, or putting a spin on events is well known, and good reporters will never take things at face value. The tendency of journalists to disbelieve half of what they are told also adds to the military's paranoia.

There is no question, however, that some journalists go too far in reporting a story, and so do some newspapers. Journalism is a profession, but it is also a business, and businesses must show profit, a situation that leads to fierce competition among the media. A scoop means sales, and sales mean profit. For a reporter, a scoop also means reputation; and if a journalist's editors were not pushing for exclusive stories, he or she would do so to enhance his or her reputation and maybe win a Pulitzer prize.

Thus, a journalist may uncover a story relating to national security that would jeopardize that security if it was made public. This is particularly true if it is on operational matters, the favorite complaint of today's officer corps. Eager to be on the front page, the journalist may disregard the security sensitivity of a story and file it to the newspaper. But that is where editors come in. They are mature professionals with long years in the business and good judgment on the implications of a story. In truly critical instances, an editor will withhold a damaging story.

The record of the American press is good, despite unsubstantiated claims made by military officers that the press leaks operational information. Two examples will illustrate the point. Newsrooms knew beforehand of the planned airstrikes on Libya in 1986 and held the news until the raids had taken place so as not to endanger the air crews. And every Washington journalist knew that the late Col. Richard Higgins had held a sensitive job in the Office of the Secretary of Defense immediately prior to his U.N. assignment in Lebanon, where he was kidnapped. Yet in hopes that his captors did not know of Higgins's unique background, no mention was made of it in the American press until after it appeared in a Lebanese newspaper.

Whether the press acted responsibly during the Panama invasion when it reported the air movement of troops on the night of the operation is the latest subject of debate. News of the airlift was on television prior to H hour, but nothing was said of a planned airborne assault. Whether anyone in the press knew for certain one was about to take place is unknown, but if it was known, nothing was disclosed publicly. The air activity was alternately reported as a buildup for military action or part of the war of nerves against the Noriega regime. The government itself actually contributed to the leak the night before when it said the unusual air movements about which they were being questioned were routine readiness exercises unrelated to Panama, only to withdraw the "unrelated to Panama" part of their statement prior to the assault the following day.

On the whole, the military was satisfied with the press coverage of its Panama intervention. Certainly it received more favorable reporting than the Grenada operation in 1983. However, the one vehicle designed to improve military-media relations during military operations, the press pool, was a failure.

The idea of a press pool emerged as the result of the exclusion of journalists from the Grenada operation. The press had howled that the people had the right to know what their armed forces were doing and the press should not be denied entry to a war zone. They concluded that they were shut out more to cover up military incompetence than to preserve operational security and more convinced of that interpretation when stories of incompetence surfaced. Press pools were established to allow selected journalists from the various journalistic media to represent the press as a whole during future operations. The pool reporters were rotated periodically and were told to be ready on short notice to accompany military units. A list of names was held at the Pentagon for that purpose. Individuals were not to be told where they were going or what was about to happen.

The system was tested in some peacetime readiness exercises, to everybody's satisfaction. But in its first real test during tanker escort operations in the Persian Gulf, reporters complained that they were isolated from the action and kept ignorant of events. Many charged that their military hosts were more interested in brainwashing them than exposing them to the news.

Panama was the second test, and again the pool concept failed. Reporters were flown to Panama but kept at Howard Air Force base and given briefings during the high points of the operation. When they were taken into Panama City, it was to view events and locations of little news value. Meanwhile, journalists not in the pool were streaming into Panama on their own and providing vivid firsthand accounts of the action. Pool reporters cried "Foul!" For their part, the military complained that the journalists made unreasonable demands for transportation and communications facilities, as well as being unmindful of the dangers involved in taking them to the fighting. Nobody was or is happy with the pool arrangement.

The pool concept suffers three fatal flaws. The first is that the military will always want to put on its best face in hopes of influencing the reporters it is hosting. When faced with the choice of taking a reporter to the scene of a confused and uncertain firefight or to the location of a success story, it is not difficult to guess which will be chosen, regardless of its relative newsworthiness. Second, because the military brought pool reporters to the scene of action, it also feels responsible for transporting them, and this may not be logistically convenient at certain times. Third, the military is protective and feels responsible for the safety of civilians they are sponsoring. Keeping the press pool isolated at an air base in Panama was a genuine reflection of military concern for the reporters' safety. It is only during long campaigns like Vietnam that the protective cloak wears thin, and then usually because journalists find ways of getting out from under the wing of the military.

Implicit in the military attitude is not only its institutional sense of responsibility but also its lack of understanding of journalists. If the pool is to work better, the services must recognize that they have no obligation to the pool other than to get them to the scene of the action and brief them on the situation. Beyond that, reporters are on their own. They are resourceful and can take care of themselves. Any additional assistance rendered to them is appreciated but unnecessary, and lack of it is certainly no grounds for restricting coverage of the story.

The press, on the other hand, should be selective in who they send to war. Pool membership should require a fit, versatile journalist who knows something about the military. Few reporters have previous military experience, and few editors can afford the luxury of a military specialist on their payrolls. But the Defense Department would be happy to provide pool members with orientations and primers on military matters so that reporters could learn some military jargon and the difference between a smoke grenade and a fragmentation grenade.

Oldtimers long for the days of Ernie Pyle and Drew Middleton, when the military and the press saw events as one and there was a love bond between the two. In those days the military could do no wrong, and when it did, a censor saw to it that the public remained ignorant. Those were the days when the nation was on a holy crusade against the evil pomps and works of fascism and nazism. In the desperate struggle, propaganda was more important that truth. Had it been otherwise, many of the World War II heroes we revere today would have been pilloried by the press as butchers and bunglers.

Today's generals have none of the protection of a Mark Clark or Eisenhower. Moral crusades are no longer the order of the day, and unquestioned allegiance to government policy died with Vietnam. The government lied too often to the American people and lost their confidence. Today the press does what Thomas Jefferson envisaged for it when he rated it more important than the army as a defender of democratic principles: it keeps a sharp eye on the military and on the government it serves.

This should not dismay the professional soldier. After all, parents have a right to know what they are doing to and with their sons and daughters and their tax money. If it is done honestly, even with mistakes, there is little to fear from the press.

This is the challenge to today and tomorrow's military leaders: they must regain the respect and confidence of the media that they once had in the dark days of a long-ago war. The press is not going to go away, but the antimedia attitude that has been fostered in young officers must be exorcised if both institutions are to serve the republic.

4
Covering the Pentagon for Television: A Reporter's Perspective

David C. Martin

I have a recurring nightmare about covering the Pentagon. It is that the U.S. cruiser *Vincennes* shoots down an Iranian airliner not, as it actually happened, on Sunday, July 3, 1988, but on Tuesday, July 5, of the same year. If it had happened on Tuesday instead of Sunday, I would have been in the Pentagon prowling the halls instead of in New Jersey visiting relatives. Almost certainly someone would have told me that the *Vincennes* had just reported shooting down an Iranian F-14. I would have quickly confirmed the tip with a second source who had seen the same report, and CBS would have gone on the air with a totally false story.

When I awaken from my nightmare, I think about how I can protect myself from making an awful mistake like that. I could have 100 sources, and it would not make any difference, since they are all reading the same incorrect report from the *Vincennes*. I could wait until the incident is officially confirmed by the Pentagon, but I know the competition is breathing down my neck and there will be hell to pay if I get scooped. I could carefully attribute my information to "reports from the *Vincennes*," but I would still be disseminating false information. There is, in short, no real protection when dealing with the short fuse of television and the inevitable confusion of combat. It is axiomatic in the Pentagon that the first reports from the field are always wrong, but those first reports are frequently all journalists have to go on.

In television, the pressure to be first on a breaking story is enormous. Journalists organize their day around it, often at the expense of pursuing other, more substantive stories. Why devote so much time and energy to reporting tomorrow's news today? The answer is that internally at CBS, scoops give me credibility. They convince the people I work for that I am plugged into the inner circuits of the Pentagon, and they are more likely to accept my judgments about what is important and what is not. In other words, scoops equal clout. But I would like to think that all the scrambling I do serves a larger audience than the handful of television executives who watch all three evening news shows simultaneously. Granted, the average viewer could not care less who breaks what story, but I think he or she does care—or, at least, should care—that the news is being reported as it happens, not after the government has had a chance to clean it up and iron out all the creases.

Breaking news is frequently confusing, particularly in military operations and the infamous fog of war. If I have learned anything in six years of covering the Pentagon for CBS, it is not to try to hide the fact that I am confused or in doubt. Not going beyond what I know is a fairly basic journalistic principle, but the time constraints of television place a premium on short, declarative statements that leave little room for ambiguity. Hiding uncertainty behind words like *might, could, apparently,* and *believe* is the easy solution to the problem, but I am not at all sure those caveats register with the audience. Sometimes the best thing to do is to keep my mouth shut.

At the Pentagon, the element of uncertainty is compounded by the fact that the stories frequently deal with matters of life and death. Wives, husbands, mothers, and children are watching to find out what happened to, respectively, their husbands, wives, children, and parents. Inaccurate reports cause needless torment. It is accepted practice not to report the names of the dead until next of kin have been notified. The dilemma is deciding what to report when told, for instance, that all the crewmen in turret 2 on the battleship *Iowa* died in the explosion. For parents who know their son is assigned to turret 2, that is tantamount to announcing his death. No reporter wants to make a mistake. I once reported the full extent of the injuries suffered by a marine officer in the suicide bombing of the marine barracks in Beirut. I subsequently learned that the officer's young son saw that report at a time when his mother was telling him daddy was going to be all right. There is no way short of silence to prevent something like that from happening, but sometimes when I am staring into the black eye of a camera, it is useful to remember that what I say intrudes into other people's lives.

"Get it first, but first get it right" is a cliché, but frequently that is what covering the Pentagon, or any other beat, comes down to. At the Pentagon, the best way to do that is by being there. Remarkably, the Pentagon is relatively open. A reporter with a building pass can roam through much of the building, stopping in offices at whim. That building pass is the Pentagon reporter's most valuable tool. Being there allows me to pick up the biorhythms and body language of the Defense Department. Some days I walk into the building and can positively hear it humming with action: doors that are usually open are closed; people are holding whispered conversations in the hallway; secretaries turn over papers on their desks when they see me coming. I know something is happening in a way I never could know if I tried to cover the building by telephone. Being there also allows me to get to know the personalities of Pentagon officials in a way I cannot over the telephone. They are my sources, and the better I know them, the better off I am. An official might be too busy to return a call, but if I am in the building I can catch him or her running down a hallway to a meeting. Besides, many Pentagon officials believe their telephones are subject to wiretap and are much more circumspect on the telephone than in person.

Like anything else, reporters can overdo it. Anyone who sees and reports the world through the eyes of the Pentagon will have a distorted view. It is not that officials in the Pentagon are deliberately misleading; rather, there is no substitute for seeing for oneself. After months of Pentagon briefings about the Sandinista threat, actually seeing the Nicaraguan army is a revelation. The army has exactly the number of tanks the Pentagon says it has, but once a reporter sees the condition they are in and the terrain they have to contend with, it is clear that they do not pose a threat to any other country. A journalist doing a story about, say, the B-1 bomber, owes it to himself or herself and to viewers to talk to the pilots who fly the plane. Not everything they say is truth—I have never met a pilot who did not think his plane was the best one ever made—but their point of view is at least as legitimate as whatever armchair critic is calling the plane a turkey. There is one other indirect benefit to travel: meeting a lot of people who sooner or later will serve a tour of duty in the Pentagon.

I travel much more covering the Pentagon for CBS than when I did the same job for *Newsweek,* for a simple reason: television required pictures to go with the story, and I cannot get the pictures without going to the scene of the story. The need for pictures forces the television reporter to get much closer to the story than a print reporter. To me, that is the most satisfying aspect of television news. And it is the only real value of the on-camera "stand-up" by the correspondent: to show viewers exactly where the reporter was when covering the story.

The need to do on-camera interviews is both a blessing and a curse of television news. The blessing is that in a world of anonymous sources, here is somebody you can actually see and hear. The curse is that a 15-second sound bite frequently does not add useful information and is used merely to keep the pace of the story moving so that the correspondent does not drone on with 2 minutes of uninterrupted narration. It is, of course, difficult to express any but the most simplistic thought in 15 seconds. Anything over 15 seconds is considered too long. The instant a television producer spots a sound bite that runs longer than 15 seconds, he or she will start looking for ways to cut it down. The sound bite has become the symbol of all that is shallow about television news. To my mind, brevity is not the real problem with sound bites. You can read a lot of newspaper stories before you find a direct quotation that takes longer than 15 seconds to read out loud. The real problem with sound bites is their artificiality.

Most stories I do at the Pentagon come from sources who will not appear on camera. Even when I find an official who is willing to talk on camera, it usually takes the bureaucracy so long to approve the interview that it cannot be done in time for the evening news. More often than not, the people who do interviews for television are not government officials but outside experts—in many cases, former government officials at think tanks like the Brookings Institution and the Center for Strategic and International Studies. The think tanks crave the exposure and have published directories listing their experts by subject matter. The tongue-in-cheek motto of the Carnegie Endowment for International Peace is "Seven scholars, no waiting." Reporters tend to choose experts not on the basis of their knowledge but on the basis of their ability to express themselves in pithy one-liners. In our internal deliberations at CBS, we refer to experts not as "brilliant" or "fascinating" but as "a good sound bite." The experts know that and pander to it. The military is just beginning to catch on, and now each of the services puts its senior officers through media training to teach them the art of the sound bite. The result is a totally artificial dialogue, but we have only ourselves to blame.

The use of 15-second bites is most troubling to me when it comes to dealing with technology. I do not have the scientific expertise to judge whether, say, an excimer laser can be used as part of a Star Wars defense against missiles. My personal opinion is that of the last person I talk to. The opinion that gets on the air will be that of the person—critic or supporter—with the best sound bite. I might not know whether that is a valid opinion, but at least I—and presumably the viewer—can understand it. The problem is that it might be scientific gibberish.

The simplest example is calculating the cost of a weapons system. Critics of the Stealth bomber program say its cost has grown from $35 billion to $70 billion, a cost increase that appears to be outrageous. In fact, the $35 billion figure is in 1981 dollars, and the $70 billion number represents the cost of the program by the time it is completed in the 1990s. In other words, the cost growth includes about fifteen years' worth of inflation, which is not the Pentagon's fault. Without inflation, the cost grows from $35 billion to $43 billion—an entirely different story. Yet members of Congress who know better still use the $35 billion increase in their efforts to defeat the plane. I, along with every other Pentagon reporter, know enough to spot that canard and ignore it. But I would not be able to spot a comparable canard about the difference between, say, short- and long-wave lasers. Over time, journalists learn who the responsible people are and stay away from those who will say anything to get on television. In the meantime, the best defense is to be suspicious of anything that sounds too good, too outrageous, or too simple to be true. Also, the more people one interviews, the better are the chances that someone will point out misleading information that some so-called expert has tried to pawn off.

The average piece I do for the CBS Evening News runs about 1 minute, 45 seconds. In that time, there is room for two or possibly three sound bites. On most subjects having to do with the Pentagon, I know who the two or three best sources are. Unfortunately, time and space frequently intervene. A print reporter's next interview is only a telephone call away, but a television reporter has to get a camera there and get the tape back in time to be edited for the evening news. If the person I want to interview is in Indianapolis that day, I may be able to persuade the local affiliate to send one of its reporters to do the interview. More often than not, the local reporter will not know anything about the story (any more than I know anything about the stories he or she is working on) and can ask only a few basic questions I have relayed over the telephone—an awkward situation, which is why journalists frequently settle not for the best but the most available expert.

One artificiality for which reporters are not to blame is the use of file footage. Television cameras are frequently not at the scene of military incidents, so we have to recreate the action using file footage. To return to my nightmare: "The guided missile cruiser *Vincennes* [file footage of the *Vincennes*] shot down an Iranian F-14 like this [file footage of an Iranian F-14] today in the Persian Gulf [map of the Persian Gulf]." Even when the facts are right, the pictures are at best only representative. We always label file footage when we use it, but I am not at all sure the distinction between file footage and the real thing registers with viewers.

We are, it seems, getting to see more of the real thing as the military records more and more of its operations on videotape. In the past few years, we have seen videotape of the raid on Libya, the run-in between Soviet and U.S. warships in the Black Sea, the *Vincennes* tragedy, the dogfight between U.S. and Libyan jets, and the explosion aboard the *Iowa*—all of it shot and released by the military. The quality is not up to network standards, and it is always subject to censorship before it is released, but it is still better than file footage. The Pentagon would never be so crass and devious as to edit footage in order to give a deliberately misleading picture of what really happened. Nevertheless, I do add a word of caution about using footage released by the Pentagon.

In television, when a reporter gets dramatic footage of military action, the pictures dominate the story in a way they do not in print. Television reporters write to the pictures. Print journalists never know what picture will run next to their story. The videotape of the F-111s dropping their bombs on Qaddafi's headquarters and on Soviet-built military transport planes made it look as though they were scoring direct hits; one moment viewers could see the target plain as day, and the next moment it disappeared in a cloud of black smoke. Since that is what the pictures showed, that is what the script said. (We have learned from the Reagan years that even if the script says something else, the pictures will be what the viewer remembers.) Not until a year later, when I finally had a chance to interview the pilots and to listen to the audiotapes of their cockpit conversations, did I find out how much trouble they had encountered and how disappointed they were with their ability to put their bombs on target. I also saw a tape that had not been released showing people running and carrying the voice of the weapons officer complaining that clouds had obscured his target. I assume that tape was not released because the combination of people running and the weapons officer's no longer being able to see his target raised the unwanted spectre of civilian casualties.

The Pentagon, like any other institution, including CBS, puts its best face forward. If it conducts a successful test of a weapon, it will release a videotape that would never see the light of day if the test had failed. But in nearly a decade of covering the Pentagon for both print and television, I have been lied to only once. That happened on the day of the attempted rescue of the American hostages in Iran when a navy admiral told me that a rescue mission was not in the cards. He called me the next day and apologized, explaining that he had to lie to me in order to protect the secrecy of the mission. I told him that he could have avoided the lie by not taking my call, but he said he was afraid even that would have aroused my suspicion.

Most military personnel would not have returned my telephone call because most of them either distrust or actively dislike the media or, at best, do not view dealing with the media as part of their job. Once while I was covering an exercise at the National Training Center in Fort Irwin, California, my army escort admitted that he had orders not to let me come in contact with the army chief of staff, who was viewing the same exercise, for fear that I would ask him a question. One army public affairs officer told me his commander had given him orders to keep the press as far away as possible. A public affairs officer in Europe told me about his experience in putting together a press guidance package for an upcoming exercise. The press guidance included what are known in the Pentagon as "Qs and As," a list of questions reporters were most likely to ask with suggested responses. The public affairs officer had submitted the package to his commanding general, who told him he wanted the questions changed. Military officers deal with the press only when they have to, and, not surprisingly, they are not very good at it on those rare occasions when they try. More often than not, they come away from their encounters with the press feeling burned or badly used, which reinforces their negative attitudes.

During that same exercise at Fort Irwin, I interviewed the commanding generals of both the 101st Airborne and the 24th Infantry divisions. The first interview was with the commanding general of the 101st Airborne, but before we could get to the second interview, he radioed ahead to warn the commander of the 24th Division that we were out to do a hit job. Apparently he had not liked my questions. At the same time the general was spreading the word that we were up to no good, my producer and I were complaining to each other that the story had no edge and was turning into a puff piece. Military and media had walked away from the same interview with totally conflicting views of what had just happened. It is symptomatic of the mistrust that dominates the relationship.

It is tempting just to write off today's senior officers and wait for a younger generation not embittered by Vietnam to come along, but my experience has been that today's captains and majors are even more hostile toward the press than their superiors. Most senior officers have been around long enough so that they know at least a few reporters they consider to be responsible. Most of today's captains and majors have never met a reporter and so have nothing to go on but the stereotype of a reporter who will do anything for a story and the myth that the press was the reason the United States lost the Vietnam War.

I recently spoke to a group of sixteen flag officers attending a joint war-fighting course and found them to be genuinely thoughtful about their responsibilities for dealing with the press. One marine major general said he had turned down a request by CBS's "48 Hours" to visit his unit during cold-weather training because he felt he had a duty to his troops not to expose them to television cameras during moments of stress. He said he had learned from experience that the soldiers who make air are the ones who break down. You can agree or disagree with the general, but that is not a cavalier dismissal of his responsibilities for dealing with the press. These senior officers voiced a number of oft-heard complaints—the compulsion to report the negative and ignore the positive, the editing of their carefully prepared statements down to 15-second sound bites, and others—and I assured them it was not a plot against the military. We do the same thing daily to their commander in chief, the president.

Those kinds of complaints explain why military officers are wary of the press, not an irrational position. What they cannot abide is the notion that reporters would jeopardize the success of a military operation for the sake of a story. They cited statements made by prominent journalists who said they consider themselves journalists first and Americans second. They said they had seen videotapes in which journalists had been asked whether they would warn an American unit it was about to be ambushed and at least one journalist had said he would not interfere with the story. To a military officer, that is an incomprehensible statement, one that calls into question not just our tactics but our values. I responded that no matter what they had heard—or thought they had heard—my own experience told me that no responsible news organization would knowingly report a story that jeopardized American lives. The emphasis, however, was on *knowingly*.

On Friday, October 21, 1983, a source told me that a carrier battle group and an amphibious task force had been diverted to the island of Grenada to stand by in the event that American medical students on the island had to be evacuated. I confirmed the story from other sources and before broadcasting it that night showed it to Michael Burch, the assistant secretary of defense for public affairs, the Pentagon's chief spokesman. Burch said he thought the story "beat the war drum too loudly" but that it was factually correct. At the time, Burch was unaware that the United States was planning not just an evacuation but an invasion as well. Had he told me that American soldiers were about to go into combat, I like to think CBS would have held the story (although we certainly would have done everything possible to get a competitive advantage by moving reporters and cameras into Grenada). As it was, the story appeared on the CBS Evening News and could well have been a factor in alerting the Cuban contingent on Grenada.

I told that story to the joint war-fighting course as a case in which I felt I had done everything right but the result had come out wrong, and I blamed the result on the excessive secrecy that kept the assistant secretary of defense for public affairs ignorant of what was afoot. I explained that regardless of my report, the only thing that kept the invasion plan from leaking was the tragedy of the marines in Beirut, who were blown up by a suicide bomber on Sunday, October 23, 1983. By then, reporters on Barbados, where elements of the invasion force were marshaling, were frantically calling their home offices with news of U.S. soldiers in combat dress. But in Washington we were so consumed by the task of reporting the deaths of 241 Americans in Beirut that reporters there did not have the time or energy to check out the reports from Barbados. The officers at the joint war-fighting course immediately wanted to know what would have happened if Sunday had been a slow news day. Would we, if not otherwise engaged, have exposed the invasion plan? The answer is that we would have done everything possible to find out what was going on in the Caribbean. Having found out, we then would have engaged in soul searching about what to report, and some would have gone further than others. The officers could not understand why we would even try to penetrate the security surrounding a U.S. military operation, never mind report it.

I then told them how on the eve of the 1986 air raid against Libya, NBC had chartered a plane to search for U.S. aircraft carriers north of Sicily. The plane spotted the *Coral Sea* going through the strait of Messina at high speed and immediately alerted NBC headquarters in New York, which in turn passed the word to their Pentagon correspondent, Fred Francis, who quickly satisfied himself that the strike was on. NBC called its correspondent in Tripoli, told him what was happening, and kept the line open. As a result, they were the first to report that the raid had begun. None of that alerted the Libyans, who had steadfastly ignored all the indications and warnings of an impending strike, but against a sophisticated enemy, those overseas telephone calls would have compromised the security of the operation. I told the story as an example of a news organization's handling explosive information in a responsible fashion, but the officers at the joint war-fighting course could not understand why NBC had gone looking for the *Coral Sea* in the first place.

The fact is that in peacetime, the military cannot move forces without the press's finding out about it. In peacetime, the movement of 2,000 soldiers to Panama, an inconsequential deployment by wartime standards, sticks out like a sore thumb. If our own sources do not tell us about it, some soldier's mother or father will call the local affiliate asking why a son has been forced to move out in the middle of the night. The exception that proves the rule is the 1980 Iran rescue mission, which was mounted in total secrecy. Subsequent post mortems determined that one of the main reasons the operation failed was excessive secrecy, which kept vital information not just from the press but from the soldiers and pilots who were supposed to execute the mission. The military would like to see the press go back to the good old days of "loose lips sink ships" in which movements of military units were, almost by definition, never reported. That will never happen.

During the 1985 hijacking of TWA 847, the networks were roundly criticized for having reported that the Delta counterterrorist force had been dispatched to the Mediterranean for a possible rescue of the passengers held aboard the plane. But by the end of the crisis, the White House was practically begging news organizations to report the buildup of ships and aircraft off the coast of Lebanon as a means of bringing pressure to bear on the hijackers. Government cannot and should not count on the press to report only those military movements it wants advertised. For the foreseeable future, we are likely to inhabit a gray zone between war and peace, and neither government nor the press has figured out yet how to deal with it.

One solution that has been put forward is the creation of the Pentagon press pool. The pool was born of the Grenada affair in which reporters were barred from the island for three days after the fighting started. John Vessey, who was chairman of the Joint Chiefs of Staff, now acknowledges that that was a mistake. But the Pentagon pool might also turn out to be a mistake. The pool would consist of a manageable number of reporters and cameramen who would be given access to a military operation on the condition that they not report anything until the operation had begun. The first exercise of the pool was a fiasco—it leaked before the reporters got to the airport—but since then, it has been exercised without leaks and is considered by the Pentagon to be a success. To my mind, that proves nothing, since none of those exercises has involved a real operation that depended on secrecy for its success. They did not leak because nobody cared. If the pool were activated on the eve of, say, an invasion of Panama, I have no doubt it would leak. At CBS, I know the reporters and cameramen assigned to the pool. If they suddenly disappear from the office in the midst of a crisis, I do not have to guess what is happening. Even if the story is never broadcast, the number of long-distance telephone calls among network executives will make hash of the operation's security. The officers at the joint war-fighting course were much less cynical about the pool than I am. One officer pointed out that once a reporter become part of an operation, he or she has as much interest in keeping it secret as any soldier in it. The difference is that soldiers have had security drilled into them throughout their career; the reporter has spent his or her entire career telling all.

Reporters, even those whose lives are on the line, tend to be less than impressed with the need for secrecy in military affairs. Partly that is a reaction to repeated instances in which secrecy has been mindlessly applied. The air force now concedes that more information should have been made public sooner about the Stealth bomber, but that change of heart is due solely to the fact that the program is in trouble. The air force initially did not intend to permit press coverage of the first flight of the Stealth bomber, not out of fear that the secret of stealth would be compromised but out of fear that a delay in the flight would lead to negative stories. They decided it was better to fly first and tell the press afterward so if anything went wrong, it would go wrong in secret. Eventually the decision was reversed, and reporters were allowed to cover the first flight but only because the air force had reluctantly concluded that members of Congress were not going to spend any more money on a plane their constituents were not permitted to see. The argument most frequently made in favor of keeping the wraps on an open secret like the Stealth bomber or the Delta force is that once reporters are given a little, they will keep pulling on the string until they have it all. You have only to look at the navy's submarine program to see what a bogus argument that is. The navy releases a great deal of information about its submarines, but what they do and how well they do it once they submerge remains a black hole.

I do not think we will ever bridge the gap between the military's desire for secrecy and the media's instinct for total exposure—nor do I think we should. The relationship between the military and the media is, after all, supposed to be an adversarial one. Journalists are hair shirts, not cheerleaders. If that makes life more difficult for military officers, it also forces them to perform their duties with a rigor that might not exist were it not for the fear of public exposure. If we cannot, or should not, close the gap, we should at least be able to eliminate some of the hypocrisy that inhabits both sides of the military-media debate. Military officers preach the need for secrecy when, frequently, what they want is to spare themselves embarrassment or inconvenience. Reporters preach the First Amendment and the people's right to know when what they want, basically, is to beat the competition. Fred Friendly, the former president of CBS News, once told me that what settled an intense in-house debate over whether to air Morley Safer's famous pictures of marines setting fire to Vietnamese huts was the fear that NBC had the story as well. What I find surprising is not that competitive pressures settled the issue—they often do—but that there was a time when a major news organization had to think hard about showing pictures which made American fighting men and women look bad. Today we would air those pictures without a second thought.

For all the controversy about military-media relations, it is important to remember that the U.S. military is the most open in the world. That assessment is based on firsthand experience with the Soviet, Nicaraguan, and Japanese militaries and on conversations with British reporters who envy Americans their freedom to roam the Pentagon in search of news. Reporters covering the Pentagon have easier access to the corridors of power than their counterparts at the State Department. Officials from the secretary of defense down to analysts in the Defense Intelligence Agency are usually accessible, and public information officers are professionals who, with a few notable exceptions, believe in helping reporters get the story. Unfavorable news stories like the *Iowa* and the *Vincennes* are as easy to get as good news stories. The degree to which Pentagon reporters are manipulated and kept at arm's length is nothing compared to what happens to reporters during an average day on the campaign trail. Not once in my experience has the Pentagon been as devious and misleading as the Reagan White House was when the Iran-contra scandal started to break. Nor have I ever known the Pentagon to disseminate misinformation deliberately and consistently the way the British did during the Falklands War. Relations between the U.S. military and the media remind me of a birthday card my wife once gave me. On the front it said, "Darling, I love you just the way you are." Inside, it said, "Just don't get any worse."

5

Covering the Pentagon for a Major Newspaper: A Reporter's Perspective

Melissa Healy

For any reporter, covering the military can be a daunting challenge. Forget for a moment that as an institution, the armed forces prize secrecy, which contributes to military success in wartime and discourages civilian meddling in peacetime. Consider instead the sheer size and scope of the U.S. military's reach, both throughout the world and into the everyday lives of its 3.8 million members.

The Pentagon is the hub of an empire so immense and so multifarious that it defies adequate news coverage. Its tentacles spread over thirty-five countries, across and under the world's four oceans, and into the smallest American communities. It has its own system of justice, its own educational institutions, its own medical and family services, its own newspapers and entertainment, and a procurement system that concludes 15 million contract actions per year. The military has become a largely separate society that parallels that of civilian America.

Has an army warrant officer been charged with espionage in Georgia? Are unexplainable deaths up at the nation's 180 military hospitals? Has a secret unit of stealth helicopters been sent to the Persian Gulf? Is there evidence of massive pilfering at a cavernous air force supply depot or contract fraud on an obscure navy missile? This is the defense beat—in effect, a separate world of high-wire diplomacy, high-stakes business interests, technical complexity, and, above all, mazelike bureaucracy. Merely to know when and where to ask the questions requires enterprise and an understanding of the Defense Department's enormity. To find the answers to such questions requires skill, perseverance, and luck. And to get anywhere on the beat, a reporter must have sources, many of them scattered throughout the far-flung empire, pried from a tradition of caution and secrecy by a reporter's appeals to personal interest, professional curiosity, and budgetary necessity.

The complexity of the defense beat and the barriers to the gathering of information are probably higher than they are on any other newsbeat in contemporary American journalism. But because of that fact—not in spite of it—the coverage of significant developments in defense can and should be better than on almost any other beat. As a practical matter, the difficulty of culling newsworthy facts on the nation's defenses also can make defense one of the most poorly reported beats in the newspaper profession.

In the hands of a newsroom scribe, Pentagon coverage can become a mind-numbing litany of budget justifications, procurement contracts, and recruitment figures—roughly all that the Pentagon's scattered public affairs apparatus readily and routinely offers. In the hands of a strategic scribbler, defense reporting can become a forbidding realm of arcane logic, complex technology, and megadeath, indecipherable to editors and inhospitable to readers. What a good reporter does is provide the bridge that explains how the prosaic, such as military contracts and budgets, relates to the larger goals of security policy and, most important, when it does not.

The challenge of reporting well on the nation's military security is to move beyond mere coverage, seizing the agenda and uncovering trends and developments early enough that taxpayers can respond to the matter and to put them in context so that there can be no doubt as to why these trends are important and where they may lead.

A good reporter uses the technique of building an article on a firm foundation of fact, such as buying plans and military capabilities, rather than on mere policy statements. This approach proceeds from the notion that defense capabilities tell more about national policy than do the government's verbal claims. The aim is to allow even the most uninitiated reader to grasp a broad picture of some major area in national security— say, strategic defenses or arms control at sea—that has begun to change, is facing a critical decision point, or is at odds with national aims or common sense. These are called enterprise stories. On the sprawling and secretive defense beat, they are among the hardest stories to report and write because there are so many priorities competing for a reporter's time, so many possible subjects to write about, and so many barriers to break down.

What do such stories have to do with breaking news, the golden coin of the realm in daily journalism? How can a reporter get scoops if he or she is off laboriously constructing what daily writers sometimes contemptuously refer to as "thumb sucks" and "trend pieces"? The answer is threefold: enterprise stories help educate the reporter (and, through him or her, the reader) about a new corner of the armed forces' vast range of concerns; they help build sources, which are the real coin of the realm in defense reporting; and, finally, serendipity sometimes strikes, and a story hits the unsuspecting reporter between the eyes. In the sprawling American defense empire, there is news hiding everywhere.

It is true, however, that even among the most thoughtful newspaper reporters who are given the time and editorial latitude to do such stories, there are competing priorities—important daily developments to be reported, scoops or tips to be investigated—and in the great competitive journalistic marketplace, other reporters' discoveries to confirm and relay. But reporters who have developed the impulse to build articles bring not only better sources but a more critical and creative eye to these everyday tasks. Breaking news, such as a shipboard accident, an aerial dogfight, or a generated nuclear alert, is placed for readers in the larger context of often-conflicting goals of national policy. It also benefits from a reporter's own observation from the field. Officials' policy statements are more often compared and contrasted to actual behavior of the military, such as deployment patterns, buying plans, and the capabilities of weapons. Enterprising reporters are less vulnerable to being cynically used by their sources. They approach tips warily, since every leaker has some political motive that may obscure the other half of a story. Leaks are checked for political content and balanced with further reporting. Other reporters' scoops are advanced with the addition of more information and reaction from officials and critics. When reporters learn to become master craftsmen, news consumers reap the benefits.

There is another reason that I am a particular advocate of enterprise stories that build a picture of larger defense priorities on the foundation of a single trend or development: they are particularly well suited to newspaper reporting and to newspaper readers. I have covered defense for a major newsmagazine at a time when even a major beat like defense was unlikely to have more than a couple of pages devoted to it per month. I have also heard my colleagues in television bemoan their struggle for a minute or two of precious airtime. Newspapers, by contrast, are ravenous consumers of copy. Moreover, newspaper reporters are called upon regularly to write a greater range of different kinds of news stories—features, interviews, profiles, breaking events, news analyses—than colleagues in either daily television or newsmagazines normally do.

Newspapers put major emphasis on reporters' developing stories on events as they are happening. On breaking news events—accidents, military operations—newspapers cannot hope to match the visual immediacy of television, and so newspaper reporters are expected to offer consumers more analysis and context than they could get by watching last night's newscast. At the same time, when newspaper reporters choose to highlight trends of national and international significance, they are expected to exercise judgment as discriminating and analysis as penetrating as colleagues writing for newsmagazines—and to do so more quickly and generally at greater length.

Because newspaper reporters are thus jacks-of-all-trades, they must anticipate some crises and cultivate potential sources. Working alone and away from the pack not only helps line up those sources; it builds a deeper sense of how the Pentagon works. It feeds the newspaper reader's voracious appetite not just for copy but for information and analysis not provided by television. And sometimes it finds the reporter in the right place at the right time to uncover a breaking story of immediate interest. Reporting enterprise stories is one of the most efficient ways to accomplish all those goals. But while greater enterprise is the ideal in reporting, the everyday reality of defense reporting offers a somewhat different picture. In the routine coverage of events of military significance, all reporters are highly dependent on a large and increasingly professional public affairs apparatus.

In many cases, the Pentagon has a virtual monopoly of information on the operations of military forces. Communities neighboring a Strategic Air Command air base can observe and share with reporters the signs of a generated nuclear alert—increased flights, cancelled leaves, a dearth of airmen in the local bar. But most reporters have few resources when, for instance, a battleship's gun turret explodes hundreds of miles into the Atlantic, as happened in April 1989 aboard the battleship *Iowa*. Similarly, when U.S. forces entered Grenada in October 1983, reporters were widely aware that an invasion was imminent, but they could not get near enough to the fighting to report on it accurately.[1]

Thus, for most stories that reporters undertake—whether a breaking story like a military operation or the plotting of some unrecognized trend—the Pentagon's public affairs office is the first stop. These men and women, both uniformed and civilian, work under the direction of the civilian assistant defense secretary for public affairs. They are the Pentagon's front door.

Especially when events are unfolding quickly, it is best to check if the most expedient way to get the facts—the front door—is open. At the same time, a good reporter will have a ring full of keys to various back doors—informal sources of information that can be used when the front door is locked. And even when the front door of information is wide open, a reporter is likely to check a few back doors to see if the picture looks the same from there or if more detail is available. On major developments, however, the Pentagon's official pronouncements, conveyed by the assistant secretary of defense for public affairs and his staff, are for most mainstream defense reporters the point of departure.[2] On less pressing stories as well, the public affairs office is often a reporter's first introduction to military officers and defense officials, many of whom will not speak to a reporter unaccompanied.

Some civilian defense officials are more politically attuned than their Pentagon co-workers and for that reason are more likely to see a reporter's interest as a potential weapon in their bureaucratic arsenal. Most, however, see no gain, political or professional, in speaking to reporters and readily follow orders: refer them to the public affairs professionals, whose jobs it is to deal with them. Having met many young military officers in several years on the beat, I have noticed that most learn early that reporters are to be treated like unexploded bombs. There is a mixture of horror and fascination at the prospect of dealing with one. But most career-conscious officers, upon encountering a reporter, remember well what the military handbook in effect prescribes: "If you see one, call a public affairs officer without delay and clear the area immediately."

For reporters with major news outlets, the assistant secretary of defense for public affairs—the spokesman for the secretary and the department—can be an important source. This official normally has regular access to the defense secretary and can be an important source of information regarding the inner workings of the Defense Department's top management, including the political and bureaucratic aims of the secretary. While this official seldom offers more information than that which is in the defense secretary's interest to release, his or her guidance (and all have been men) helps form a picture of who in the government stands where relative to what issue.

In my own experience, newsmagazines are among the media best serviced by this important source, perhaps because their interest in such stories—and in the political machinations of government—is greater than the television networks' or newspapers' interest. But where does one cultivate sources that will provide the crucial back-door keys to power, sources to whom a reporter can look to unlock information with or without the cooperation of public affairs?

First, enterprise stories, which often begin with an introduction from a public affairs officer, help create sources. For reporters who do not take the time or have the opportunity to do workmanlike (some say pedestrian) stories between national security crises, the defense beat means lurching from crisis to crisis as a captive of the Pentagon's official spokesmen. For those who have bothered to make the effort, such stories create a stable of potential sources whose trust has been won before the crisis began.

Second, defense reporters lean heavily on sources outside the Pentagon. In the years of the Reagan buildup, when vast sums of money were being spent quickly on defense programs, a cottage industry of watchdog groups, many of them highly critical of the Reagan administration's spending priorities, sprouted up around Washington and elsewhere. Some of the groups concerned themselves mainly with narrow procurement issues, others concentrated on larger issues of nuclear policy, and still others specialized in specific programs like the Strategic Defense Initiative.

Many of the groups were left-leaning, mainly because they sprang up in protest of the policies of a conservative administration. But in the "star wars" program particularly, conservative watchdog groups often provided thunder from the right, warning reporters of changes in the program's structure and priorities that had important policy implications. The watchdog groups in general provided defense reporters with resources that few old-guard journalists had enjoyed; reporters were the beneficiaries of full-time experts, digging into the diverse details of increasingly complex subjects, whose overall orientations and political motives were generally well advertised.

Probably no other watchdog group had more impact on the nature of defense coverage during the early Reagan years than the Project on Military Procurement, which began as a taxpayers' interest group. The project's practice of releasing internal Pentagon documents on the cost, testing, and proposed acquisition strategies of weapons systems created a lively news market for stories sometimes so arcane that they once would not have made it past the pages of the trade papers and into the major general circulation press. That fact notwithstanding, many of the programs lambasted by the project were important examples of the waste, fraud, and abuse of taxpayers' dollars and trust that are likely to occur when budgets increase by more than 40 percent in fewer than ten years.

The project fostered enterprise on the part of some reporters, who suddenly saw an opening short of Watergate for their investigative talents and were introduced through the project's work to knowledgeable and independent thinkers, many of them hidden deep within the Pentagon's bureaucracy. Others were content to write up the project's releases on a sole-source basis, as if they had been just another—more newsworthy—press release from the Pentagon. To be sure, the latter was a reporting style that the organizers of the project themselves discourage, but for some scribblers, old habits die hard.

Other groups sprang up to bemoan the erosion of U.S. adherence to the 1972 antiballistic missile treaty, the Reagan administration's reluctance to negotiate limits on new weapons, and the nation's growing reliance on computer-based weaponry. Each boasted analysts versed in the issues, who combed diligently through congressional hearing records, which were and remain one of the best sources of information coming out of the Pentagon. Many maintained sources of their own in the bureaucracies whose work they surveyed. As a result, these analysts have come to serve many functions. During the Reagan years, they offered a critical measure of balance for daily stories, rebutting or offering alternatives to the administration's initiatives. They became useful sources and sounding boards for larger policy stories that attempted to stand back and analyze the meaning of the administration's initiatives. And they became important sources of second-hand tipsters, extending a reporter's own network of sources to relay views and information from their own sources. For reporters willing to check out their leads independently, the results often made front-page news.

Yet another group of sources carries news from the Pentagon to reporters: the vast numbers of defense industrialists and study contractors (the so-called beltway bandits whose offices line the artery surrounding

Washington). During the Reagan administration's defense buildup, when the Pentagon turned increasingly to defense and study contractors to find ways to spend new money, they became critical nodes in the defense news network.

Defense contractors work with a strong and easily identifiable agenda. They are generally less forthcoming to reporters than they are to lawmakers and their congressional staffs, whose power of the purse is a strong incentive. But for reporters who take the time to coax industry officials into conversation, some can be important sources of information on their own programs and initiatives and also on the shortcomings of competing programs.

The national laboratories fit here also. Virtually autonomous entities funded by Department of Energy contracts, they have strong stakes in promoting pet projects. To the workers who are researching these new defense technologies, they are endlessly interesting research and engineering challenges for which funds and political support must be found. Potential congressional patrons are sought out for briefings; scientific and laboratory publications tout their potential applications; and inquiring reporters are often ushered in quickly to interview the scientists.

For lawmakers, defense officials, and reporters, these technologies sometimes promise to solve longstanding military problems and pave the way for new strategies. Often, however, they open Pandora's boxes of wasteful and provocative military capabilities that make for sensational and significant news stories. For example, a few of the controversial products of research in the national laboratories promised to revolutionize Western military strategies. Among them are the neutron (or enhanced radiation) warhead, lasers proposed for use in Star Wars missile defenses, and many of the powerful conventional warheads that, when paired with improvements in accuracy, would make it possible to strike deep behind military lines. All were terrific news stories.

By far, however, most reporters' best sources are on Capitol Hill, where prerogative, pride, and pork barrel politics conspire to make nearly anything available to the reporter who bothers to look. Recognizing the Congress's power of the purse, the Defense Department, the national laboratories, their defense industry contractors, and all manner of special interest group flock to Capitol Hill to plead their cases. Lawmakers and their staffs eagerly pick up information on Pentagon plans and programs, and their motives for sharing that information with reporters are as varied as the programs themselves.

Reporters in search of a promising lead in defense can do no better than to pore over the transcript records of congressional testimony, which have long been a major resource for scholars. They are a source of information on programs for which the Pentagon is seeking funds. They reveal, through the questioning of committee members, which are most politically controversial and why, and they often expose material that has not been revealed elsewhere, since some of the hearing records are of committee sessions that were closed to the public. Although classified information has been removed, that process is spotty and often allows a reporter to piece together previously unknown facts about U.S. military capabilities or operations.

What, meanwhile, has happened to the military services themselves as sources of information? Interservice rivalry was once a hardy perennial as a news story and an everyday source of information. Senior military officers of one service, disgruntled with its share of the defense dollars, would unload on the pet projects of another service. For reporters, the competition was not only good sport—there is nothing like a public squabble to draw the press—it was a great behind-the-scenes source of information. But that once-rich source of conflict and of news appears to have largely dried up. Congress's 1986 defense reorganization identifies the problem most succinctly as logrolling—the growing tendency among the services to divide up missions and resources and implicitly agree never to question the priorities of a competing service or its effectiveness in performing missions assigned to it.

For defense reporters, and probably for the nation as a whole, the advent of logrolling in the Pentagon is a shame. For reporters, that kind of rice bowl politics ("you mind your rice bowl, I'll mind mine") removes the clash of interests that makes for some of their best and most significant stories. It removes thoughtful, knowledgeable dissent from the marketplace of ideas in which reporters so thrive. We are all a little poorer for it.

The Pentagon's public affairs organization, dubbed by one Senate critic as "The Pentagon Propaganda Machine," has changed considerably since the days of the cold war and Vietnam.[3] So have most defense reporters, whose response to propagandization is more often to write about the sudden hard sell than to pass it along unquestioningly to readers. Throughout the 1950s and 1960s, as Senator J.W. Fulbright (D–Arkansas) documented, the Defense Department and the military services spent hundreds of thousands of taxpayers' dollars to produce and distribute films warning of the threat of communism, extolling the virtues of patriotism and military life, and offering views of the Vietnam War that were unrealistic.

To Americans watching these widely circulated films today in war documentaries and in movies like *The Atomic Cafe*, the Pentagon's efforts are shamelessly propagandistic. To modern eyes, they also appear quite crude. Pointing to such abuses, Fulbright called for legislation setting a ceiling on the Defense Department's public relations spending and regular reports on the Defense Department's public affairs initiatives. "Of course the military needs an information program," Fulbright wrote. "But it should be designed to inform, not promote or possibly deceive."[4]

The men and women in the Pentagon's public affairs apparatus seem to have taken to heart their more limited mandate. On the whole, they are quick to respond to reporters' specific questions with facts and to arrange interviews. They do so cheerfully and, for the most part, quickly. But that is all they do. In the upper reaches of the military and its partners in the defense industry, more subtle efforts at propaganda continue: after years of secrecy, information on the $70 billion B-2 bomber program grows from a trickle to a torrent on the eve of crucial congressional votes; one of the nation's top three defense contractors advertises itself by showing a classroom scene, accompanied by a reading of a passage from one of Lyndon B. Johnson's most moving tributes to the value of education; and the navy, beset with requests to use battleships for music videos and aircraft carriers and submarines for major motion pictures, develops a community of slick film liaisons. The greater subtlety of their techniques may be insidious. But beyond placing reasonable limits on the use of taxpayers' money, I would advocate no moves that would further limit the public affairs apparatus. The marketplace of ideas and information has already been shrunk too much by secrecy and such practices as logrolling.

It is the proper role of defense officials, as those entrusted to spend taxpayers' money for the nation's defense, to make the case for the weapons they wish to buy and the strategies they plan to use them for. They should do that as aggressively as they can within their budgets. The reporter's role is to see those arguments for what they are, to use them in context, and to balance them with opposing views. A reporter whose unflagging sense of enterprise has hardened him or her against the seductive flackery will know what to do with the Pentagon's arguments when they are offered.

6

Media Coverage of the Military: A Soldier's Critique

Philip E. Soucy

The current defense establishment in the United States is the very embodiment of the horrors spoken of by former President Dwight Eisenhower when he warned of the dangers in the military-industrial complex. The Pentagon's procedures and practices are rife with waste, fraud, and abuse of the public trust and public monies. Weapons and their support systems are "goldplated"— made to the maximum profit of industry—regardless of their military utility or the deadly consequences of their poor performance in battle. Military officers tasked with the development of these weapons are far more interested in furthering their military careers than in ensuring that the proper weapons are produced. In order to secure promotions, they continue the research and development of fatally flawed systems rather than incur the ire of their superiors in the service and the dislike of those really in charge— the unholy alliance between a powerful defense industry and members of Congress who believe they were sent from their districts to go to the national treasury with wheelbarrows and cart it home.

Military systems are never subjected to any form of rigorous testing, certainly never under conditions approximating combat. When such tests are finally mandated by the few members of Congress altruistic enough to face up to the real issues (that is, they have no military posts or significant defense spending in their districts), the military is likely to circumvent the testing or so rig the tests that either success is guaranteed or the results are faked—even if they have to load the target up with gasoline and wire it with explosives. Were it not for a very few brave whistle-blowers like Ernest Fitzgerald and retired air force colonel James Burton, the taxpayers' money would be frittered away on $600 toilet seats, $300 hammers, armored vehicles that are deathtraps, and command and control systems so unmanageable that the soldiers assaulting Grenada had to use AT&T credit cards and a commercial telephone line to get the attention of their superiors to an immediate problem. There are so few of these public-minded citizens who are willing to step forward and take the heat—the pressures of industry are so inexorable—that the process continues in the main to produce substandard products like the Bradley Fighting Vehicle, a 25-ton armored infantry fighting vehicle whose sole practical utility is as an armored car in which to convey $1.2 million safely from the Treasury to FMC Corporation, after which the military may do as it pleases with it.

The young men and women in the service are wonderful, but they are being handed weapons too complicated to use and impossible to maintain on the battlefield. Some of them will die because of this profligate use of public resources to line the pockets of rich capitalists and careerist officers, many of whom are feathering their future nests with jobs in industry after they retire. The solution to this problem is to build simple weapons and systems, inexpensive and effective, and a lot of them. The solution is to take the procurement of military systems out of the hands of the military and put it in the hands of a separate civilian agency. It will take time to wrest control of this process from the dead hand of the fat cats and the venal Pentagon bureaucracy; in the meantime, the best we can hope for are a few brave souls inside the system with the courage to speak, a few stalwart members of Congress willing to face down powerful industry, and a watchful press ferreting out malefaction wherever it is found.

I submit that this is the general view held by much of America concerning the Pentagon. This view is accurate insofar as it represents the only conclusions that can logically be drawn from the evidence presented to the public on an almost daily basis. It is woefully inaccurate in that the evidence presented to the public is incomplete, generally out of context, and presented not in a direct effort to inform but more as byplay to a completely different game. The players in this game use the public forum in ways the public is unaware of, to purposes at times inimical to intelligent discussion.

The military—certainly the army—seems to have a poor understanding of the purpose of public relations and how to use it effectively. It does not do a particularly good job of directly and succinctly engaging its antagonists in public, particularly if they are from Congress. The press is a victim of the pressures inherent in the media world, and it seems not to make sufficient effort to understand what it is reporting on. Some members of the Congress misuse the military's compliant and generally submissive public posture. The net result is a lot of negative shouting in the public ear, without the public's being presented adequate information to make its own judgments in a balanced fashion.

I do not believe that everything is perfect within the military, that mistakes have not occurred and continue to be possible, and that oversight should not be exercised. But I do believe that the public should realize that it is getting an incomplete picture and understand how and why that incompleteness comes about.

In this discussion of the military and the media, I run the risk of committing the very sin that I will charge and convict others of: addressing extremely complex and important issues in a simplistic manner that often brutalizes and deforms the issue beyond recognition. I accept that risk; it is time to face the bad parts of this interaction head-on.

I have the context of nearly four years as one of the media spokespersons for the secretary and Department of the Army. During that time, I handled a wide variety of subjects: environment, base closures, chemical weapons and their destruction, weapons systems, testing, research and development, procurement, and the army budget. I have been a tactics and doctrine instructor and an infantry officer for twenty years. Most of my comments are based on my experience in the army; whether those comments are representative of the rest of the defense establishment, I will leave to the reader's judgment and experience.

The public is poorly served by the quality of the public debate conducted on defense issues by the military, the Congress, the amorphous pool of outside experts, and the press. Complex, important, and incredibly expensive issues of national significance are made trivial by accusatory quips, facile generalizations, rhetorical posturing, uninformed and increasingly inexperienced reportage, and the manipulation of issues for purposes that have little to do with defense and more to do with personal power and influence. The lack of rationality in the process by which the public is presented defense issues in the United States is appalling.

Both the military and industry oversell systems, partly because bravado is a warrior's posture and partly because Congress forces that kind of inflated language just to get heard. Congress runs amok, castigating the Defense Department for its free-spending ways and then reinstating the funding for projects like the V-22 Osprey in spite of the opposition of the Defense Department. But Congress does know better than the Defense Department what is good for their districts. In other words, everything is normal in this very untidy thing we call a democracy. But it could all be done slightly better. None of those participating in the debate can escape a share of the responsibility for the current state of misinformation and misunderstanding in the mind of the public. The groups I have mentioned are all guilty of sins.

It is important to note at the outset that most of the people involved in the military-and-the-media issue are good people. The dishonest reporter who deliberately misuses facts, invents quotations, or takes them out of context deliberately for effect, consciously writes from a bias, or refuses an opportunity for a full airing of the facts is rare; I have met only three out of hundreds. The member of Congress whose handling of defense issues is based solely on personal political gain heedless of the truth or the outcome is similarly rare; I have dealt with only four out of the hundreds. The general who truly believes that his or the army's decisions should be questioned only by someone higher in the hierarchy he inhabits is not as rare as should be but is by no means commonplace or the norm. Rather, it is the cumulative effects of the weaknesses of all these groups interacting among themselves that brings about the poor state of the debate on national defense issues. It is a perverse imitation of the engineering version of Murphy's law that states that in a machine or project with several subcontractors or manufacturers, tolerances will accumulate in the direction of impossible to assemble.

The Army

Public relations in the military is referred to as public affairs, a euphemistic bow to Congress and others who believe (wrongly) that public relations smarts of the slick marketing that makes big lies believable. Unlike the air force and the navy, the army does not have dedicated public affairs officers; that is, no one comes on board as a second lieutenant of public affairs and serves an entire career in various positions in that field. There are many jobs in the army that the army does not want inexperienced younger officers doing, jobs that require some basic experience in and of the army to do effectively, like financial management or operations research. Somewhere around the eighth year of service, officers choose or have chosen for them an alternative military specialty, to be added to their basic branch. They receive training in that specialty and thereafter alternate assignments between their two specialties. They are expected to maintain themselves current in both areas. Thus, an infantry officer with public affairs as an alternate specialty could spend three years as the public affairs officer for a 15,000-soldier division and then be assigned back to the infantry for three years, and so on.

Thus, the army's public affairs officers are not just observers but participants. They can generally speak from a conviction born of experience. Although they may not reach the level of public affairs expertise that their peers in the navy and air force might, it also means that they can be of more use to the commander, the press, and the public in efforts to translate things army into terms easily understood by a general audience.

Public affairs officers work for the commander they are assigned to, not for the chief of public affairs at Department of the Army headquarters in Washington. Some local commanders, however, have a dismal understanding of public relations. They believe that only the positive and uplifting are the proper province of the public affairs officer. (They share that deplorable view with a large segment of leaders in the military, who have no trust of the press.) It must be observed that the vast majority of the leaders in the army spend the great part of their adult lives inhabiting a different world. Drive onto any military post and the change is obvious: growing things are manicured and clipped; there is no trash lying about; everything has a well-maintained look. Military posts are open, but their societies are closed. They are largely self-sufficient, with some even generating their own electrical power. It is possible to live on a military post and have little to do with the surrounding civilian community. Posts tend to be fully articulated communities, with schools, churches, libraries, shopping centers, recreational facilities, a police and fire department, building and grounds keepers, and road departments—and over it all a hierarchy of military leaders and a single executive empowered to run the entire community autocratically. However democratic and approachable that single executive may be or appear to be, it is an option, not standard equipment.

The wonderful part of this system is its capacity for reacting with a coordinated, total commitment of the entire community when something needs to be done. Whether it is the refurbishment of a neighborhood playground, snow removal, or reaction in the aftermath of a natural disaster, the military has no parallel in its ability to galvanize and organize its own community. There is a sense of family and community on post that unites residents all the time, not just in crisis, a quality often lacking in the surrounding civilian community. The on-post atmosphere, however, is somewhat sterile. Moreover, they are used to protest that is polite, dissent that is demure, and questions asked only in private, particularly if they are hard or unanswerable.

In contrast, the press, the Congress, and the public are raucous, undisciplined, and relatively unbridled as well as iconoclastic. The usual reaction of the military leadership is to hunker down. They fail almost universally to realize that questions can be asked, that those questions need not be polite, and that most of them must be answered—preferably forthrightly, intelligently, in easily understandable and quotable terms, and now.

For servicemen and servicewomen who may have to go to war, there is the very real issue that we, as a people, should not freely tell potential opponents about exploitable deficiencies in our systems, and we should not look kindly on those who do. A Washington bureau chief recently said, "It's not my job to keep your secrets; if I get one, and it's a good story, I'm going to print it." Think about how soldiers would react to this; for this fellow, the real difference between convicted spies such as Jonathan Pollard receiving jail terms or Pulitzer Prizes is not who they told but how they did it. If they had been smart enough to write for him, they would be on the speaker circuit instead of taking recreational walks in a guarded yard.

Some mistrust of the press is warranted, as is mistrust of members of

Congress, but a large measure of the disrespect for, mistrust of, and reluctance to cooperate with the press that most senior leaders in the army feel is actually a reflection of their own lack of understanding and inexperience; their attitude is the result of a situation where their control is tenuous. The natural reaction where talent or experience is lacking is avoidance, and that has been raised to an art form.

As the new public affairs officer for the 8th Infantry Division in Germany, I received my first set of guidance from the equally new division commander when I informed him at an evening staff briefing that Drew Middleton wished to interview him (hardly an attack with an unfriendly weapon for those familiar with Drew's style and philosophy). I was told "never to miss a golden opportunity to keep both your and my mouth shut." And I did not miss one for another fifteen months. This edict included even the routine press release of training deaths—those sad (fortunately rare) but inevitable consequences of working in and around huge machines and death-dealing weapons. I finally convinced them that they had only two choices: a one-inch story on page 23 of the *Stars and Stripes* at the time of each incident or a three-column story on page 1 or 2 of the *Washington Post* when it came out (as it would) that the division had been "covering up" its training deaths. For the most part, however, the press was turned away, and the division was so difficult to deal with that even Headquarters, U.S. Army Europe, could send down only a fraction of the press that was our due on major exercises like Reforger and its attached Autumn Forge series maneuvers. Months later, the now-seasoned division commander asked through the chief of staff why he never saw the division in the *Stars and Stripes* and civilian press; I reminded the chief of staff that he had been present as a brigade commander when I had received the only operating guidance I had. He smiled and changed the guidance.

The bankruptcy of this kind of refusal to deal with the real world becomes most apparent at the top, at Department of the Army level, in Washington, a one-industry town: government, power, influence. Washington is like a huge Van der Graaff generator laid on its side down the Mall between the Pentagon and Congress. The press stands in the middle, keeping the slide moving back and forth. As expected, the whole process produces a large amount of voltage, but very little amperage. It makes your hair stand on end, but you could not illuminate a light bulb with it. Rhetoric is the coin of the city; quotability is its currency. If you are not making news, you do not exist, a political reality that will become a physical reality come the next election.

The amount of available power and influence is relatively fixed. In order to get more, you must take it from someone else. Moving, jostling, and posturing are constant. This makes Washington a reporter's heaven; there are so many agendas, so many prima dons and donnas, so much intrigue, banality, venality, and outright charlatanism, not to mention actual criminality, that I am surprised that reporters need do much more than sit on any street corner with a sign out.

Faced with the reality of the cacophonous chaos, the army leadership reduces the size of their problem by pretending that there is only one problem: Congress. They do this because they take seriously their responsibility to provide the American people and the president of the United States with an army, fully trained and well equipped. But the long-term impact of public opinion and attitudes on their ability to do that pales to insignificance and indirection compared to the near-term, direct impact of a healthy (or poor) relationship with Congress. They view it as their job to go to the Congress and get the money and the support necessary to do what they believe is in the long-term best interest of national defense. Generals and other officers are sent over to the Hill to brief, to inform, to respond to questions, and occasionally to testify; the one rule is not to anger the congressman or congresswoman. No matter what is said, where it is said, or how ludicrously inaccurate it is, the officer's response is expected to sound like a dramatic reading from the D.C. metropolitan bus schedule. There are striking exceptions; Lieutenant General Don Pihl is masterful in his ability to speak directly and simply to the understanding of complex issues by the public and press, as well as by Congress.

Usually, though, it does not matter whether the inaccuracy or twisted logic comes from a "friend" or an "enemy"; the response comes out as gray, lengthy, and unquotable, often in the worst army staff talk. The army is so compliant that some congressional harangues are preannounced. I can recall occasions when I knew the army had been told by a congressman that he was going to savage the army the next day in the press or on the floor of the House, "but not to worry; it's all form and no substance—I just have to do this. You'll get the money."

This creates what should be recognized by even the most naive member of the press as laughable, ridiculous exchanges between supposed intelligent adults. On April 17, 1988, retired four-star general Donn Starry, armor officer, veteran of service in war, father of the current doctrine of the U.S. Army, member of the board of directors of Ford Aerospace, intelligent and knowledgeable, appeared in an open session of the Conventional Forces Subcommittee of the Senate Armed Services Committee before Senator Carl Levin (D–Michigan).

The subject was the importance of the recent deployment of reactive (self-protecting explosive) armor on some Soviet tanks in Eastern Europe. After a portion of the lengthy exposition of how reactive armor would lessen the effectiveness of chemical-energy antitank rounds, the senator leaned into his microphone: "Excuse me a moment, general. [pause to allow press pencils to go to the ready] Are you telling me that if we went to war, our bullets and missiles would bounce off Soviet tanks?" Starry paused a moment and replied, "That's correct, senator." The groan from the army officers in the room could almost be heard aloud.

The truth, is that nothing was going to bounce anywhere; if a chemical-energy antitank round struck a Soviet tank, a tremendous explosion would take place. Reactive armor would reduce some of the effectiveness of that explosion—enough that the army needed to request additional funds in order to pay to move already planned improvements forward. Both Levin and Starry knew how things were supposed to turn out; that had been explored in advance by staff, and Levin had been found to favor the proposed additional funding. General Starry simply played out his part of the game by rules he knew all too well. Headlines and stories in almost all the publications that covered that hearing featured Levin's characterization as the lead. America was misinformed. The quality of intelligent discussion of an issue was lessened. Levin got the exposure he wanted; the army got the money it needed.

The army in the Pentagon believes that it is not in its best interest to join the battle. It prefers the OCLL (Office of the Chief of Legislative Liaison) position: quietly work the halls of Congress, talk to staffers, see what deals can be made, find friends in Congress to fight the battle for the army. Public affairs is viewed as an adjunct to the Hill fight and important only insofar as it contributes to the final outcome in Congress. That the public is listening, reading, and watching seldom occurs to them and even more rarely concerns them. The army has no idea how the public feels about it, the level of support it has, and what the population knows about how different it is from the army of their memory. Most of America's impression of the army is an admixture of Vietnam, John Wayne films, a book they have read, and, for some, the warm remembrance of becoming a man in the army. Army public affairs and the army leadership have not commissioned any recent serious research into public opinion of and knowledge of its army that I know of, other than the Recruiting Command, which has a rather limited interest—eligible 18 to 22 year olds.

Public affairs is not thought of as a staff function with an independent audience, expertise, and an important contribution to make; it is thought of in the same terms one thinks of the mailroom—as a conduit or clearinghouse essential to the dissemination and proper distribution of communications but in no way contributing to or influencing the content of messages, except negatively by garbling the message. Since the only problem being addressed is the congressional one, public affairs is viewed as simply another conduit to deliver a message to Congress; if anyone else eavesdrops, that is not a matter of concern.

Press releases and responses to queries are prepared in public affairs on everything from upcoming announcements to issues that blew up today. By the time they have gone through staffing procedures, the lawyers, and OCLL, one is lucky if they do much more than state that "today is

Tuesday and it appears from past experience, not confirmed, that tomorrow will be Wednesday, but the army hastens to point out that Pope Gregory was not in the army, or employed by the army, at the time the calendar was developed." Answers will get longer or shorter in the process and start sounding like a poor translation into English. Professional public affairs officers know they cannot talk like that to the press or the public, but the army thinks it can. The public affairs men and women with whom I associated in the army had among them some of the brightest and most dedicated people I have known, who worked long and arduous hours under great pressure and cared about the outcomes. But whether they were heeded among the staff was a product of personalities, not function.

Perhaps an example will clarify what the army thinks of its public relations efforts. A recent chief of public affairs (CPA) was chosen because he was a Medal of Honor recipient and presumably had talked to a Kiwanis Club luncheon or two. He was deserving of honor and respect for what he did on the battlefield. But these are not proper criteria for selection to this position. He replaced a respected man of great experience. The newer CPA had no experience in issue-oriented public debate, did not routinely read any newspapers or watch the nightly news (not unusual for generals; they are still at work at 6:30), and told his first gathering of public affairs professionals that he had no idea why he had been chosen (a thought now almost universally shared). He believed that telling a reporter that a subject was classified would cause the reporter to back off from the story. Alternatively, he believed that telling a reporter that we "had nothing for him on that subject," the current version of "no comment," resulted in the reporter's having no story "because we're the only ones with real information on the subject and they couldn't publish without talking to us." On another occasion, referring to reporters, he said that he didn't "understand why he was the one who had to deal with these bastards."

The Press

The press is far less monolithic. Most of the reporters I have dealt with are honest, hard working, enterprising, and possessed of a healthy skepticism. They have usually been patient and long suffering when I insisted on telling them how a watch was made when all they had asked was the time.

The press inhabits a different world from the military. The traditional view that the press and government are natural adversaries is certainly true. However, this view is being forced to carry too much of the freight of mistrust between the media and the military. But let us explore the relationship before wandering into new explanations.

How are the press to be dealt with? My contacts with the press have been amicable and straightforward. The average reporter is usually clear and candid about what information is wanted and why it is wanted. The exception are self-described investigative reporters who, though they may achieve the occasional success in routing out someone caught with their hand in the till, generally fail miserably in achieving any kind of meaningful context.

Some discussion is necessary regarding what the press is looking for when it approaches the military—or any other story for that matter. In statistical terms, the press is looking for stories that are in the tails of any distribution, that is, the unusual. As P.T. Barnum once said, "You can lead a horse to water, kid; when you can get him to float on his back, come back and see me." That the army functioned perfectly normally this week, that it is in general adequately trained, sufficiently equipped, and mostly in good spirits is dull, uninteresting, and unprintable. It does not attract readers, viewers, or listeners and does not sell newspapers, which does not prompt advertisers to send in their money. What the press is looking for, as one former television reporter told me, are "stories with bite and grab": conflict, crime, fraud, weapons that do not perform as advertised, waste, and abuse.

The problem with this approach by the press comes in the routine lack of context, scale, and understanding in their stories. The military is an arcane, specialized world, far too often difficult for the average layperson to understand. It speaks in jargon and talks seemingly casually about death, dying, and killing. Soldiers are easily accused of being sick, grown men in love with killing; they are often portrayed in Hollywood films as brutal, cold psychotics, eagerly seeking someplace to try out their weapons, someplace where they can exercise their deadly penchant unbounded by the rules of civilized society, throwbacks to more barbaric times. This is not the case. In my twenty years in the infantry, I met far more ordinary civilians who wanted to "nuke someone 'til they glowed in the dark." Just because they study warfare and tactics and advocate the development of more powerful weapons does not make the military enamored of war any more than the doctor is in love with disease and suffering or the police officer thrilled by crime. Soldiers are tasked with defense, the stopping of an aggressor, the prevention of war through deterrence—yet a surprising number of reporters give every indication that they believe the opposite: that soldiering is warped.

An intelligent reporter realizes that preconceived notions have little place in accurate reporting, and editors usually require more than gut feelings as the basis for conclusions in articles. Where a subject is difficult to understand, reporters assigned to that beat on a routine basis usually strive to acquire some background expertise. And it is difficult to imagine a wire service, network, or major newspaper hiring someone randomly and assigning them to cover, say, the stock market. Yet when the *Balti-*

more Sun was casting about recently for a reporter to replace their veteran Pentagon correspondent, they specifically looked for someone with no prior military experience. It is not that I believe only reporters with military experience can understand what is going on; but the implied judgment that only reporters who start out knowing nothing about the subject can report in an unbiased fashion is shocking.

I can count only a handful of reporters who, in four years, called or came in and asked, with the intention of learning more about the military, to be taught about tactics and doctrine. The days when phalanxes crossed the open field and battles were decided by simplistic but hopefully clever tactics are long gone. Warfare is now complex. It is also an art form, not a science. This is a lesson the army spends a great deal of time and effort convincing its junior leaders of: decisions about what to do on battlefields are dependent on the situation, not mathematically arrived at by simple formulas or though the rote application of simple rules. The captains I taught in their advance course usually took three months to stop asking what the "school solution" was for the tactical problems we were presenting to them and started realizing the huge matrix of factors that influenced how they would successfully complete their mission. No less than these captains who are tasked to complete their missions, reporters have an obligation implicit in their position as translators, purveyors of the truth, to seek to understand what they are reporting. The services would cooperate gladly in the education. Think about how many simple, enraging mistakes could be avoided.

Throughout the almost two years that the Bradley Fighting Vehicle was under concerted attack from a seemingly endless array of faceless congressional aides, pseudo-experts, and one air force officer, I can recall only four print reporters and one broadcast network producer-reporter team who said, "So, tell me how mechanized warfare is going to be prosecuted and how this vehicle will participate." More often, simple questions were posed on the basis of the latest accusation, however absurd or bereft of context, and any answer that did not reply directly was discounted or simply cut off as unresponsive.

Stupidity is not the reason for this. Reporters are not stupid. But they are generally hard-pressed for time for breaking stories; they have to do a tremendous amount of research in a brief span of time and reduce it to close, compacted prose that is understandable and saleable. I have a great deal of respect for the professionals among them and understand how awesome it must be to tackle something so hidebound, other-worldly, and complex as the military. One of the great difficulties facing captains in the army finds echoes in the problem facing the press: in the army, it is difficult enough to write an operations order that can be understood, but the real art of a professional is to write one that cannot be misunderstood. I often marveled at the consistently accurate way in which stories were reported by hard-nosed journalists like Norman Black of Associated Press, Vernon Guidry of the *Baltimore Sun,* Deborah Polsky of *Defense News,* Tony Capaccio of *Defense Week,* and broadcast reporter-producer teams like Fred Francis–Naomi Spinrad of NBC, Dave Martin–Roxanne Russell of CBS, and Carl Rochelle of CNN. They were good stories, in context and full of hard-won understanding, some that everyone liked and some that ripped our face off on those occasions when it was deserved.

Aside from the problem created by having so few reporters with any military experience at all, partly because the draft has been dead for more than a decade, there are other problems inherent in the media that have nothing to do with the supposed role of adversaries that they occupy in our society. One has to do with who they are as individuals. Reporters tend to be people who work best alone. They develop their skills in some isolation from each other, though I am sure they learn from each other and from their editors, and work best when left alone and given sufficient time. Though they may be in a large corporation, they are not of that corporation. They prefer not to be part of management; most never want to be in management. Most have not worked on team efforts of more than two or three reporters. Very few have ever been in charge of more than their pencil and pad.

This is not a criticism, just an observation. Journalists have no visceral understanding of the limitations imposed by people working in groups. Particularly the young ones do not understand that doubling the number of people does not halve the time required to completion—at best it is three-quarters of it—and that tripling or quadrupling the number of people working on a project in fact adds to the time and effort required for completion. Of course, this means that in any human effort where the project is large or the number of people involved is great, there will be inefficiencies—certainly as a consequence and perhaps as a design characteristic. If one sets out to focus only on the slack in any endeavor, one is assured of finding some. One also runs the risk of easily missing the significance of what is going on.

Several years ago, Bell Helicopter of Fort Worth, Texas, signed an agreement with the army whereby it paid (returned) $81 million to the government, covering a two-year period during which a very poor computerized accounting program accumulated at least that much of the government's money. Bell would have you believe that one of their accountants was rummaging in the back of the safe and found the money in a shoe box, whereupon Bell immediately informed the army. Though that was hardly the case (government audits for almost the whole two years had warned Bell that transactions were accumulating in one direction), no substantive evidence was found at the time that Bell was consciously criminal in intent or that any of the money had been used wrongly. The army finally stopped progress payments to Bell until it shut that computer program down and substituted a new one acceptable to the government. Five months later, Bell and the army began the process of disassembling every transaction run during the almost two years that program was used. The final nonduplicative total was the $81 million Bell returned in cash and purchased parts. This occurred at the time of one of the periodic flare-ups of waste-fraud-and-abuse-in-the-Pentagon seizures, and Bell was tarred with that brush.

Because I was beginning to wonder about American industry, I asked staff what the total dollar amount of the two years' worth of disassembled transactions was. The answer was $2.1 billion, of which $81 million was found to be in error. I realize that $81 million is a huge sum, but compared to the volume of business, in context, it means that errors occurred in only 3.85 percent of the transactions. Certainly any error should be corrected and errors involving this amount of money are unacceptable, but I now wonder about the analyses of the state of American business and the gratuitous smearing of the defense industry that fill the pages and screens of the news media. I told a number of reporters what I found out, not in Bell's defense but because I found it interesting context; to my knowledge, none included it in their stories.

Of particular interest is a subculture within the media called investigative reporting, done by investigative reporters, represented by television programs such as "60 Minutes" and "20/20" and various print reporters. They work on their articles for weeks, and even months. Their work is arduous and tedious, often done without the willing help of the investigated. The results are sometimes startling revelations like the Wedtech scandal in New York or the series on mast bumping on UH-1 helicopters that earned Mark Thompson a Pulitzer Prize. Theirs is a secretive art. I understand it when actual criminality is being investigated and there is a very real possibility that the guilty will run or destroy the evidence; I do not understand it when the institution is willing to cooperate with the reporter.

Generally investigative reporting is done according to a recipe that tells the reporter to file Freedom of Information Act requests for everything on a subject, believe nothing the government public affairs people say, and rely on outside sources for facts and analysis. The investigative reporter will usually submit a series of specific questions tapping into a subject. He or she will not usually allow you to know what he or she is being told by others but will place your quotes and information in juxtaposition as if an open and free debate had occurred on the subject. The outside party is told what the government had to say but not the reverse.

A classic example occurred with a series of articles on the Black Hawk helicopter and electromagnetic interference (EMI), a phenomenon in which outside electromagnetic signals are picked up by the electronic circuits of equipment and cause unintended, sometimes untoward, reactions by the machine. It was apparent from the questions that the reporter's knowledge was detailed in some aspects but lacked an overall understanding of the subject, its effect on the Black Hawk, and its overall significance in a combat setting. Six times the reporter was offered the opportunity to discuss with army experts what he knew and what it led him to believe; then he could write what he pleased. EMI is not a subject easily understood beyond the basic concepts. He refused every time. The articles came out filled with alarm, innuendo and loaded language, leading casual readers to conclude that the army had a serious, debilitating fault in its helicopter; that the army "forced the helicopters back into the air"; that deaths were attributable to EMI; that the army was covering this up and endangering its pilots and soldiers in callous disregard for their safety because "stray radio transmissions" could bring these helicopters down.

He was not correct. Research had shown that only transmissions on specific frequencies at specific and high levels of power might affect the particular subsystem susceptible to that phenomenon. The army was well aware of the phenomenon and had kept its pilots informed of what it knew that affected the safe operation of their aircraft and the lives of themselves and their passengers. Compensatory procedures had been established that worked, and minor modifications had been made to allow pilots to correct for untoward movement of the control surface in question. Told in its full context, the story would have been of interest to a trade journal and of almost no interest to the general reader. The helicopters had been around for ten years and had flown hundreds of thousands of hours. Surely if the allegation that stray radio transmissions could bring them down was true, the countryside would have been littered with them.

What surprised the army was that this reporter would not avail himself of an opportunity most other journalists would have leaped at. When I expressed my frustration with his hit-and-run questions and refusal to allow us a full hearing on the subject, the reporter told me that the army should not have been surprised, that I "knew the rules when I signed on."

Whenever we would take exception to a story, particularly one done by an investigative reporter, as we did in this case, the rejoinder invariably was "show me a factual error." There were several, such as calling the Black Hawk a "fly-by-wire" aircraft. The Black Hawk is a standard aircraft, flown by means of cables, bellcranks, and pedals; only one subsystem was controlled only by electronics. But it was not with the facts but with their assemblage and their context that the conclusion that we had a problem was shoved in the face of readers. That sounds like a difference of opinion, which, as the saying goes, honest people may have. I assure you that no honest person, informed on this subject, would find the articles reflective of the true state of affairs. Nevertheless, when articles like these get a political ball rolling and the service is forced to react because it has been made politically impossible to do otherwise, that reaction is used as evidence that the stories were true.

A word must be said about lexicon. I have noted over a long time that critics seem to "say" or "state," while the government seems to "contend" or "reply." My favorite two words in this lexicon are that government "acknowledged" or "admitted." I realize that reporters tire of using "said" when writing and that these words all have "say" in their definition. But these are loaded words with generally accepted ellipses; "acknowledged [reluctantly, after it was dragged out of them]" and "admitted" always mean "admitted guilt" to everyone.

What are some reporters seeking? I was once told by a reporter for a Washington defense publication that specializes in the truth behind the truth that there was a poster hanging in her office that said, "There is no truth; there are only good stories."

The Congress

In the last fifty years, Congress and politics have become a creature of the media. Much like the tree in the forest that falls with no one there to hear it, there appears to be some question in the minds of members of Congress whether they will receive credit for actions taken on the Hill without press coverage. Accordingly, there is a vying for the attentions of the press probably unparalleled in modern times. This produces an environment in which pithy quotes, gross oversimplifications, and rhetorical devices replace deliberative thought, meaningful investigation, and well-thought-out funding decisions on matters of vital national importance.

Despite some of the appearances to the contrary, there is a limit to the amount of money available to the Congress. The fierce competition for dollars between sectors of our society, between projects within a department such as Defense, produces an atmosphere in which only perfection can be bought. The slightest flaw in a program can result in a storm of criticism that drowns out reasonable thought. The propensity for the media to jump on a breaking story and produce cloned stories, especially if a congressional member is yelling at the Defense Department for some depredation, has resulted in a simple but effective recipe for getting your favorite congressional member into the limelight. Aides to congressional members "turn reporters onto a story" with cleverly leaked "facts" or simply selective release of material provided by the Defense Department. It is best if the reporter can be shown actual documents, so the words in it condemn without need of other evidence. The trick here is to get the story going and feed its progress over the course of a couple of weeks, all without revealing that the source of the material is the aide and the reason for the release is the congressional member's desire to make a splash later. After several weeks of this, the congressional member announces, publicly that he or she can no longer ignore "the spate of stories in the press" and will ask for an investigation of the truth behind the allegations.

The brouhaha over the Bradley Fighting Vehicle started just that way. At the core of the maelstrom were five or six people—not a conspiracy but symbiosis. Every one of them was getting something that they wanted: for the congressman, influence, power, a chance to kill another big program, and with that a reputation that would last forever; for the aide, the certainty that those inside the hothouse of the Hill would know that he had really done it (his boss not being that clever); for the air force colonel, spurned by the professional testers, a chance to vindicate his opinion and force the service to follow his ideas; for others involved, a chance to get even with their former employer who had fired them (the obligatory disgruntled employees). And there were genuinely better ways to have gone about the testing of this vehicle. What was wrong here was the abuse of facts, the misleading of the public, to private purposes and the somewhat shameful practice of sniping from the obscurity of "sources said."

Among the first allegations was that because the aluminum armor of the Bradley burned, the vehicle was a firetrap. A simple check with the Aluminum Association of America would have revealed that aluminum does not burn in any ordinary sense of the word; it cannot be set afire to join the conflagration. In fact, the way metallurgists work with this aluminum armor is to play an open flame on the ingots. This armor will deform in sustained fires at very high temperatures (above 1,000 degrees Fahrenheit), but it is not burning. Why would this ridiculous allegation even see the light of day? Why would it not work to discredit the "source"? I do not know. I only know that it did not. Why doesn't the press expose this process? As one veteran reporter explained to me, the first one to do that would not get any more telephone calls from the Hill and would "die on the vine swinging slowly back and forth in the wind."

Congressional members accused the army of rigging the tests. Facts in the testing were taken out of context and either willfully or stupidly misused in spite of the fact that the testing procedures had been laid down and agreed upon by all parties. Why did such tactics work against the army and the vehicle? The reaction of the army was to wander around in a daze, feverishly write point-counterpoint papers (and do little with them), and hold endless meetings—all the while bleeding badly in the public eye. For a long time, the army got the best defense three lieutenant colonels and a major could muster. The central problem in the beginning was that there were excellent and telling replies that could be made, but no one of consequence was willing to do so. Later, the stories had a life of their own. Finally, the army galvanized into action and fought a fairly good rear-guard fight. The army won the battle with Congress—it got the money and support to continue Bradley production—but then declared a victory and retired; it lost the battle in the public sector because it refused to fight there.

Congress was not inactive during this fight. During the battle, Senator William Roth, Jr. (R–Delaware), published an article that correctly stated that the army had twice run a full-scale battle simulation, the defense of a position—once with a force of tanks and M-113 armored personnel carriers and once with a force of tanks and Bradleys. The Bradley is supposed to be a much-improved replacement of the M-113. Roth correctly stated that more Bradleys were lost when they were employed than 113s when they were used. He drew strident conclusions. He failed to mention that when the Bradleys were used, the position was held, and when the 113s were used, the position was lost, which was also in the report. This is not a small point. The Bradleys contributed tank-killing capability and were on the front line doing that, where they could be hit; the 113s, armed with only a .50-caliber machine gun, did nothing against tanks and were correctly positioned off the front line. This is not simple oversight but intellectual dishonesty and conscious pollution of public debate.

This is not to say that the services do not oversell weapons. But Congress does not listen to 70 percent solutions; one cannot go over to get money for systems that are not "with this we win, into the 21st century, without it we lose." That kind of overselling contains its own minefield. But the blame for the services' getting trapped in that kind of rhetoric lies partially with Congress and congressmen.

Congressional members do not like the army to stand up and vigorously defend itself, particularly if that occurs at their expense. Their reaction is swift and blunt. Congressman Ron Wyden (D–Oregon), a protégé of Congressman John Dingell (D–Michigan), after absolute silence on the subject, suddenly stepped out into the press making statements laced with factual errors on the Bradley Fighting Vehicle, presumably believing or having been told that the army was lying panting on the ropes and it was therefore free publicity. He was probably surprised when the next day, a Department of the Army spokesman, Lt. Col. Craig MacNab, was quoted in the newspaper saying, among other things, that the congressman "was spectacularly uninformed on the subject" and that although the army was used to that among congressmen, Mr. Wyden "had exceeded the norm." The reaction was swift and came from Dingell, not Wyden. In the view of his staff, what MacNab had said was chargeable under article 88 of the Uniformed Code of Military Justice (the manual for courts-martial), which forbade speaking against Congress. Even the most cursory reading of the text in the manual about article 88 would reveal that the stricture was against speaking ill about Congress as a body, and it specifically stated that this did not apply to the speaking about the members individually. Court-martialing MacNab was not the issue; silencing him was. Dingell knew that; so did the army.

Conclusion

What is to be made of this whole process wherein the military and the media find themselves in close association with each other? All parties to the interaction need to take a close look at how they operate in the public forum on defense issues and seek to correct their deficiencies. If any of the parties takes offense at my focusing on the negative aspects of their part in the public debate, then I can only remind them that management by exception should be the rule. Fix only the things that are broken; try not to break anything else during that repair.

The army needs to take much more seriously the training of its officers to recognize their responsibilities and roles outside, as well as in, the army; it is the public's money, the public's defense, and their sons' and daughters' lives that are at risk, and they have a right to a full exposition of the unclassified facts in terms they can understand. Public affairs professionals are in place, but they have to be listened to. The services must engage themselves thoroughly in the public debate on issues affecting them. For the media, it means acting on their responsibility to the right of the people to know to seek to understand their subject and fully expose those facts—that is, to further the public understanding of the issues. Full disclosure of the facts implies not only a willingness by the services to speak but of the press to listen. To Congress, I offer the following: "It is my firm belief that if the Army [and the other services] represent an organic part of the people—as is the case [here]—it is inadmissible to rob the Army of political rights given to every citizen by the Constitution." Those words were spoken recently by Dmitri Yazov, minister of defense of the Soviet Union, about his army's right to speak out on issues of concern to it. For the rest of us, the public, I can only offer the proverbial "everything I read in the newspaper [see on television news] is true, except for the occasional story or two with which I happen to have some acquaintance."

Where are we? Probably about where we can be. We have lasted this long as a republic. The nation is well and vigorously defended by dedicated people, for all of the deficiencies that defense possesses. The public is receiving some information on significant issues. But all of it could be done better.

7

A Culture of Incompetence: Why the Daily Press Covers Defense So Poorly

Fred Reed

Most reporters who cover the military believe that they do a creditable job. But students of the military outside of journalism believe that coverage is usually incomplete, often factually inaccurate, poorly understood by the reporter, and seldom put into adequate context. They are correct. The result is that the public cannot acquire a reasonable understanding of military news. In particular, if my anecdotal experience with the public is any guide, people think the military is far more irresponsible, stupid, ill-managed, and dishonest than I have found it to be.

The defects of coverage are not primarily a matter of political bias. Conservative papers are as consistently wrong as liberal papers, although the direction of their cheerleading differs. Instead the problem is that the weapons named do not exist, the tactical employment of existing weapons is not grasped, the technology is misunderstood, and the historical background is negligible. Journalists indeed have an amusing tendency to get things precisely backward, and they do not seem to improve much with time.[1]

The defects of coverage are far more obvious to those outside journalism than to those within. When I joined the press, having majored in chemistry and therefore having the habits of mind natural to the hard sciences, I was astonished by what seemed to me the intellectual slovenliness of military coverage. When I tried to point out defects to my editors, the attempt elicited either irritation or uncomprehending stares. They did not disagree with me; they just had no idea what I was talking about.

Why is there such consistently poor work?[2] After seventeen years in the trade, I have concluded that the reasons are chiefly cultural. Journalism seems to attract a type of personality well suited to doing something else. More precisely, the better a reporter is suited to some parts of the job, the less well suited he or she will be to others; this is a trap without an easy exit.

The cultural homogeneity of the big league media exacerbates the problem. Reporters tend to be the same kind of people, and they tend to think the same things. The press has become a self-perpetuating culture sharing certain attitudes that are no more questioned by journalists than the Incarnation is questioned by a colony of monks. Among these attitudes are a contempt for the military, a distaste for industry and commerce, a disinterest in technology that verges on resentment, a powerful egotism, and a discomfort with blue-collar people, such as soldiers.

The nature of the work further screens reporters, driving out all those who do not have particular qualities that, while useful in filling a newspaper, are not necessarily conducive to insightful or even intelligent coverage. Reporters must work well under intense pressure, whether of deadlines or incoming artillery. They must be detail-minded and lacking in fastidiousness; for example, they must be willing to immerse themselves day after day, month after month, in tedious details of stories that have at best transitory importance. They must be combative to thrust aside the countless attempts to influence them or keep them from getting information. And they must be satisfied with rushed research channeled into superficial, anecdotal treatments.

The result is a reporter who is brave, reasonably intelligent, aggressive, skeptical, self-reliant, and given to quick decisions and action. People having these qualities are almost inescapably anti-intellectual, disinclined to engage in big-picture thinking, little interested in serious study, poor at analysis, and very sure of themselves. The sort of personality needed to get the news is almost inevitably incapable of understanding it.

Eleven Deficiencies

There are at least eleven basic weaknesses in the way the press covers the military that are sufficiently frequent to warrant discussion.

First, journalists exhibit a near-perfect technical illiteracy. Students of the hard sciences do not often go into journalism. Most reporters therefore know nothing of physics, engineering, electronics, or computers. They consequently cannot read technical journals or textbooks; indeed, most have so little background that they could not learn without starting with high school algebra.

Yet much of military coverage deals with the design, engineering, testing, maintenance, and application of formidably complex machinery, especially computers. Merely talking to engineers and pilots about their weapons requires a strong layman's grasp of a large number of technologies, which can be kept up only by constant study. Reporters seldom know enough to know that there is anything to know.

For example, to discuss sonar, one needs a grasp of convergence zones, phased arrays, resolution versus aperture, shadow zones, thermoclines, ducts, and perhaps a dozen other ideas. To talk radar, one needs a conversational grasp of frequency agility, doppler beam sharpening, synthetic apertures, the inverse-square law, side-lobe deception techniques, range-gate pull-off, and so on. These ideas, a week's pleasant reading for a sharp chemistry major, are mysteries to most reporters.

Without such a grasp, the reporter is dependent on simplified analyses and descriptions from people who typically have agendas other than informing the public. The technically illiterate reporter cannot recognize obvious nonsense, does not know what questions to ask, and lacks access to original sources. Furthermore, people who know their subjects often refuse to talk to those who do not.[3]

Second, reporters seem to have a strong aversion to intellectual work and to lack engagement with their subjects. They tend to be interested in being reporters but not in the fields they cover. They do not read about the military in their spare time, and they do not discuss serious military questions at the after-work bar. The military is interesting, but they do not notice.

Here again, the trade requires people of action, who by nature are not studious. They will put in long hours in the office or spend months in the bushes of Chad, but will not learn what Kursk was, how a tactical reserve is employed, or what a phase shifter does. They do not care about these things. Their orientation is to the immediate, the present, and the concrete. One often gets the feeling that a reporter knows everything that has happened in his field since he or she came on the beat but nothing that went before.

Third, journalists characteristically avoid structured theoretical thought. They do not instinctively inquire about the fundamental principles of their fields and then seek to understand events in reference to those principles. This is certainly true of military reporters. Usually they do not even suspect that such principles might exist. Being disinclined to tie their thinking to fundamentals, they necessarily are poor at abstract or synthetic thinking and do not readily pull together information from disparate sources to notice a pattern.

They have no idea how odd this seems to others; in fact, they have no idea that the condition exists. A chemistry major, upon being told to cover, say, submarines, will find books on underwater acoustics, submarine design, the history of submarines, the structure of the major oceanic basins, and the theory of modern tactics. This person is unhappy unless he or she has mastered the overall logical framework of submarines. This, after all, is how he or she studied chemistry.

The reporter, by contrast, will read clippings in the morgue on submarines, learn the navy bureaucracy dealing with submarines, and determine which congressional members stand to gain by contracts. He or she learns not submarines but the politics of submarines—and probably little else. The result is that this journalist never really understands what he or she is writing about. Neither do the editors.

Fourth, newspapering is forced, by the crippling pressures of deadlines, into anecdotal thinking, to which the literal-minded reporter is already attuned. The basic unit of journalistic coinage is the story. In the incessant scrabbling to fill the paper by deadline, no one has the responsibility to ask whether the paper's coverage makes sense, whether the stories add to a coherent whole, or whether the important pattern is being missed in preference to the trivial detail. The overwhelming focus is on assembling by deadline a catchy capsule of information called a story. The system rewards those who can produce stories. It does not reward understanding or accuracy.

The pressure is deadly, particularly on wire services and understaffed papers. In high-stress reporting, the journalist grabs not at the fundamentally important story but at the easy story or at anything that is new and will get attention. He or she rewrites a press release with a few quotations added, pads hard with old material, goes repeatedly to the same sources because there is no time to do anything else, and sometimes publishes what he or she knows to be nonsense as long as it is attributed. Anyone unwilling to do this leaves, so those who remain are willing.

Thus, one may see a story asserting that the Stinger missile is too complicated to use and the next day a story, not inconceivably by the same reporter, that the Afghans, good thirteenth-century peasants, are using the Stinger to defeat the Soviet air force. The obvious fact that one of these stories must be wrong does not occur to anyone.

Because those whose intellectual bent is for coherency and understanding depart in frustration, the paper soon has no one capable of big-picture thinking and no one who knows why it is important. The result is that the press almost never notices the larger currents in military affairs, the emerging patterns that are critical to understanding the rapid evolution of the field.

Consider the popular notion that weapons are becoming too complex for soldiers to use. In the late 1960s and 1970s, this was substantially true of some weapons for reasons embedded in the evolution of technology. Now the problem is that weapons, because of highly reliable and internally sophisticated but easy-to-use electronics, are becoming so simple that anybody can use them. Witness the use of the Stinger by the Afghans, the Exocet by the Argentines (the missile that hit HMS *Glamorgan* was fired from the back of a truck) and the destruction of Libyan tanks by barefoot Chadians. Such weapons are also becoming available on the international arms market. The highly significant consequence is that major powers find it increasingly difficult to intervene in the Third World. The press has not noticed.

Fifth, superficiality of treatment is devastating to good coverage. It arises partly because military reporters have no deep interest in their subject and partly because of the lack of time. In many cases the consequence, if deliberately cultivated, would amount to lying.

Suppose that a reporter discovers that the Pentagon has bought a hammer for $400. (Actually the Pentagon normally discovers the problem, and the reporter discovers the discovery.) This becomes a major story, accompanied by all manner of indignant editorials. Other reporters scramble to find their own hammers. Furor and outrage briefly ensue. Then the press goes on to something else. The public is left to think that hammers routinely cost $400 in the military.

By contrast, a chemistry major asks: Was the hammer an anomaly or the norm? How many hammers does the military buy a year, at what average price? Does the overpricing occur only on support equipment or also on the General Services Administration (GSA) schedules from which almost all hammers are bought? Is the average overprice 1 percent, in which case it is negligible; 15 percent, in which case it is a problem; or 1,000 percent, in which case it is a crime? Who is at fault: the contractor or the service? Who, assuming that the malfeasance occurred, is responsible? Are we to believe that the chief executive officer of an enormous corporation called a warehouse clerk and said, "Hey, this is the Big Boy. Let's stick it to the navy today for a hammer. How does $400 grab you?" In short, is there a story at all, and, if so, what is it? Reporters do not ask these questions; they apparently do not realize that there is anything to ask.

There is an element of pure irresponsibility here. A newspaper should make sure that the crimes it exposes have occurred. Often they have not occurred, but the press often does not bother to find out the truth. In the majority of the outrageous-price stories I have looked into, the facts were grossly misreported.[4] For example, the notorious $3,500 coffee pot, which most people now seem to believe to be just that—a glass container with a handle—was in fact an elaborate stainless steel contrivance to make coffee and so on for an aircraft crew. Was it overpriced? I do not know. Clear comparisons with similar products for civilian airliners were not drawn so far as I know. But the object did not remotely resemble a coffee pot.

Sixth, reporters increasingly lack military experience, a difficulty that can be overcome with effort but usually is not. Too many prestigious papers now hire Ivy League students who not only have never worn army boots but have had little contact with the lower- and lower-middle-class men who typically become soldiers. The effects of this inexperience are not easily proved, but they are real.

A hitch in the army gives an idea of what troops can and cannot do, of how they must be led, of their technical limitations, of the real-world behavior of real-world soldiers. If one has watched a platoon learn to fire half a dozen weapons in training, one knows whether a given new weapon is beyond the capability of trained soldiers. (Typically it is not; an inexperienced reporter looks briefly at a weapon whose manual he or she has never read, whose principles he or she barely grasps, and decides that if he or she cannot understand it instantly, neither can a soldier who has trained with it for six months.)

Arguably far worse, the reporter inexperienced with the military often lacks sympathy for soldiers. An Ivy League journalism major is likely to be at best quietly contemptuous of kids who grew up in the hills of Tennessee, a world about which he or she knows nothing. Seeing soldiers as abstractions, the journalist may unconsciously regard them as expendable or at least not think much about their welfare. The result is further isolation of the armed forces from the press.

Indeed, Washington reporters come close to forgetting that soldiers actually exist. The tendency in the capital is to think that the military consists chiefly of generals with a few colonels thrown in to make coffee. A man with time in service knows very well that there is another military: families living in broken-down trailers because their pay is inadequate, ghettoes of oriental wives who huddle together by day because they do not speak English and cannot go downtown, tanks that malfunction because the spare-parts budget is inadequate.

Seventh, bad research—particularly an unwillingness to go to original sources—is the norm in military journalism. Good research takes time and reasonably high intellectual standards, neither of which reporters have. The lack of background knowledge makes research much harder. As an example, consider the debate over the M-1 tank. The story was a major one, running for years and involving billions of dollars. Serious charges were repeatedly made against the tank, such as that it was so dependent on its electronics that it would not fire if the computers went down and that the stabilization system for the main gun "did not work." I still occasionally see these assertions. (The stabilization is much less criticized because few reporters know what it is.)

When I looked into the M-1 story, well after it had become national news, I asked the army for the operator's manual, certainly an obvious first step. The manual contains detailed, step-by-step descriptions of everything the tank will do. Furthermore, it had to be correct in most respects because, unlike slanted documents prepared for Congress, troops use it. The Pentagon told me that I was the only reporter to ask for it. Incredible? No. The same thing has happened to me in writing about any number of controversial weapons. Reporters for the major media do not bother to read the manuals.

I discovered from the manual that if the electronics fail, the tank becomes a perfectly good hydraulically operated tank. If both the electronics and the engine fail, the tank can be fired by means of hand cranks, optical sight, and a piezoelectric firing mechanism. It works; I tried it. The criticism was false.

Similarly, when I went to Fort Knox to test drive the tank, the criticism of the stabilization proved wrong. Having read books on tank design, having studied the M-1 manual to the extent of knowing what every switch was for, having used stabilization on various other vehicles, I could tell how good it was. This was not particularly admirable on my part; anybody can read a few books. Reporters do not.[5] I could fill pages with such examples.

Eighth, reporters, lacking time, knowledge, and interest, rely on journalistic shortcuts. Following the general principle that any organization comes to be structured chiefly for the convenience of those within it, these shortcuts come quickly to be regarded as responsible journalism. One such shortcut is the view that reporters are fungible—that any good reporter can cover anything if given a few weeks to learn the beat. He or she can, to a limited extent—and this extent is almost the limit in what military reporters will learn.

Another shortcut is to confuse covering the Pentagon with covering the military, a desirable illusion because the Pentagon is convenient to Washington. Since there is nothing at the Pentagon but paper, the press covers paper instead of people and equipment. This saves infinite work, but it overlooks the fact that what one hears in Washington and what one sees in the field often bear no resemblance to each other.

Another pernicious shortcut is the assumption that a report, or any statement by someone whose name the public might recognize, constitutes a story in itself. For example, if the General Accounting Office (GAO) releases a report that a weapon is too complex for soldiers, the report itself is covered substantially as a fact. This fits the reporter's need for the anecdotal and the easy. Genuflecting subliminally toward the notion of verification, the reporter will call the Pentagon and "get some comment," which in practice means that an unprepared public affairs officer will say, in desperation, that "the military has done all that is appropriate and the weapon is the best in the world."

The reporter does not check carefully to see whether GAO, notorious for finding what the requester of a report wants it to find, produced the report honestly or even with the help of employees who knew what they were doing. Nor will he or she spend a few days training with the weapon or talking at length with troops who use it. The report is a story. Whether it is accurate is irrelevant.[6]

Another shortcut, used by smaller papers, is reliance of the press on the press. The worst form of this journalism is Nexis, a computerized data bank of major newspapers. The *Washington Post*, for example, once published a miscomprehended story saying that Divad in testing had failed to shoot down a large number of drones. The story was nonsense; there had never been any drones. (It probably was printed because of the author's or an editor's not knowing that "false target" in radar jargon means not a drone but a blip that looks like a target but is not.) It got into Nexis and then appeared in yet more garbled form in an editorial in the *Chicago*

Tribune. Journalists from other papers, doing research on a story, typically look in Nexis (few papers have bureaus in Washington), read the *Post* and the *Tribune,* and write their own versions from these. Soon every paper assumes that since every other paper has carried the story, it must be true. They are all writing from each other.[7]

Ninth, many reporters seem prepared to believe anything that reflects badly on the military. The unexamined assumption that the military is guilty as charged, almost without regard to what is charged, permeates the press. The assumption is journalistically useful, protecting the reporter from having a story evaporate. In the great majority of cases, the military's misdeed either did not occur at all or is not nearly so clear-cut as it seems if unexamined. No reporter likes to see a punchy story dissolve into murky questions of trade-offs in procurement. For example, a $600 "toilet seat" turns out to be a complex injection-molded fixture with various elements of plumbing built into it. The question then becomes whether the price is reasonable for such a contrivance in the small quantities made or whether the airplane for which the seat is made should have been designed with a different sort of toilet—a dull story. A wildly overpriced toilet seat is so much more fun.

The combination of automatic assumption of guilt with the refusal to risk checking frequently leads to absurd charges that never seem to die. Consider the idea that aluminum armor burns. How can anyone believe that if it did, the engineers would not know it—aluminum being, after all, a common metal? Or that army generals would be willing to design a death trap for soldiers? Why not call a trade association of the aluminum industry and ask? For that matter, does one believe that engineers designing a tank, in conjunction with tankers, would not ask such an obvious question as, "What happens if the electronics fail?" The worst form of this bias is the frequent assertion that the military has cheated in testing weapons, an assertion I have yet to see verified.

Tenth, the press has no effective mechanism for self-criticism in military coverage. On other sorts of stories, columnists help maintain standards. A political reporter who writes nonsense about a conservative position is likely to find the story dissected agonizingly in William Buckley's column. No such corrective exists for military stories. Reporters can write almost anything and get away with it.

Eleventh, an assertion obvious to many but one that will be furiously challenged by reporters, is that the press is easily manipulated on military questions. To a reporter who has no factual or conceptual grasp of the subject, mood and ideology must serve as guides. He or she must choose which sources to believe rather than find out which charges are correct. For people who understand the weakness of the press, managing ignorant and overworked reporters is not difficult.

A masterful job is done, for example, by the military reform movement—perhaps the worst source of military information I have encountered and certainly the most cynically dishonest but widely believed by the media.

The techniques of the reformers, and of others like them, are simple. They acquire, say, an internal Pentagon document that mentions or seems to imply problems in the development of a weapon. Difficulties occur in the development of anything complicated, civilian or military, but the reporters do not seem to know this. Alternatively, the reformers produce an assertion by someone who seems to be an unbiased authority that some weapon is poorly designed.[8] Or they manage to suggest that the military is cheating in testing a weapon.[9]

These are tempting stories. The reformers always have documentation of a sort, so the reporter does not have to do research. Their charges are presented in simple form, predigested. They fit the reporter's preconceptions, need for the easy, and taste for the simple. Above all else, the reformers are friendly and accessible. They return calls. They offer telephone numbers for sources who are helpful, funny, give snappy quotes, make stark and fascinating charges, and do not say anything the reporter cannot understand. They are wonderful copy, and they give the inexperienced reporter a delightful feeling of having penetrated a mystery.

In contrast, the Pentagon—stodgy, terrified of saying the wrong thing, bureaucratized to the gills, and not journalistically sophisticated—takes days or weeks to answer and does a poor job. The reformers get the ink; it is not unusual to see half a dozen reformers, and no one else, credited as sources. The reporter has no idea that he or she has been used like a wrench.

Can Coverage Be Improved?

What can be done to improve coverage of the military? Much could be done by any publication that wanted to improve it; however, none do, or they would have done it long ago. Few of my criticisms here are new or original. Most of them are regularly contained in irritated letters to editors.

But why should we in the press want to change? We have no incentive; we have it made as it is. Reporters are people of enormous privilege, perhaps unequaled elsewhere in society. There are surprisingly few things that we cannot do when we want to, as we want to. We are feared, pandered to, cultivated, and coaxed. Our favor is solicited by the high and mighty, our needs taken seriously. There is no one to correct us, no penalty for poor work, and no one to laugh at our solemn self-importance. We do not have to know anything. The chief of staff of the air force will talk earnestly (even desperately) to a fool if he or she represents the *Washington Post*.

People outside the trade perhaps do not understand how much we are able to throw our weight around. A comparatively minor journalist, writing, for example, a military column for a few dozen papers and doing occasional pieces for a major magazine, can tell the air force he wants to ride in a fighter plane, and the air force will immediately arrange it. Who else can do this? If the airplane is suffering criticism in the press, the air force will spontaneously ask him to fly in it. Generals and chiefs of staff will give interviews. A reporter who wants to tour bases in Korea or Germany has to pay his or her way there but then gets a personal escort who will spend a week showing him or her anything. The White House returns his or her calls and faxes documents. Industry instantly provides tours, private showings of new weapons, and interviews with laboratory heads.

Is this because of the reporter's merits? No. It is because the White House does not want its military policy to be savaged in publications on Capitol Hill, which influences the opinions of important people. The reporter's access to print, not ability, intimidates them. Actually, the less competent and responsible the reporter is, the more he or she will be feared. The less responsible the publication is, the more feared it is.

It is insidiously easy for journalists to become smug, to mistake this fear of our uncomprehending attacks for fear of our great insight, to confuse our unquestioned power with our highly debatable competence. Power does corrupt, and it has. As columnists, we are privileged to tell the rest of the world what is really going on. We succumb easily to the belief that we truly understand and that our critics have merely been wounded by the terrible barb of truth.

Added to this conceit is the fact that defense reporters do indeed know more about defense than almost anyone they meet, which encourages their belief in their superior wisdom. Most of their knowledge is of the bureaucracy, of Congress, of essentially nonmilitary considerations, but they have it. Any military reporter for the *Washington Post*, for example, can talk at length of the machinations regarding various weapons in the various armed services and appropriations committees, of this testimony and that testimony, of this leaked document and that ploy by the air force to influence legislation.

This peripheral knowledge impresses people at Washington's cocktail parties, impresses editors, impresses the reporters themselves, indeed impresses almost anyone except those who know what they are talking about. An angry and inarticulate sergeant who writes a letter saying that the reporter does not even know the purpose of the weapon is easy to dismiss.

Add, finally, that reporters are not by nature independent thinkers. The press prides itself on its independence of government, but it is highly dependent on itself. Few reporters dare say that their colleagues are writing nonsense, even when the nonsense is easily demonstrable. Fewer editors believe in correcting their own writers in print or even the writers of other publications. Reporters tend very powerfully to write what their colleagues are writing.[10] Change is therefore unlikely. Nonetheless, a few recommendations are appropriate:

- A paper of any size should make an effort to have on staff at least one technically competent writer assigned to stories having to do with hardware. To the extent possible, this person should read hardware stories by other reporters to catch obvious mistakes. This would improve both the paper's reputation and the reporter's standing in the Pentagon.

- Heterogeneity of staff should be promoted and divergence of political outlook tolerated so that not all reporters share the same background and biases.

- Papers should have an explicit policy of presenting the views on major stories of all sides: critics of the military, the Pentagon, and industry (almost never given a hearing).

- Reporters should be expected to read carefully about their subjects, to spend time—not their own time, but their paper's—on background investigations that have no immediate payoff in stories. Knowledge of their subject should be tied to promotions and raises. This is crucial: the attitude at papers today is that study is all right, provided that it does not interfere with work.

- Reporters should be assigned to cover the military only if they have a genuine interest in the military, as distinct from a desire for a glamorous beat.

- Larger papers should require that reporters have military experience or spend a month living with an infantry company or aboard a ship. By "living with," I mean standing watches, making the marches, freezing in tanks, suffering the boredom, learning the equipment and its foibles. The experience should be repeated at intervals.

- A paper should refuse to print nonsense and should correct it prominently if it slips up. Discovering whether aluminum armor burns requires only a telephone call.

- Reporters should be expected to check stories—not just gesture at objectivity by a perfunctory call to the Pentagon but make a careful evaluation of the Pentagon's responses on their merits. Many stories run for weeks or months and easily allow for research.

- Some means needs to be found to provide thoughtful analysis of military news. Political, as distinct from military, news is analyzed at great length on editorial pages by columnists covering the spectrum from Mary McGrory to George Will. Fundamental political ideas receive ample attention. By contrast, military matters get almost no informed analysis. They are treated by political columnists who haven't the foggiest idea what they are talking about. Surely more informed commentators are available.

This is not a particularly ambitious list of reforms. The nation's great newspapers certainly have the resources to improve their military coverage. The question is whether they care enough to do so.

8
U.S. Defense Reporting:
A British Perspective

Lionel Barber

The British reporter observing how defense is covered in the United States soon suffers shell shock. American journalists talk about constitutional rights, freedom of speech, access to government, and the adversarial nature of the job, all predicated upon the free flow of information. The most striking impression is how the American media expect to be treated, and are treated, with a respect and deference more usually reserved for Oxford academics.

Back home in London, the British defense correspondent rarely attains such prestige. Unlike the Pentagon, which reserves a correspondents' corridor with mounted photographs of the American defense correspondents, there is no permanent place of abode for reporters covering the Ministry of Defence. British reporters belong to a specialized, almost exclusively male band, all operating within a limited framework. Despite the presence of British combat troops, Northern Ireland is, by and large, off-limits since it is considered the preserve of the Belfast correspondent. Domestic defense stories that mushroom into controversy are more than likely plucked by the national political correspondents, who can point to their network of contacts at Westminster and Downing Street. The Thatcher government may well have accentuated this trend by centralizing the flow of official information and consciously politicizing defense for electoral purposes.

In their search for column inches and airtime, defense correspondents can still find some glimmers of hope. The reduced size of the British armed forces, which have shrunk from 720,000 to 320,000 in thirty years, has led to increasing collaboration with European allies in terms of both defense strategy and defense procurement. This has lent the job an increasingly international flavor, with reporters concentrating on news generated by a variety of sources, such as the defense industry, technological advances, the North Atlantic Treaty Organization (NATO) defense policy, and nuclear arms control.

Yet the most important fact remains that British defense correspondents operate in a domestic environment that is not conducive to the free flow of information, a secretive and anonymous world that puts in perspective American journalists' complaints about the difficulties of penetrating the Pentagon. It is a world best summed up by a senior British civil servant: "You must understand that, in the United States, the government operates on the basis of the public's right to know. We in Britain operate on the basis of the public's need to know." Thus, in the United Kingdom and the United States, the ground rules for defense reporting are very different.

In exclusively national terms, defense in peacetime Britain lacks the same interest it commanded, say, thirty years ago. In 1957 Harold Macmillan's Conservative government carried out the first major defense review of the postwar era. In addition to phasing out conscription, which touched the majority of British families, the minister of defense, Duncan Sandys, elected to concentrate on small mobile forces and the nuclear deterrent. In 1964 the Labour government, this time with the ebullient Denis Healey in the chair at the Ministry of Defence, cut down the nuclear force and canceled Britain's fighter bomber, the TSR2. By 1967 he began withdrawing British forces from east of Suez—the tangible evidence of what had long been suspected (and accepted) by the public that Britain's imperial role had drawn to a close.

Since the 1960s British forces have been slowly integrating with their allies on the European continent.[1] The old British army colonels—the "Blimp" class caricatured by their bull necks, diminutive brains, and domed foreheads—have all but disappeared, replaced by professional officers paying duty to the NATO command. This applies not only to the British army on the Rhine, where contacts have traditionally been close with German and U.S. troops, but also to Royal Navy–U.S. Navy links, as shown during the Falklands War. For all the occasional jingoism, collaboration with Europe is increasing. The Western European Union is slowly emerging as a forum for collective defense and security. Perhaps more important in the medium term are the pan-European groups set up to reduce the risks and costs of major weapons systems, such as the Independent European Program Group (IEPG) and NATO's Conference of National Armaments Directors (CNAD). Increasingly the adroit British defense correspondent will turn to these organizations for stories on procurement and the international defense industry.

There still is, however, a relatively high level of national defense spending as a proportion of gross domestic product (GDP) in the United Kingdom. In 1985–1986, even excluding the spending for the defense of the Falkland Islands, the defense budget had climbed to more than 5 percent of GDP, 28 percent higher in real (inflation-adjusted terms) than in 1978–1979.[2] In 1986–1987 defense spending was still running at 4.6 percent of GDP, though the trend was slightly downward as spending in education and health continued to rise.[3]

This spending was designed to fulfill three broad aims: the provision of independent strategic and theater forces for the direct defense of the U.K. homeland, a major land and air contribution to the European continent, and the deployment of a major maritime capacity in the eastern Atlantic and the English Channel.[4] Indeed, the nation's defense priorities appear to have remained fairly constant since 1981, when the Thatcher government made its controversial decision to contract the surface fleet, though the government subsequently did its best to avoid a debate on national defense strategy and priorities, as several British commentators have pointed out.[5]

This is the essential background for the nation's fifteen hard-core defense correspondents, all but one of them male. The only female is Adela Gooch, a former Reuter correspondent working for the *Daily Telegraph* whose favorite story is how she requires special dispensation from the First Sea Lord before staying overnight on a Royal Navy vessel. The other core correspondents work for the national, rather than the provincial, press. Almost all are regarded as specialists, and many share a common culture with links to the officer class. Aside from Gooch, they range from John Keegan, a distinguished military historian and Sandhurst lecturer recently hired as chief defense correspondent of the *Daily Telegraph*, to David Fairhall, the long-serving defense correspondent of the left-leaning *Guardian*. Their common curse is that they have to work in a country where, in the words of Max Hastings, a distinguished war correspondent who is currently editor of the *Daily Telegraph*, "it is considered legitimate to conceal large amounts of information."

Until 1990 the government could resort to the equivalent of a blunderbuss: the 1911 Official Secrets Act, the basic law covering illegal disclosure of official information, to deter journalists from probing too deeply into the activities of the executive branch. In 1958, for example, two Oxford students were jailed for an article they wrote for the university magazine *ISIS* based on their national service experiences. They suggested that in order to accumulate information about Soviet military activities, British forces often behaved in a manner dangerous to peace and contrary to international law—something that, presumably, the British public had a right to know about.[6]

In theory the 1911 act barred publication of something as innocuous as the Ministry of Defence canteen's menu. In practice the law began to fall into disrepute once the government sought to persuade the courts they should use the act to crack down on journalists and their informants. In 1977, for example, three journalists trying to bring out into the open the activities of the General Communications Headquarters in Cheltenham were given mild sentences (two were discharged, another was given a suspended sentence). Some of the information published, such as the location of the listening posts, was available in public telephone directories.

In 1984 a middle-ranking Ministry of Defence official, Clive Ponting, was prosecuted for passing documents to a Labour member of the House of Commons relating to the sinking of the Argentine vessel the *General Belgrano* in the Falklands War. The documents appeared to cast doubt on the Conservative government's argument that the *Belgrano* was steaming in a threatening manner toward the British fleet. In fact, Ponting was acquitted by a jury. The year before, however, a Foreign Office clerk, who passed a document to the *Guardian* newspaper revealing the arrival date of cruise missiles, was successfully prosecuted and sentenced to six months in prison. This outcome caused great hand-wringing at the *Guardian,* whose editor had originally agreed to hand over the relevant document to the government. The move, in retrospect, shut down many of their Whitehall sources on the grounds that no civil servant would wish to risk jail if the newspaper was not willing to protect its sources.

There are other outside pressures on defense journalists such as the D notice system, which carries no legal force but was set up in 1912 to guide journalists away from the pitfalls of the Official Secrets Act. The D (for "defense") notice committee comprises civil servants and editors. It covers sensitive areas such as the intelligence services, photography, radar transmission, navy operations capability, and classified military weapons. Though rarely invoked, D notices in the past have presented problems to journalists, as Andrew Wilson, a former defense correspondent of the *Times,* explained: "As a defense correspondent you could be denied all Ministry of Defense facilities, such as visits to military establishments, transport in service aircraft, and most important of all the off-the-record talks in Whitehall. Without these facilities, most correspondents would find it extremely hard to do their job."

From time to time, a correspondent must ask whether the system is being used to cover up the facts that he or she believes the public should know—for example, a particular practice by a security organization or performance deficiencies in a weapons system for which Parliament is voting large sums of money. When that happens, good journalists obey their conscience. They may get away with it through skillful use of words or by passing the information to an overseas colleague (not subject to D notices) and then reprinting the story.[7]

Although the Official Secrets Act has long been discredited, it took the Thatcher government ten years to come up with an alternative. Before that, the Labour government made a half-hearted effort at reform, but the sad truth was that it suited both major parties to fudge the issue, so both Labour and the Tories proclaimed a willingness to reform while trying to ensure that the authorities retained maximum discretion in interpreting and enforcing the law to protect their definition of national security. It was classic British hypocrisy.

Some believe the recent reforms may, however, have done little to remedy the principal faults of the 1911 law and may even tighten reporting restrictions on certain areas that an American journalist might consider information to be disclosed in the public interest. For example, the new law makes it a criminal offense to publish unauthorized information on security, intelligence, defense, or international relations in any case where the government can prove that harm, broadly defined, results. "Harm" includes anything likely to jeopardize Britain's interest abroad or the ability of the armed forces to carry out their tasks. Moreover, the Thatcher government's reform specifically rejected a national interest defense for whistle-blowers and also a defense based on prior publication.[8]

The last clause dealing with prior publication seemed a deliberate effort to plug the gaps created by the legal battle over *Spycatcher,* the book detailing alleged abuse by the British intelligence services that was written by a former member of MI5, the domestic counterintelligence agency. Mrs. Thatcher ordered injunctions against seven British newspapers, as well as newspapers in Hong Kong and Australia, in an effort to stifle publication of excerpts from the book. When the trial opened, the government even discussed barring news reports about the court proceedings.

The Law Lords, the highest court in the land, eventually ruled, in principle, in favor of the government's argument against publication, but they withheld punishment on the grounds that the material was already in the public domain. The case therefore hardly amounted to a victory for the press. Some commentators noted that in instances where it suited the government to have sensitive material published about the intelligence services—such as the exposure of Soviet spies, real and imagined, by Chapman Pincher, defense correspondent of the *Daily Express*—the long arm of the law was notably restrained.

From a working defense correspondent's point of view, the most deleterious effect of the act has been to encourage a climate of secrecy among civil servants.[9] Unlike their American counterparts, who are political appointees, senior officials in the executive branch are professional civil servants who are camera-shy individuals and have little experience in dealing with reporters or, for that matter, governmental public relations. The argument British defense reporters employ is that the permanent civil services' reluctance to talk to reporters leads often to grossly misleading reportage. Hence, the recent refusal of the Ministry of Defence to say anything about the likelihood of Britain's accepting increases in the U.S.'s F-111 bomber force led to frenzied speculation by the British press—and a great deal of misinformation.

Most assiduous defense reporters nevertheless work hard to reach these reclusive civil servants because they are in a position to provide useful information. The terms of engagement are, however, strict. A journalist applying to the Ministry of Defence press office for background briefings can usually use the material only without attribution, which means no clear identification of the source. The result is usually an anodyne collective code word such as "Whitehall sources" or the knowingly coy "it is understood that" (though the latter is fading out). Though this may not appear to be that different from Washington's use of "a senior administration official," the upshot is that British ministry officials are able to maintain the largely fictitious premise that they are speaking on behalf of Her Majesty's Government rather than their own individual government department.

The British correspondent's primary sources in the Ministry of Defence (MoD) are likely to be the defense secretary accompanied by his junior ministers, all of them elected members of Parliament (MPs) or peers from the House of Lords. One veteran correspondent says it is vital to build up a working relationship with the ministers because they have the confidence and the authority to speak on subjects of immediate news interest. These ministers can, on occasion, be reached in the House of Commons. This can sometimes present problems for the defense correspondent who does not enjoy the same degree of access in the Commons salons as the national political or "Lobby" correspondents—though, in practice, a good working relationship with the Lobby correspondents can easily overcome these obstacles and can even lead to useful two-way traffic in political and policy gossip. More often, however, because there is very little parliamentary business dealing with defense, the ministers are holed up in the MoD or out in the field with the armed forces. This makes daily stories such as "Minister praises troops" or "Minister tests troop morale" favorites among national, and certainly local, newspapers and television.

The real question is how reporters penetrate the executive branch, where policymaking and decision making take place. The American model, where the legislative branch can often prise open the activities of the executive, does not apply in the United Kingdom, partly because the defense budget submitted by the government is not liable to drastic revision as has been the case in the United States. But there have been improvements. The creation in 1979 of parliamentary select committees, which monitor specific government departments, was a welcome step toward more government accountability. The defense select committee has done some useful work in focusing, for example, on the mismatch of commitments and resources, as well as stimulating debate on major weapons systems, notably the Trident missile. The committee also deserves credit for prodding the government into providing annual information on big defense projects, which in turn has helped journalists present better informed stories.

Elected members do have the right to put down questions to ministers, which are then passed to civil servants to draft replies. The process is double-edged; in practice, the MoD press office, knowing that a parliamentary question has been put down, informs the inquiring journalist that any disclosure of detail would amount to a breach of parliamentary privilege. In practice, parliamentary questions rarely get to the nub of the affair, unless the government so wishes. In 1948, for example, a Labour MP agreed to plant a question in the House of Lords on the quality of Danish beef sold in British shops, which led to the momentous announcement that Britain was building an atomic bomb. When the Labour MP gingerly inquired whether the defense minister could supply further information on the development of atomic weapons, he was told: "No, I do not think it would be in the public interest to do so."[10]

There are exceptions that test the rule, notably the Public Accounts Committee (PAC), which is 120 years old and historically has kept a close eye on the public purse. The PAC, working with a journalist from the *Times,* winkled out enough information about the super-secret Chevaline project to force the government to disclose the cost of the plan to modernize the Polaris nuclear missile system. Chevaline received ministerial approval in 1974 and again after the 1975 defense review. Estimated to cost $175 million in 1972, Chevaline's price tag ten years later was $530 million at 1972 prices—$1,000 million in cash. And yet it was not until January 1980 that Francis Pym, then defense secretary, revealed its existence and its true cost in a Commons debate on nuclear weapons.[11]

The public debate over the Trident missile system—the replacement for Polaris in the mid-1990s—was a good deal more enlightening. With antinuclear sentiment in the United Kingdom rising and the former Labour-Conservative consensus on nuclear weapons (at least between party leaders) breaking down, the ruling Conservative government could not stifle debate about the strategic merits of Trident, its cost, and the status of Britain as an independent nuclear power. The interparty row over Trident was matched by the controversy over the siting of nuclear-tipped cruise missiles in the United Kingdom—part of NATO's dual-track negotiating stance, which provided for deployment of new theater weapons as well as negotiations with the Soviet Union on their elimination.

British newspapers covered the cruise and Trident debates with acres of newsprint. With the majority of the U.K. press supportive of Mrs. Thatcher and lukewarm about the Labour party's antinuclear bent, the Conservative government was given an easy ride on cruise missiles. But commentators were more skeptical about the cost of Trident, which at the end of the decade was calculated to take up 6 percent of the defense budget and 12 percent of weapons spending. (In fact, the cost turned out to be lower than expected by 1989, taking up 3 and 12 percent, respectively.)[12] Yet there were also questions about the necessity of Britain's retaining an independent nuclear deterrent when the country's status was far removed from the military or economic power it enjoyed in the immediate postwar period, when the decision was initially made to develop nuclear weapons.

The Thatcher government's response was instructive. A special committee of civil servants was formed; named Miscellaneous Secretariat 17, it was an ad hoc group of government officials whose job was to discredit the Campaign for Nuclear Disarmament (CND) and argue the case in favor of nuclear missiles and the independent deterrent. Defense correspondents, perhaps unwittingly, became the tools for government propaganda directed by the British defense secretary, Michael Heseltine, who, with his mane of blond hair and sweeping good looks, earned himself the nickname Tarzan. Heseltine's official unit in the Ministry of Defence, working with private, unofficial campaign groups, made nonsense of the official notion that civil servants are apolitical creatures.

Nevertheless, the unit's work had an immediate and rapid impact on public opinion in the run-up to the 1983 general election. The popular press, selling more than 10 million copies a day, the bulk of the national newspaper market, lampooned mercilessly the protesters of Greenham Common, site of the cruise missile base. In the columns and cartoons of the tabloid press, the antinuclear protesters at Greenham were depicted as self-indulgent members of the educated middle class, rabid feminists, and "peaceniks." The CND movement did itself few favors by continuing to associate with far left and Soviet front organizations.

At the same time, as defense became highly politicized and the Conservative government recognized its potency as an election weapon against the opposition Labour party, the prime minister's office became increasingly involved in the presentation of defense policy. Bernard Ingham, Mrs. Thatcher's chief spokesman, worked the lobby correspondents and took a close interest in Misc. 17. From the Conservative government's point of view, this was not only inevitable; it was sensible because it offered the opportunity for greater control over what was being published or aired on television (just as the Reagan White House sought to dominate coverage). Yet the co-opting of the Whitehall apparatus appeared to be a new and disturbing development to some civil servants.[13] Indeed, the official machine proved so efficient that the Foreign Office set up a similar operation in 1987, prior to the general election, to preach the virtues of the government's defense and arms control policies.

A separate example of the growing power of Number 10 Downing Street concerned the NATO dispute over the modernization of the alliance's short-range nuclear missiles, which pitted West Germany against Britain, with the United States assuming, after some hesitation, a mediating role. Within days of the Bonn coalition government's announcing that it wanted to link modernization to early negotiations with the Soviet Union on short-range missiles, the Ministry of Defence told inquiring reporters that it was no longer handling questions "because it has now become a political matter," and Downing Street therefore assumed control. While it was true that the SNF did have political ramifications, it was also true that the defense aspects of the dispute (were these weapons vital to NATO's forward defense, what were the alternative nuclear strike weapons, and how did they fit into NATO's conventional arms strategy?) were also very important. Judging by subsequent reporting, in strictly domestic political terms, it suited Mrs. Thatcher's advisers to cast the prime minister as the resolute defender of the NATO alliance and nuclear weapons.

What happens when other departments with an interest in defense resist the trend toward centralization? The best and most recent episode occurred with the Westland helicopter affair, which led to the resignation of Michael Heseltine, as well as another cabinet minister and, on some accounts, presented Mrs. Thatcher with the worst political crisis of her second term. The affair revolved around a cabinet battle over the respective merits of separate rescue plans for Westland, Britain's sole remaining helicopter maker. The company's chairman, Sir John Cuckney, backed by Mrs. Thatcher, supported an American rescue by Sikorsky, a subsidiary of United Technologies. Heseltine favored a European solution and almost singlehandedly directed a London merchant bank to put together a consortium led by British Aerospace, Aerospatiale of France, Messerschmidt-Boelkow-Blohm of West Germany, Agusta of Italy, and GEC of Britain.

In the last few weeks of 1985, Heseltine transformed the Westland rescue into a debate about British dependence on American technology, about the imbalance in the two-way street on defense sales across the Atlantic, and about the need for Britain to put its faith in Europe through a European venture, which, he argued, could herald greater defense and technological collaboration among the West European allies.

Viewed four years later, Heseltine anticipated almost perfectly the arguments about Britain's role in and commitment to Europe. At the time, however, most journalists recognized that, however fervently he preached his message of greater European collaboration, Westland was more an excuse for a political challenge to Mrs. Thatcher. What is surprising is how journalists accepted at face value his assertions about the viability of the consortium. In fact, further questioning of other parties involved, particularly among the consortium partners and the financiers, would have revealed what a ramshackle partnership it actually was.[14]

Instead the press reveled in the political battle and the far more unusual public warfare between the Ministry of Defence and the Department of Trade and Industry. Civil servants, acting under ministerial direction, leaked information anonymously to reporters, even to the extent of a botched effort to discredit Heseltine personally. The strictures of the Official Secrets Acts were discreetly forgotten. Yet even at the height of the fray, the civil service attempted to preserve the fiction of cabinet unanimity, inviting correspondents to official briefings on condition they did not identify the source of attack. Only after Heseltine resigned (staging a theatrical walkout of a cabinet meeting in Downing Street) were order and prime ministerial authority restored.

The Westland episode represented a rare story where a great deal of information about the inner workings of government and policymaking became public, American style. One obvious reason was that the story offered a multiplicity of sources, and this represents perhaps the biggest difference in reporting on defense in the United States and the United Kingdom.

In the United States, defense correspondents are never short of someone they can telephone for a quotation or even an official document. Washington, where the dozens of Pentagon correspondents are based, is best described as an information bazaar where a multitude of think-tankers, lobbyists, government officials, and congressional members ply their wares daily, competing for the attention of journalists to a degree that can be intoxicating.

In the United States, the law works in favor of the inquiring journalist. Libel, which can be a million pound problem in Britain, does not present the same preemptive threat to publication or broadcasting that it does in Britain. In the United States, the executive and the legislative branch share information to a degree unimaginable in the United Kingdom. They rank as co-equals in what all concerned recognize as a public debate, and they therefore court journalists incessantly. Such public debate, accompanied by constant leaks, half-truths, and trial balloons, may not necessarily be the best way to make policy, but it certainly makes life for American journalists a good deal easier.

The constant flow of information in Washington ought to make for better-informed reporting. In the case of experienced journalists, it surely does. But the sheer amount of material available must raise questions about how effectively journalists can process it, interpret it, and present it in a fashion comprehensible to readers and viewers. In my view, this applies to those American journalists who place particular emphasis on disclosure of information rather than seeking to put that information in context.

During a recent current affairs radio show, an American journalist defended disclosure for disclosure's sake on the grounds that it was important to get the information "out into the public domain so it can be discussed." The danger in such journalistic theory is that it turns the reporter into a passive receptacle for information passed on by officials or legislators rather than preserving the journalist's most important function: a thinking transmitter of news and information. One of the most striking recent examples was the coverage of the Justice Department's "Ill-Wind" investigation into bid rigging and fraud in Pentagon procurement during the late 1980s.

To read the stories at the time, it would be easy to infer that the vast majority of federal defense contracts were tainted and the bulk of the U.S. defense industry compromised. So obsessed were reporters in naming names and hanging suspects out to dry in public that they failed to raise questions about the timing and nature of the Justice Department's disclosure of the investigation. In fact, Ill-Wind was revealed on the direction of Ed Meese, the U.S. attorney general, whose own reputation was so tainted by an independent prosecutor's inquiry (again prematurely leaked) that he was prepared to do anything to prove himself the toughest, cleanest lawman in the land.

The emphasis on scandal—whether the $700 coffee pot or the defective Aegis air defense system—permeates American defense reporting. To some degree, it is the inevitable result of the $2 trillion defense buildup under the Reagan administration, which lacked any sense of forward planning or future budgetary reality. The huge flows of cash into the industry guaranteed waste, abuse, and fraud.

For all the words spent on the procurement scandals of the early 1980s and the preoccupation in 1988 with Ill-Wind, the general public's knowledge of the problems does not appear to have been enhanced. Even Governor Michael Dukakis of Massachusetts, the 1988 Democratic presidential candidate, showed himself to be ill briefed and ill informed in the campaign. During one of his final television interviews, this time with Ted Koppel of ABC News, Dukakis struck his familiar theme about cleaning up the Pentagon and cracking down on procurement fraud. "Well," said Koppel, "do you know how many people they have over at the Pentagon responsible for preventing fraud and abuse?"

The governor shifted uncomfortably. "The answer is 26,000," said Koppel who, almost apologetically, proceeded to disclose that he too had not known the correct number of auditors and inspectors until one of his researchers turned up the information while preparing for the Dukakis interview. Pentagon officials reckon he might have done better to have driven home the argument that more auditors, while making bigger headlines, might not necessarily help cure procurement abuses and might even make the problems faced by contractors worse.

An awareness of the causes of such abuse sometimes turns into the sort of world weariness that characterizes an annual bill of $300 billion, surely nothing to fall asleep about. In February 1988, for example, Robert Costello, the Pentagon's top procurement official, told defense reporters that the Department of Defense wastes twenty to thirty cents of every dollar on defense procurement—an estimated $50 billion a year. The news made one paragraph in the *Washington Post* at the end of a long article on army personnel cuts. The *New York Times* thought it so unremarkable as not to be worth mentioning. None of the newsweeklies, the media outlets that are supposed to give readers the news and the interpretation that the daily newspapers and television are too busy to offer, saw fit to publish the information, let alone analyze what it meant and what the Pentagon was doing to rectify it.

When Richard Cheney and his deputy Donald Atwood unveiled a twenty-seven-page management review setting out the guidelines for improving the running of the Pentagon, tightening up procurement procedures, and breaking down distrust between the civilian and military branches, the news conference received little coverage in the major U.S. press. One reason was that select parts of the report had been leaked prematurely; another was that the Cheney-Atwood review was just another effort at reform done in good faith but doomed to failure just like the more than thirty previous postwar reports, starting with the Hoover commission in 1949.

Yet during their news conference, Cheney and Atwood provided some eye-catching information about one of the chief sources of trouble in the Pentagon budget process: the Congress, with its desire for comprehensive oversight and its propensity for micromanaging the procurement of weapons. Cheney told reporters that every day the Pentagon receives 400 written requests and 2,500 telephone calls from Capitol Hill. Defense Department officials, he added, spend on average 17 hours a day testifying to any number of the fifty-seven congressional committees and subcommittees that claim oversight over the Pentagon. In 1970, the Pentagon submitted thirty-seven reports to Capitol Hill; in 1989 the figure had grown to 661 separate reports, each costing an average of $50,000.

It is tempting to suggest that U.S. reporters covering defense tend to pull their punches with regard to Congress because it is there that some of their best and most important sources lie. Most American journalists deny this strongly, pointing out that no good reporter relies on one source. The next response is to point to other equally valuable repositories of information in Washington, such as the think tanks, many of them populated by former government officials who are both knowledgeable and quotable (a major television concern). Yet some Washington correspondents would probably empathize with the advice given by David Hoffman of the *Washington Post*, who told a new recruit at the White House that he would get "good press" if he offered access and talked, just like James Baker (Don Regan's predecessor as White House chief of staff). Those who did not talk to the press, like William Casey, director of Central Intelligence, would not be given the benefit of the doubt in case of trouble or scandal, warned Hoffman.[15]

Congress, of course, does provide valuable research and information to journalists, starting with the productive Les Aspin (D–Wisconsin) of the House Armed Services Committee who seems to pump out press releases almost daily on subjects ranging from the B-2 Stealth bomber to an "end-of-term grading exercise" for the allies that contributed to the Persian Gulf escort mission in 1987–1988. Again, the striking impression is how plentiful resources (and staff) are on Capitol Hill compared to the single secretary and, maybe, a research assistant employed by the hard-pressed British MP.

The trap for the American defense reporter based in Washington is that it becomes too easy to treat the subject as a political game, a story where deals are cut and budget maneuvering takes on a life of its own. The risk is that the defense reporter based in Washington becomes a pawn in this game, ignoring the larger reality of the armed forces whose job it is to defend the country and the American public (including, presumably, the reporter). Several Washington reporters I interviewed for this chapter complained that their newspapers do not allow them enough time to spend covering the troops, the navy office, and the air force. One senior correspondent said that of all the articles he wrote in two years, his favorite was a description of two nights on a mock war game exercise in the Mojave desert. There he spent time with combat troops, and he could assess their skills, character, morale, and fighting spirit.

It is probably fair to say that British defense correspondents are somewhat closer to the armed forces. Newspapers and television are willing to give plenty of coverage to subjects such as bullying (even buggery) in the forces. Other recent stories included alleged racism in the army and the exposure of the color bar in many British regiments. This in turn led to a reasonably informed debate about the "demographic trough," whereby the British armed forces face shrinking pools of available recruits and therefore may turn more to minorities.

Similarly, it is striking how much coverage the future of the Gurkha forces, now based in Hong Kong, have commanded the British press in 1988. The obvious reason is that it is linked to the future of Hong Kong, which has become of intense interest in the aftermath of the massacre of students and workers at Tiananmen Square in Peking ordered by the Chinese communist government. But the press and television are also making a calculated and correct gamble that the British affection for the Gurkhas, from their World War II feats to their performance in the Falklands War, guarantees them a place in the public affection. They might be superfluous in strict military terms, but in British eyes, that is no reason to send them back to their native Nepal.

British defense reporters' proximity to the armed forces may be the most important contribution they have to make to the coverage of their subject. They may not match their American counterparts in the amount of information they provide or the accuracy with which they present it. That is because of the restricted and narrow system within which they are forced to work and which is far inferior to the open and more accountable system operating in the United States. But when it comes down to the life-and-death part of defense—the men and women involved—the British reporter is usually on the spot.

9

The Department of Defense Media Pool: Making the Media-Military Relationship Work

Jeffrey J. Carnes

A fundamental principle of the American political system is the use of checks and balances to ensure a free society despite the divergent needs and interests of its people. The system must reconcile many conflicting goals in order to function, and the relationship between the military and the media presents an important example. This relationship is characterized by an inherent conflict of interests stemming from the press's desire for full disclosure of government activities and the government's need for secrecy in national security matters. Former Secretary of Defense Caspar Weinberger once observed that "the nature of the relationship between a free press and government in our society is constant competition, an additional check and balance within the democratic process. It is a healthy and historically sound situation."[1] Few people would disagree with him, but some would question whether an appropriate balance between the needs of the media and the government is being achieved. This chapter examines that question through a review of the history of military-media relations and an analysis of the most recent efforts to improve the relationship by creating a media pool for coverage of sensitive military operations.

The media pool concept was specifically developed as a means of improving the deteriorating military-media relationship. The pool was designed primarily for use during the initial phase of surprise operations or for coverage of military actions in restricted or remote areas. All U.S. military operations since the Vietnam War have exhibited at least one of these characteristics, thus highlighting the importance of the media pool concept. Furthermore, the Department of Defense media pool has been employed in every significant military action since its inception in 1985, so there is sufficient information to analyze whether the pool approach has resulted in any improvement in military-media relations.

History of the Military-Media Relationship

Most writings on the history of military-media relations recognize the Civil War as the first American conflict to be covered by true war correspondents. There was a great deal of animosity between the military and the press during the war. The causes of poor relations were many, but they included events such as reporters' hiding in bushes near command posts and the publishing of operational secrets like the breaking of the Confederate signal flag codes.[2] Union general William Tecumseh Sherman expressed the prevailing attitude of military leaders toward the press:

> War correspondents are a nuisance and a danger at headquarters and in the field. . . . All such accompanying the expedition were and should be treated as spies . . . because their publications reach the enemy, [and] give them direct and minute information of [*sic*] the composition of our forces. . . . Napoleon himself would have been defeated with a free press.[3]

Military-media relations improved during the Indian wars that followed the Civil War, mostly because there were few reporters in the field and their reports on the actions of the military were usually favorable. This improvement in relations did not last. The commander of American troops in Cuba during the Spanish-American War, Major General William R. Shafter, disliked the presence of reporters.[4]

World War I saw the establishment of an official Allied policy of censorship. General John J. Pershing, commander of the American Expeditionary Force, preferred controls on the press. Reporting was generally favorable to the Allies but often lacked detailed factual content. Because of the high degree of censorship, no Allied reporters wrote about one of the most important events of the war, the French army mutiny in 1917.[5]

Relations between the military and the media improved significantly during World War II, for many reasons, including increased recognition by military leaders of the valuable role the media could play if properly handled (especially in morale building), closer personal contacts between the media and the soldiers on the field, a public consensus about the morality of the U.S. involvement in the war, more lenient censorship policies, and increased military cooperation, especially in disseminating news quickly. New methods of regulating the press included government accreditation of reporters and signature of affidavits agreeing to military regulations (including censorship). Correspondents had to waive all claims against the government for injury or death, and reporters were assigned to public relations assistants and specific military units.[6]

The increased cooperation between the military and the media in World War II is sometimes seen as the peak of military-media cooperation. Curiously, the Korean War marked a downward turn in these relations despite a relaxation in censorship. With this decreased censorship of news reports came a new form of censorship at the source; military leaders like General Douglas MacArthur withheld all information about impending military operations. This is normally attributed to a lack of faith in the less constrained news media's ability to exercise self-restraint when dealing with sensitive operational secrets.[7]

Despite the introduction of nearly total freedom of movement for the press without censorship, Vietnam was a war during which military-media relations seriously deteriorated. The use of censorship at the source reached an all-time high.[8] News reporting became more speculative, arguably contributed to by the lack of information available from the tight-lipped military, which in turn resulted in an agitated press, increasingly critical of military activity.

Drew Middleton, a veteran *New York Times* reporter who covered World War II and all subsequent U.S. conflicts, believes that the lack of censorship or other controls over the media fostered distrust among military leaders concerned with maintaining operational secrecy. Their natural reaction was to shut out the media, thus creating animosity between the two groups.[9] He also identifies a lack of education and experience on the part of both reporters (concerning military operations and security sensitivities) and military personnel (understanding media deadlines and technical intricacies) as another factor in the deterioration of military-media relations in Vietnam. The natural results were increased inaccuracy in reporting due to restricted release of the facts by the military and lack of understanding of existing information on the part of reporters.[10]

If both groups had been better educated concerning the needs and concerns of the other, there probably would have been more trust and cooperation during the Vietnam War. Instead, the breakdown of military-media relations that occurred during that war left indelible scars in the minds of reporters and military personnel alike.

Grenada: Crisis in Military-Media Relations

Although it was a small operation compared to the other conflicts discussed in this chapter, the October 1983 military operation in Grenada, code-named Urgent Fury, was an important watershed in military-media relations. The decision to send U.S. forces into Grenada is itself a fertile subject of debate, but the initial exclusion of all media personnel from the operation was the one decision that had a critical impact on the military-media relationship.

In the short time frame during which Urgent Fury was planned, options that would allow press coverage of initial operations were omitted. The decision was defended by the government on the grounds of military security and safety of reporters. Neither reason was acceptable to most members of the press. Media representatives argued that history did not support either of the explanations for their exclusion cited by the government.[11] The media were not allowed onto the island until the third day of operations, after most of the significant battles had been fought.

There is little question that the memory of Vietnam and the distrust it evoked influenced the military services and their civilian superiors in the decision to exclude the media. The media, however, saw this as "an unparalleled act of censorship that forced the public to rely on the Government's self-serving accounts of the action."[12] Virtually all major news organizations and professional institutions responded by sending strong letters of protest to the government. The Department of Defense recognized that a crisis situation had been reached in its relations with the media. Accordingly, the chairman of the Joint Chiefs of Staff, General John W. Vessey, Jr., commissioned a study in response to the media's complaints.

Media-Military Relations Panel

General Vessey appointed retired Major General Winant Sidle chairman of a special review panel whose purpose was to make recommendations to the chairman on the following central question: "How do we conduct military operations in a manner that safeguards the lives of our military and protects the security of the operation while keeping the American public informed through the media?"[13]

The Sidle panel, named for its chairman, was formed in February 1984 to draft guidelines on press access to military actions. The original intent was to have a panel composed of military public affairs and operations experts along with representatives of the major news organizations, but all of the latter groups declined to participate on the grounds that journalists should not serve on a government rule-making body.[14] As a result, retired journalists and professors of journalism were sought to represent the concerns of the media.

The final composition of the panel was as follows:

Major General (retired) Winant Sidle, former army chief of public affairs.

Richard S. Salant, former head of CBS and now president and chief executive officer of the National News Council.

Barry Zorthian, senior vice-president of Gray and Company.

Scott Cutlip, former dean of journalism, University of Georgia.

A.J. Langguth, professor of journalism, University of California.

Wendel S. Merrick, retired war correspondent for *U.S. News & World Report.*

Keyes Beech, retired war correspondent and Pulitzer Prize winner.

Colonel George Kirschenbauer, U.S. Army, Office of the Joint Chiefs of Staff (OJCS).

Captain James Major, U.S. Navy, OJCS.

Colonel Robert O'Brien, Jr., U.S. Air Force, deputy assistant secretary of defense for public affairs.

Billy Hunt, Office of the Chief of Public Affairs, Department of the Army.

Captain Brent Baker, U.S. Navy, assistant chief of information for operations, Department of the Navy.

Tom Halbert, assistant chief of public affairs, U.S. Air Force.

Major Fred C. Lash, Office of Public Affairs, U.S. Marine Corps.[15]

Prior to meeting, the chairman of the panel invited a number of news organizations to address the group during its public sessions and sent questionnaires to these groups requesting their views on key topics the panel would address. Some of the questions included what the media thought were its rights under the First Amendment, the type of access they thought was required during military operations, their thoughts about the use of media pools, and other questions concerning the technical details of media coverage in military operations.[16] The responses of the media were distributed to the members of the panel prior to its official meetings.

The fourteen-member panel met for five days commencing on February 6, 1984. The first day, a closed-session organizational meeting, ended with an agreement that the media should have access "to the maximum degree possible consistent with the security of the mission and the safety of the troops." Further, the panel decided it would not address the legal issue of whether the press has the right to be present at military operations but would concentrate on recommending specific procedures for the military to utilize in allowing media coverage.[17] The remaining four days of panel meetings were open sessions for receiving presentations from and discussing specific issues with news organizations.

The long-awaited report of the Sidle panel was released in August 1984 after review and approval by the chairman of the Joint Chiefs of Staff and the secretary of defense. The final report presented eight recommendations on how best to fulfill the needs of both the military and the press. Following is a summary of the more significant items:

- Public affairs planning for military operations should be conducted concurrently with operational planning, and this should be institutionalized in written guidance or policy as soon as possible.
- When it becomes apparent that news media pooling is the only feasible option for early access to an operation, planning should provide for the largest press pool possible and minimize the length of time before full coverage replaces the pool.
- A basic tenet governing media access to military operations should be voluntary compliance with ground rules established for each individual operation, and violation should mean exclusion of the correspondent(s) concerned from further coverage of the operation.
- Public affairs planning should provide qualified personnel, sufficient equipment, and communications and transportation support to assist the media in covering the operation adequately.
- Routine meetings between key media and military leaders should be established to address ways of improving the military-media relationship, and existing programs for educating military and media personnel in each other's methods and responsibilities should be greatly expanded to foster improved understanding and cooperation.[18]

The final remarks in the report focused on the need for both the military and the media to commit themselves to improving and maintaining sound relationships with each other:

> The optimum solution to ensure proper media coverage of military operations will be to have the military—represented by competent, professional public affairs personnel and commanders who understand media problems—working with the media—represented by competent, professional reporters and editors who understand military problems—in a non-antagonistic atmosphere. The panel urges both institutions to adopt this philosophy and make it work.[19]

In general, the Sidle panel report was well received by both the military and the media. As soon as it was released, it was announced that the Pentagon had already implemented many of the recommended actions. Completed actions included the rewriting of exercise and contingency manuals and the establishment of a public affairs office within the Office of the Joint Chiefs of Staff.[20]

The media generally applauded the panel's recommendations but nevertheless voiced some concerns over how the military would select pool members and what role escorts would play in pool activities.[21] The question of how the pool would be selected was quickly answered by the release of a proposed nominal pool structure by the Office of the Secretary of Defense. The pool would normally consist of about twelve people:

two news agency reporters, one radio correspondent, four television reporters, a camera operator, a sound technician, a still photographer, a magazine writer, and at least one newspaper correspondent (originally no newspaper reporters were included, but this was quickly changed).[22] Concerns about how well the concept would work could be answered only by trial and error in eventual exercises of the press pool.

The Pentagon also moved quickly to establish a basic set of ground rules for press participation on the battlefield. The rules were similar to those of Vietnam, which excluded specific censorship but provided certain guidelines about what not to print (future plans or operations or size of units engaged in the operation, for example). This was qualified with a warning that reporters who did not follow the rules would lose their accreditation to the area of operations. One important addition to the ground rules, compared to those of the Vietnam era, was the right to submit complaints to the on-scene commander as well as to the Pentagon itself.[23] It is not surprising that the press had little quarrel with these relatively simple rules.

One member of the panel, Barry Zorthian, wrote an editorial after the report was released focusing attention on the most important factor in implementing the panel's ideas. The thrust of his editorial was that both sides must now act in good faith. He added that since the Pentagon had basically accepted and appeared to be implementing the recommendations of the panel, the focus was now on how the press would respond to the challenge.[24] The challenge was clearly centered on exercising the proposals in future training or actual events.

The Pool at Work

The first test of the pool concept came in April 1985 when the Department of Defense secretly activated the pool to cover an exercise deployment and mock invasion in Central America. It was termed a failure by both the media, who could not get dispatches released in a timely manner, and the military, which was surprised that word of the pool's activation was leaked within twenty-four hours. Although both sides complained that they were disappointed by the operation, the Pentagon vowed that it was committed to try the concept again.[25] One media participant actually went as far as saying he suspected the exercise was meant to be a failure "to prove . . . the press can't be trusted." Despite the problems and animosities uncovered by this first attempt, the Pentagon went on with plans to correct those problems identified in preparation for further tests of the system.[26]

Five months later, in September 1985, a second secret deployment of a twelve-member press pool was executed in conjunction with a training exercise in Kentucky. The test was declared successful, with few complaints about the mechanics of media pool operations. Secretary of Defense Weinberger boasted about the success of the concept and promised continued testing of the system.[27] The feasibility of the press pool concept appeared to have been verified but had yet to be tested in an actual situation.

The confrontation between the United States and Libya in 1986 provided the first true test of pool operations although in a different scenario from that which many had envisioned. The hostile action was sudden and basically unpredictable when compared to the invasion scenarios of Grenada or previous media pool exercises. Additionally, the short periods of actual combat took place over the horizon from the far-flung U.S. fleet or at night. Actual shooting occurred only during several days over nearly four months of operations.

The military tried to give the media some opportunity to view the fleet in operation by flying rotating press pools to the aircraft carriers. One pool missed the first hostile action by only a few hours, but the next crew was satisfied with the candid, unencumbered interviews they were permitted with the pilots and sailors immediately following the action. The media reported that despite the difficulties of the unpredictable operation, few reporters had any complaint about the level of cooperation they were receiving from the military.[28]

An attempt by four U.S. television networks to get coverage of the Libyan confrontation outside the structure of the press pool highlighted one of the possible dangers of freelance incursions into a combat zone. This occurred when the networks chartered a plane to fly over the U.S. fleet. The plane was intercepted and escorted out of the combat zone by U.S. fighter aircraft. Both network and government sources agreed that the plane could have been shot down by either Libyan or U.S. forces if it had not been identified and escorted away from the scene by the fighters.[29] These attempts ended after the media recognized that they could get more information from the military media pools than by taking independent action and that the risks of such flights were extremely high.

The experience gained by media pool employment in the 1986 Libyan confrontation provided additional evidence that the pool concept had many merits, even in the type of unique situation in which it was nearly impossible to predict when shooting would break out and where modern over-the-horizon or night air strikes were employed beyond the view of the battle group. But since no reporters were actually lucky enough to be in the right place at the right time, the use of media pools in this situation did not receive as much publicity as could be hoped for.

The media and the military continued to work together under the media pool system in the spirit which was intended by the Sidle panel. In March 1988 another pool was activated to cover the show of force in Honduras during the Nicaraguan incursion into contra havens inside the

Honduran border. By then the pool concept had been exercised and continually fine-tuned in eight training deployments and the Libyan confrontation.[30] The most successful demonstration of the flexibility and usefulness of the media pool concept was yet to come.

The threat to U.S. interests in the Persian Gulf during 1987 and 1988 provided another opportunity for the use of the media pool. A media pool was secretly deployed to the Persian Gulf in July 1987 to cover the first transit of a convoy of U.S. Navy warships escorting Kuwaiti-owned tankers that had recently been reflagged under the U.S. flag.[31]

The United States and Iran had been exchanging political rhetoric, full of warnings and threats, for months leading up to the beginning of what was called operation Earnest Will, designed to provide military escorts for convoys of U.S.-flagged tankers past the Silkworm surface-to-surface missiles, naval combatants, and small high-speed attack boats that Iran had been employing for years to threaten and attack unarmed shipping. An additional threat came from Iraqi warplanes that were conducting an aggressive campaign against Iranian oil tankers that had resulted in the tragic mistaken attack on the USS *Stark* several months earlier when thirty-seven U.S. servicemen were killed. It was clearly an important event with high media interest and the potential for significant military action.

The pool was activated out of concern that hundreds of media representatives might try to cover the transit of the convoy using their own boats or aircraft, creating additional security risks for the navy as well as the reporters who entered the volatile war zone. The ground rules for the pool were similar to those of previous ones: all information gathered by the pool was to be shared and widely disseminated; the pool could move freely about the bridge, the combat information center, the captain's quarters, or just about any other place except the secure communications space; pool members could interview anyone they wished, could listen to radio circuits, and even could view the radar scopes and navigation charts.[32]

Clearly one of the benefits of this type of media pool is the close interaction between the reporters and the servicemen and servicewomen. Carl Rochelle, a Cable News Network reporter and member of the pool, summed up the positive aspects of pooling: "We shared the feelings of the crew, the fears and sometimes even the anger. We watched the whole thing. We didn't just get a slice of it; we got all of it. That's the way to report a story."[33]

Although there were several serious delays in transmitting the first several press pool releases, the overall conclusion drawn by both the military and the media was that the first Persian Gulf media pool had been a success.[34] The Associated Press's Tim Ahern said, "As far as I'm concerned, the pool's chief test came Friday, after the *Bridgeton* hit the mine. The story I filed was the first word released at the Pentagon." Mark

Thompson of Knight-Ridder Newspapers added: "First and foremost, [the pool] had been a success inasmuch as our audiences were better served for our having been there, rather than at our Washington desks, and for having covered the escort operations, albeit under unusual conditions."[35]

Operation Earnest Will was designed to last indefinitely, and the threat of further military action did not disappear. As a result, new territory was broken in the use of media pools as a continuous, rotating group of correspondents in the gulf region. The popularity and feasibility of prolonged pool operations was affirmed by the successful implementation of no fewer than twenty-eight media pools in the nine months following the start of Earnest Will.[36] The only change to pool procedures was the reduction in size to four or five members; this took into account limited shipboard space and improved the mobility of the pool.

The twenty-eighth Persian Gulf media pool was activated for a routine embarkation for a tanker escort mission. While preparing to rendezvous with the merchant ships, the pool received word on board their host ship that another U.S. ship, the USS Roberts, had struck a mine. A series of logistics moves brought the pool to the scene of the incident, and video footage of the damaged ship was transferred via an unprecedented linkup with an NBC helicopter based in the region. The videotape was transferred from the navy ship to the NBC helicopter and transmitted via shore facilities for same-day coverage in the United States. This was applauded as a fine example of media-military cooperation.[37]

The next morning the pool again transferred ships and was informed by escort officers that U.S. forces were preparing for action planned in measured response to the Iranian mine laying that had damaged the *Roberts*. Later pool members were briefed concerning U.S. operational plans for what was code-named operation Praying Mantis. The operation would be the first real test of the media pool concept in a planned hostile military action.[38]

Combat action on April 18, 1988 was extensive compared to previous U.S.-Iranian confrontations, but because it was far-flung, covering hundreds of square miles of ocean, the media representatives could not witness all the action. The problem was compounded by extensive use of modern missiles and other guided munitions that struck targets over the horizon. Nevertheless, pool members were overwhelmed by the mass of information they were privy to while listening to the tactical radio communications of the battle groups.[39] Once again, media pool members shared the exhilaration, anxiety, fear, and frustration that the servicemen alongside them were feeling in the battle.

The pool did film several surface-to-air and surface-to-surface missile firings later in the day. The surface-to-surface missiles were launched against an Iranian frigate, the *Sahand*, just over the horizon, about 20 miles away. The reporters felt and heard the impact of the missiles, as well as secondary explosions that disabled and eventually sunk the *Sahand*.[40] Footage of these missile shots, including the sights and sounds of the crew members during several tense but exciting moments of combat, would be seen back home—probably the first such footage of modern U.S. naval warfare ever recorded.

One account of the pool's experience called it "cordial, cooperative, and unforgettable." It listed the following summary of accomplishments for the pool:

> Pool accomplishments during this [eleven day] activation included over 2,000 miles traveled, ten ships embarked, six helicopter transfers, four small boat transfers, fourteen print reports, six television scripts filed, 600 minutes of videotape, eighteen rolls of still film, and three ship-to-shore transfers of pool material. . . . This deployment clearly demonstrated the essential value of the pool and the military's ability to coordinate challenging pool requirements without significant impact upon operations or security.[41]

Because of the great interest generated by the fortunate timing of this press pool, the many improvements in military-media relations were well covered in postoperation news reports. The civilian news helicopter linkup, previously an unauthorized means of transferring videotape ashore, was accepted as an approved method of transfer. Media wire reports were sent out over military communications channels via immediate precedence (the third highest of four levels of precedence), and the commanding officer (CO) of the USS *Williams*, the ship the pool was riding during the attacks on April 18, dedicated a word processor and operator to media pool reports. The media also made concessions, agreeing not to print anything the CO said over the ship's loudspeaker system, thus permitting him to talk frankly with his crew.[42] Such levels of military-media cooperation are hard to find in any other operations since World War II.

Although routine deployments of the Persian Gulf press pool continued after April 1988, nothing significant was noted from these increasingly routine operations.

Despite the many successes of the media pool during the Persian Gulf operations, the December 1989 invasion of Panama challenged the viability of media pool concept. The invasion, nicknamed operation Just Cause, was primarily a ground operation, much like the many exercise deployments where the media pool had been tested previously. A media pool was activated for the invasion, but it was a resounding failure.

The stage for operation Just Cause was set by several years of increasing conflict between the regime of the self-proclaimed Panamanian dictator Manuel Noriega and the U.S. government. The United States had

issued indictments against Noriega on drug trafficking charges, while Noriega consolidated control over the Panamanian government by removing
the previously elected president and installing loyal political and military
officials. He eventually agreed to hold free elections, but he annulled the
results after it became apparent that opposition candidates were winning
the election.

The final weeks before the invasion were marked by increased harass-
ment of U.S. personnel and dependents and the murder of an off-duty U.S.
serviceman. The increasing threat to U.S. citizens and property, combined
with Noriega's rejection of the democratic process, led to President Bush's
decision to undertake operation Just Cause.

The Just Cause media pool was a failure from the start, arriving in
Panama four hours after the invasion began—well after most of the initial
heavy fighting had ended. Secretary of Defense Richard Cheney's concern
for secrecy delayed activation of the pool until it was too late to deploy it
with the advance forces. When the pool finally arrived in Panama, military officials did little to rectify the situation, often refusing to cooperate
with or support the pool. The cumulative failures in organizing and supporting the pool all appeared to stem from a lack of thorough advance
planning.[43]

Pool members later expressed total frustration during the four days
the pool was in operation. One photographer complained that the first
pool picture was not transmitted until 17 hours after the invasion began.
The pool spent much of the first day on a U.S. base watching CNN
coverage of the invasion outside. The on-scene commanders told them it
was too dangerous for them to visit combat areas. By the end of their
ordeal, one pool member drafted the motto, "If it's news today, it's news
to us," underscoring the pool's inability to cover the invasion.[44]

Responsible military and Defense Department officials regretted their
failure to implement and effectively support the Just Cause media pool.
Defense Department spokesman Pete Williams initially accused U.S. military leaders in Panama of "incompetence" as the reason the pool failed
but later recanted and accepted full responsibility.[45] The chief public affairs official in Panama, air force colonel Ronald Sconyers, said the Panama command's inability to support the press contingent adequately was
the most "professionally embarrassing" time of his demanding two-year
tour.[46]

The media and the military addressed the Just Cause media pool
failure shortly after it ended, looking to save the pool framework. Fred
Francis of NBC News claimed the media shared some of the blame with
the military due to lack of experience among pool members and a security
lapse. He noted that a national newsmagazine had searched for a correspondent to go with the pool during its office Christmas party. As a result,
the staff and its guests learned the invasion was imminent, seriously

breaching operational security hours before the invasion.[47] Despite the poor performance of the pool in this instance, one report claimed that many news executives believe the media pool is a distinct achievement and should be preserved and improved.[48]

The Pentagon's report on why the Just Cause media pool failed placed the majority of the blame on Defense Department officials. The "Review of Panama Pool Deployment" report was written by former Associated Press reporter and Pentagon deputy spokesman Fred Hoffman, who helped establish a national news media pool after the Grenada fiasco. Secretary Cheney's excessive concern about security, fueled by White House signals to be wary of the press corps, was cited as one factor in the failure. Pentagon spokesman Pete Williams, however, was singled out for failing to plan properly for the pool, failing to push Secretary Cheney on activating the pool early enough to deploy it, and failing to ensure the pool was properly supported after it was deployed.[49] Hoffman's recommendations primarily emphasized that the media pool idea demands the full support of political and military leaders and requires advance planning. The report suggested the secretary of defense issue a policy directive requiring full military support for media pools, which the Pentagon agreed to in principle. Moreover, media pool planning should be included in all Joint Chiefs of Staff war plans, according to Hoffman.[50]

In retrospect, the failure of the Just Cause media pool could have spelled the end of the pool concept, but both the military and media appear committed to continued development of it.

An Assessment

Several points stand out in this historical review. First, a major source of animosity between military and media personnel is a lack of mutual understanding. Second, censorship is a double-edged sword; too little can yield the same result as too much—a lack of information due to the unwillingness of the military to release information to an unrestrained press. The lack of authoritative information affects the accuracy and availability of news for the public. Third, no two military actions are the same; thus military-media relations must be based on flexible, clearly defined ground rules. Finally, the media pool initiative requires the commitment of media and military leaders alike if it is to survive and succeed. What are the best ways of approaching these problems?

There are innumerable studies and articles on the dangers of uneducated media and military representatives. Veteran correspondent Drew Middleton offered the following opinion in an interview several years ago: "I don't think there has to be a reason for the military-media controversy. Ignorance contributes to it as it does to everything else."[51] Military officers also recognize this problem. A recent questionnaire given to 105 senior officers attending the Army War College asked how the army could improve military-media relations. The most common answer was, "Do more to educate army officers and the media about each other."[52]

Another study proposes an additional problem that exacerbates the lack of understanding between these two groups. The Twentieth Century Fund, a research foundation, commissioned a study on journalists and military leaders that concluded:

> The divide between the military and media is in danger of widening. Each tends to attract different personality types and to foster different sets of values. Of necessity, military people are schooled to respect tradition, authority and leadership; obedience is an inescapable part of military life. In contrast, because journalists on occasion have the job of challenging official wisdom, their ranks tend to be filled with those who are more free-wheeling, irreverent and skeptical of authority.[53]

This may be too stereotypical and a little exaggerated, but the point remains that there are many sound justifications for increasing the mutual education of military officers and media personnel. The most logical means of accomplishing the important goal of educating such large professional groups is coursework in the schools of journalism and the academies of the armed forces. Educational courses should be supplemented through postgraduate seminars and panel discussions.

A complementary method of elevating the media-military base of mutual understanding is to promote close interaction between the two groups. One of the most productive ways of promoting understanding, and even a sense of camaraderie, is to encourage close, continuous cooperation on the battlefield. History shows that personal relationships develop, trust is fostered, and a rapport is established when these two groups live and work together. Improved military-media relations ultimately benefit the American public, which gets more and better news. World War II and the Persian Gulf media pools are good examples of this phenomenon, and similar positive reports were noted in Britain's experiences in the Falklands.[54]

The next problem noted in the history of military-media relations is the role of censorship. The term automatically triggers cries of First Amendment violations, yet many veteran correspondents and military officers believe that a complete absence of censorship can be as bad as, if not worse than, routine official censorship. The Vietnam experience is a good example; military leaders appeared to withhold information since they had no guarantee that the press would act responsibly in choosing what was suitable for print. This censorship at the source bred contempt and greater distrust among military leaders and the media. Additionally, reduced access to the facts, a natural by-product of this form of censorship, hinders the press's ability to understand the overall context of operations, leading to more speculation and greater inaccuracies in reporting. Speculative reporting and any attendant errors normally cause the military to develop an even greater distrust of the media.

The best form and amount of censorship for a healthy military-media relationship is difficult to define, but the answer lies somewhere between the extremes of World War I (nearly total censorship) and Vietnam (no formal censorship). The basic ground rules developed for the media pool concept, as recommended by the Sidle panel, appear to be an effective compromise. Although these rules do not implicitly direct censorship, the control exercised by the military in selecting members of the pool and the role the military plays in transmitting or transporting pool products back to the users provide an effective yet low-key form of censorship.[55] The examples of media pool relations in the Libyan and Persian Gulf operations appear to support the proposition that the military and the media were both comfortable with the ground rules and minimum military control that represented this new form of censorship.

The final key point to be drawn from the history of military-media relations is that no two conflicts are alike. The beginning of the American military-media relationship was developed in fairly large-scale military conflicts, wars generally supported by the public under official declarations of war. Most recent military actions have been the subject of increased political and public debate, have not been covered by official declaration of war, and are usually classified as low-intensity conflicts.

It is impossible to predict where the next military challenge will occur, how much public support it will have, whether it will be primarily over land or sea, and how accessible the area might be to modern press technology. The only way to be prepared for such uncertainty is to remain flexible, clearly a requirement for both the military and media. The extreme differences in the planning and logistics for the sea-based Persian Gulf media pool as opposed to the land-based Panama pool demonstrate the need for flexible planning to prepare for future media pool deployments. Innovative ideas like the news helicopter and navy ship rendezvous used in Persian Gulf media pool operations set a healthy example of mutual cooperation and flexibility between the news correspondents and their military hosts. It is exactly this kind of combined effort that is necessary to face and overcome the many unknown situations the future may bring. That is the heart of the military-media commitment the Sidle panel called for and is an essential element in the process of improving and maintaining sound military-media relations.

The problems highlighted in past failures of the military-media relationship were clearly evident. There were extensive writings on the crisis in the relationship during the period between Vietnam and the watershed Grenada operation.[56] The fact that the problem was allowed to fester reflects the culpability of all concerned for having failed to take action to correct the unneeded animosities that existed between the media and the military. The ultimate loser in this situation was the American public, which had a right to be accurately informed. It appears that the relations are now improving because of the responsible action by both media and military leaders.

Conclusions

Phillip Knightley began his 1975 history of war correspondents with a quotation from Senator Hiram Johnson: "The first casualty when war comes is truth."[57] This does not have to be the case. Honest men and women following the Constitution and legal interpretations, intent on serving the public, and dedicated to finding solutions to problems can ensure that truth is protected.

The sound recommendations of the Sidle panel and the obvious efforts of both the media and the military to act in good faith on the panel's recommendations have resulted in visible and substantial improvements in the military-media relationship. The most important factor promoting further development and maintenance of this new, more productive working relationship is a continued total commitment by all involved in military operations and news reporting. The lessons of Vietnam and Grenada, the nadir of the military-media conflict, must not be forgotten.

The success of the media pool concept provides a strong basis for continued cooperation in future military operations. It has developed a good track record, and the time has come to stick to one course, in sharp contrast to the inconsistent policies of the past. No plan is perfect, but the current arrangement between the military and the media is strong enough and flexible enough to survive indefinitely. Most important, continued utilization of the concepts implemented since the Sidle panel will ensure that truth does not become a casualty of an unnecessary struggle between the media and the military.

10

Constitutional Concerns
in Denying the Press Access
to Military Operations

Marshall Silverberg

In the early morning hours of October 23, 1983, U.S. military forces led a multinational invasion of the island of Grenada.[1] Despite a long history of members of the media accompanying U.S. military forces into combat,[2] in the Grenada operation the press was denied access to the island for the important first two days of the invasion.[3]

The decision to exclude the press was made by the American commander of the invasion force, who acted with the support of the Reagan administration.[4] Senior U.S. officials announced that the exclusion of the press from the battlefield was necessary to ensure the secrecy (and thus probably the success) of the mission,[5] to support the tactical conduct of the action without distractions from the media,[6] and in consideration of the safety of reporters.[7] Once these objectives were accomplished (after two days), members of the press were allowed onto the island.[8]

The media were outraged.[9] Newspaper editorials strongly criticized the decision to deny access to reporters.[10] In the wake of that criticism, a special Department of Defense panel was convened to review press access to military operations, chaired by Major General Winant Sidle, a former military spokesman in Vietnam.[11]

The Sidle panel made various recommendations that were adopted by Secretary of Defense Caspar Weinberger[12] and largely applauded by the media.[13] Distrust between the two sides continues to exist,[14] however, creating the possibility that the military might choose to deny the press access to future military operations.

This chapter focuses on the constitutional concerns raised by such an exclusion of the press. These concerns are important because in any future exclusion, the press will likely seek injunctive relief from the federal courts.[15] And such relief, if granted, would force the Department of Defense to provide press access at least to particular phases of the operation or even to the entire conflict.[16] The constitutional concerns are complex, with a variety of commentators reaching different conclusions. At the center of the controversy are competing concerns between the First Amendment's guarantee of a free press[17] and the national security interests of the government.[18] For reasons discussed below, these issues should be analyzed under the prior restraint doctrine and the emerging right of access.

The Prior Restraint Doctrine

The prior restraint doctrine is usually invoked when government restrictions are imposed before the expression protected by the First Amendment has occurred. Courts are extremely reluctant to allow prior restraints[19] and, with one exception, have struck down all such restrictions because of the First Amendment.[20]

The argument that the prior restraint doctrine should be invoked here is based on a theory that "a press exclusion, like a suppression on publication, prevents the press from reporting the news to the public."[21] That argument, however, does not recognize that in Grenada, the government did not try to prevent the publication of the news as it did in the other prior restraint cases;[22] rather, it merely decided on whether the press had a right of access to the military operation. Skeptics would respond that denying access is nothing more than an extreme form of censorship, and thus the prior restraint doctrine should apply. Such an argument, however, does not recognize that in other situations when the Supreme Court has considered whether the media had a right to access, it did not invoke the prior restraint doctrine.[23] The Court thereby has recognized that determining whether the press has access to a particular situation is not the same as deciding whether to prohibit the publication of already gathered information by correspondents.[24]

Even if one disagrees with this conclusion by asserting that the prior restraint should apply to instances of press exclusion during military operations, the national security exception to that doctrine should apply. This exception was first established in dictum in *Near v. Minnesota*[25] in which the Supreme Court stated, "No one would question but that a government might prevent actual obstruction to its recruiting service or the publication of the sailing dates of transports or the number and location of troops."[26]

This national security exception to the prior restraint doctrine was implicitly reexamined by the Supreme Court in *New York Times Co. v. United States*,[27] commonly referred to as the Pentagon Papers Case. In that case, the Court examined a request by the U.S. government to prevent the *New York Times* and the *Washington Post* from continuing to publish the contents of a classified Defense Department study, "History of U.S. Decision-Making Process on Viet Nam Policy." The government argued that an injunction was necessary because continued publication of the report presented a "grave and immediate danger" to the security of the United States.[28]

In a brief per curiam opinion, the Court noted that "any system of prior restraints of expression comes to this Court bearing a heavy pre-sumption against its constitutional validity."[29] And because the govern-ment had not met its burden in the facts before the Court, the Court denied the government's request for an injunction.[30]

The case also was unusual because all nine justices wrote separate opinions. Of these, Justice William Brennan focused most directly on the national security exception established by *Near v. Minnesota:*

> Our cases, it is true, have indicated that there is a single, extremely narrow class of cases in which the First Amendment's ban on prior judicial restraint may be overridden. Our cases have thus far indicated that such cases many arise only when the Nation "is at war", Schenck v. United States, 246 U.S. 47, 52 (1919), during which times "no one would question but that a government might prevent actual obstruction to its recruiting service or the publication of the sailing dates of trans-ports or the number and location of troops." Near v. Minnesota, 283 U.S. 697, 716, (1931).[31]

Justice Brennan then added:

> Only governmental allegation and proof that publication must inevitably, directly, and immediately cause the occurrence of an event kindred to imperiling the safety of a transport already at sea can support even the issuance of an interim restraining order.[32]

Justice Brennan's opinion, and other subsequent decisions by the Supreme Court, thus stand for the proposition that the national security exception to the prior restraint doctrine continues to have legal vitality.

In *Haig v. Agee,*[33] for example, the Court examined the government's decision to revoke former Central Intelligence Agency employee Philip Agee's passport and stated:

> The revocation of Agee's passport rests in part on the content of his speech: specifically, his repeated disclosures of intelligence operations and names of intelligence personnel. Long ago, however, this Court recog-nized that "no one would question but that a government might prevent actual obstruction to its recruiting service or the publication of the sailing dates of transports or the number and location of troops."[34]

The Court then added:

> Agee's disclosures, among other things, have the declared purpose of obstructing intelligence operations and the recruiting of intelligence per-sonnel. They are clearly not protected by the Constitution. The mere fact that Agee is also engaged in criticism does not render his conduct beyond the reach of the law.[35]

Even more recently, the Supreme Court has cited approvingly the national security exception: "This Court on many occasions has recognized that certain kinds of speech are less central to the interest of the First Amendment than others . . . Near v. Minnesota ex rel. Olson, 283 U.S. 697, 716 (1931) (publication of troopships sailing during wartime may be enjoined)."[36]

These cases make it clear that if the media had obtained information about the proposed invasion of Grenada and intended publishing the information while the ships were about to embark or were already at sea, then the national security exception to the prior restraint doctrine would apply; that is, the government could obtain from the courts a temporary restraining order prohibiting publication of such information.

Beyond that relatively clear-cut scenario, however, it becomes increasingly difficult to determine what types of information and under what circumstances the government could restrain from publication. If correspondents had been allowed aboard the invasion fleet, would they have been allowed to begin reporting after the ships reached Grenada and the troops had landed? This question is especially problematic because contemporary news reporting is often accomplished in real time; that is, unlike in previous wars, reporting in Grenada could have been transmitted to American homes while the fighting was ongoing. Such transmissions might endanger the soldiers (and the correspondents) because the enemy could adjust targeting based on the newscasts. One can almost imagine an enemy commander watching Cable News Network and using the information imparted by that continuous news telecast to position his forces to attack the Americans better. The news reports could become an invaluable source of intelligence for the enemy.

In past wars, such problems were avoided by military censorship. Indeed, the history of military censorship has been described as follows:

> Several clear lessons emerge from the history of censorship in military emergencies. Congress has never statutorily enacted direct domestic press censorship. The government effectively employed censorship, however, through statutory control of cable traffic and the mails. Mandatory field censorship was also used until the Vietnam War, where it was physically impossible. . . . History suggests a general, if uneasy, acceptance of censorship as a necessary feature of being at war.[37]

Because of the technological advances that enable the media to develop a real-time reporting capability, military censorship through the "control of cable traffic and the mails" is probably no longer possible. Times have changed. In order to accomplish the same primary goal that it had in the past—the success of the operation—the military has had to reevaluate its capabilities regarding the presence of the media. It may no longer be possible for the military to allow the presence of correspondents and still hope to accomplish its mission. The national security exception to the prior restraint doctrine seems to control any decisions, judicial or otherwise, in this area.

Therefore, if the press is to succeed in arguing that it has a constitutional right to accompany military forces in the field, it needs to rely on a theory different from prohibition against prior restraint. A better analysis might be based on an emerging doctrine, the constitutional right of access.

The Right of Access

The right of access to information is believed to have been first stated by James Madison: "a popular Government, without popular information, or the means of acquiring it, is but a Prologue to a Farce or a Tragedy; or, perhaps both."[38] The Supreme Court, however, has recognized the right of the press to collect information only in relatively recent times. In 1972 in *Branzburg v. Hayes*,[39] Justice Byron White wrote for the Court: "We do not question the significance of free speech, press, or assembly to the country's welfare. *Nor is it suggested that news gathering does not qualify for First Amendment Protection; without some protection for seeking out the news, freedom of the press could be eviscerated.*"[40] Justice Potter Stewart, while dissenting from the Court's holding, agreed with Justice White's statement about news gatherings being protected under the First Amendment: "A corollary of the right to publish must be the right to gather news. The full flow of information to the public protected by the free-speech guarantee would be severely curtailed if no protection whatever were afforded to the process by which news is assembled and disseminated."[41]

These statements, however, did not herald an age of unrestrained press access. Just two years later, in the companion cases of *Pell v. Procunier*[42] and *Saxbe v. Washington Post*,[43] Justice Stewart, writing for the Court in both cases, concluded that the press did not have unlimited access to prison inmates:

> It is one thing to say that a journalist is free to seek out sources of information not available to the public, that he is entitled to some constitutional protection of the confidentiality of such sources, and that the government cannot restrain the publication of news emanating from such sources. It is quite another thing to suggest that the Constitution imposes upon government the affirmative duty to make available to journalists sources of information not available to members of the public generally.[44]

The issue of press access was considered again in 1978 by the Supreme Court in *Houchins v. KQED*.[45] A deeply divided Court could not agree on the right of press access to a jail that was allegedly in poor condition. Three justices found "no discernible basis for a constitutional duty to disclose, or for standards governing disclosure of or access to [government] information."[46] Three other justices believed that there was a right of access, arguing that without "some protection for the acquisition of information about the operation of public institutions such as prisons by the public at large, the process of self-governance contemplated by the Framers would be stripped of its substance."[47] The tie-breaking vote, authored by Justice Stewart, agreed with the former three justices in concluding that there was no special right of press access: "The Constitution does no more than assure the public and the press equal access once government has opened its doors."[48] Yet Justice Stewart also wrote, "Terms of access that are reasonably imposed on individual members of the public may, if they impede effective reporting without sufficient justification, be unreasonable as applied to journalists who are there to convey to the general public what the visitors see."[49]

Justice Stewart's concurring opinion in *Houchins* thus seemed to indicate that potentially a plurality, if not an outright majority, of the Court would support the right of press access in an appropriate case. Indeed, despite a temporary setback in *Gannett Co. v. DePasquale*,[50] a plurality emerged two years later in *Richmond Newspapers, Inc. v. Virginia*,[51] to hold that "absent an overriding interest articulated in findings, the trial of a criminal case must be open to the public."[52] Chief Justice Warren Burger's plurality opinion for the Court was based upon "unbroken, uncontradicted history" of public trials.[53] He further found that "the right of access to places traditionally open to the public, as criminal trials have long been, may be seen as assured by the amalgam of the First Amendment's guarantees of speech and press."[54]

The Chief Justice also noted in a footnote, however, that the facts before the Court were different from those in *Pell* and *Saxbe* because those cases "were concerned with penal institutions which, by definition, are not 'open' or public places."[55] Notwithstanding that reservation, Justice John Paul Stevens declared that "this is a watershed case. . . . [Today] for the first time, the Court unequivocally holds that an arbitrary interference with access to important information is an abridgment of the freedoms of speech and of the press protected by the First Amendment."[56] Justice Stewart, whose concurrence in *Houchins* seemingly began this process, also concurred in this case, but he noted that "in conspicuous contrast to a military base, . . . a trial courtroom is a public place."[57]

The *Richmond Newspapers* plurality opinion was followed two years later by *Globe Newspaper Co. v. Superior Court*,[58] in which the Supreme Court, for the first time, had a majority conclude that there was a constitutional right of access. In an opinion by Justice Brennan, the Court stated that the First Amendment required a right of access to criminal trials because "the criminal trial historically has been open to the press and general public"[59] and because "the right of access to criminal trials plays a particularly significant role in the functioning of the judicial process and the government as a whole."[60] The Court thus established that the press and the public must be admitted to trials unless "the denial [of access] is necessitated by a compelling governmental interest, and is narrowly tailored to serve that interest."[61] And in the facts before it, because Massachusetts had not sufficiently demonstrated that its statutory requirement to close all courtrooms during testimony by a minor victim of a sexual offense was narrowly tailored to serve the state's interest, the statute was invalidated.[62]

The right of access was again considered when the press was excluded from jury selection in a murder case. Chief Justice Burger, writing for the Court in *Press Enterprise Co. v. Superior Court*,[63] stated that the "presumption of openness [of any part of a criminal trial] may be overcome only by an overriding interest based on findings that closure is essential to preserve higher values and is narrowly tailored to serve that interest."[64] Under the facts at issue, where the trial court had neither articulated any specific findings nor considered alternatives to closure of the trial, the Court held the closure improper.[65]

What do all of these Supreme Court decisions mean in terms of whether the press has a right of access to military operations? The answer is not clear. On the one hand, it could be argued that the right of access may be alleged to challenge almost every government decision denying such access to government facilities and operations.[66] That position, however, would seem to open the floodgates to litigation for access to a broad range of government activities. Such a possibility was cautioned by Justice Brennan in his concurring opinion in the *Richmond Newspapers* decision,[67] and it seems contrary to the intent of the Court's majority.

A close examination of the different opinions in *Richmond Newspapers* indicates that the Court's holding should not be unduly broadened. Chief Justice Burger and Justice White distinguished the question of access to criminal trials as being different from prisons because prisons "are not 'open' or public places."[68] Justice Stewart agreed that trials stood "in conspicuous contrast" to military bases, jails, or prisons.[69] Justice Stewart's successor, Justice Sandra Day O'Connor, also agreed that the Court's decision in *Richmond Newspapers* does not "carry any implications outside the context of criminal trials."[70] Moreover, Justice William Rehnquist, now chief justice and arguably the most influential member of the contemporary Court, believes that there is no First Amendment right of access.[71] Thus, although one could fairly argue that at least three justices believe there is a broad right of access,[72] there is no basis to contend that that view is shared by a majority of the Court.

Moreover, in other cases in which the plaintiff sought access to government facilities or information, the Court did not find such a right. In *Baldrige v. Shapiro,*[73] the Court upheld the government's refusal to disclose certain census data under the Freedom of Information Act.[74] Similarly, in *FCC v. ITT World Communications,*[75] the Court held that negotiations between the Federal Communications Commission and its foreign regulatory counterparts did not have to be open to the public. Also, in *Members of the City Council of Los Angeles v. Taxpayers for Vincent,*[76] the Court held that the First Amendment does not guarantee access to utility poles for communication simply because they are owned or controlled by the government. Finally, and perhaps most important, in *Department of Justice v. Reporters Committee for Freedom of the Press,*[77] the Supreme Court held that under the Freedom of Information Act, the media have no right of access to any criminal history records maintained by the Federal Bureau of Investigation regarding persons alleged to have been involved in organized and improper dealings with a corrupt congressman.[78] In that case, the Court did not even address the question of whether under the First Amendment, instead of the Freedom of Information Act, the media had a constitutional right of access to the information.

These latter cases, when considered in conjunction with the different opinions in *Richmond Newspapers* and *Globe Newspaper,* surely indicate that the right of access should be construed narrowly. Thus, rather than automatically concluding that the press has a First Amendment right of access to military operations, it must be determined whether there are guidelines that can be applied in making that determination.

The cases suggest that a tripartite test can be used. First, the party seeking access to a particular government facility or operation should prove that the place "historically [has] been open to the press and general public."[79] Second, the right of access must "play a particularly significant role" in the operation at issue and of the government in its entirety.[80] Even if both of these tests are met, however, access may still be denied if the government proves that "the denial is necessitated by a compelling governmental interest, and is narrowly tailored to serve that interest."[81]

This test provides a framework by which particular access issues may be addressed.[82] It is based on the Supreme Court decisions and is more accurate and supportable than a mere comparison of the public's interest in obtaining the information versus the government's interest in denying it, as others have suggested.[83] By not distinguishing between the right of access for the media, as compared to that of the general public, the test not only applies the specific language of the *Globe Newspaper* decision, it also incorporates the recent pronouncements of the Supreme Court in *Department of Justice v. Reporters Committee for Freedom of the Press,* which explicitly rejected the media's claim that they had a greater interest in the government's information than members of the general public.[84]

While the test is applied to the issue of press access to military operations, it becomes apparent that there is no such First Amendment right. Under the first part of the test—whether there has been a historical right of access to military operations—it must be recognized that the *public* never has had such access and the media have had only a very limited one. While the media's historical access to military operations has been described elsewhere,[85] it is sufficient to note here that such access was provided at the discretion of the military and usually specified conditions, such as the registration of correspondents, the approval of their credentials, and the retention of a right to censor significant operational information.[86] The media have not been given unrestrained access to military operations as in criminal trials.

Moreover, the Supreme Court has frequently recognized that in many circumstances, military activities are different from civilian ones in relevant constitutional concerns. For example, in *Greer v. Spock,*[87] the Court noted that it is "the business of a military installation like Fort Dix to train soldiers, not to provide a public forum. A necessary concomitant of the basic function of a military installation has been 'the historically unquestioned power of [its] commanding officer summarily to exclude civilians from his area of command.' "[88] The *Greer* decision quoted *Cafeteria Workers v. McElroy,*[89] which noted that commanding officers historically have enjoyed broad authority to exclude civilians from areas under their command.[90]

Indeed, if the military has broad authority to exclude civilians from its bases for national security reasons and the Supreme Court decisions have so held, then it should be undeniable that a military commander engaged in a military invasion or a similar maneuver should have absolute discretion in deciding whether to exclude civilians in his area. His primary responsibilities must be to ensure the success of the mission. And if, in his judgment, the success of that mission would be jeopardized by correspondents' roaming around the field of battle, then he has not only the discretion but the duty to exclude those reporters from his field of operation. Anything less would be a failure in his responsibilities as a military commander. Thus, in such circumstances, it should be clear that the media have no right of access to the military operation.

It should be noted anyway, however, that the second part of the test—whether the media have played "a particularly significant role" in military operations—is far less clear. Some commentators have argued that the press has played a significant role in requiring the military to provide accurate information about a military conflict that is untarnished by political considerations.[91] Other commentators have claimed that the media actually have damaged significantly the success of military operations.[92] Still others believe that the significance of the media in military operations is overemphasized.[93] Whatever view one takes about the role of the media in military operations, it should be undeniable that with respect to the operation itself, the media cannot possibly assist in the success of the mission (unless the correspondents are also willing to serve as combatants) but can quite possibly contribute to the failure of the mission, a possibility that has become more acute with the emergence of real-time news reporting.

Finally, this concern about the effect of real-time news reporting should also be considered in applying the last part of the tripartite test: whether the denial of the media to military operations is necessitated by a compelling governmental interest and whether it is narrowly tailored to serve that interest. There should be no doubt that the government has a compelling interest in maximizing the potential for success of its military operations. Indeed, the media themselves recognize that they have no right of access "to lightning fast in-and-out military engagements such as the Iranian rescue mission, or access to extended covert action which is not publicly known."[94] Part of the controversy with the Grenada operation was that it was not clear whether it was a blitzkrieg-type of commando attack or whether it was a more traditional type of invasion to which the media historically have had access.[95] Because of the length of the operation, during which the first two days were the most important, it is difficult to categorize it definitively in either fashion.

When there is such a doubt, however, it should be the decision of the military commander, as it was in Grenada, to decide whether for operational reasons the media must be denied access. That decision subsequently should receive broad deference because the exigencies of battle are far removed from the arenas of public debate.

It is for these reasons that courts, if not correspondents, have usually given broad deference to military decisions. For example, in *Chappell v. Wallace*,[96] the Court stated that "judges are not given the task of running the Army. . . . Orderly government requires that the judiciary be as scrupulous not to interfere with legitimate Army matters as the Army must be scrupulous not to intervene in judicial matters."[97] Even more recently, the Supreme Court noted that "courts traditionally have been reluctant to intrude upon the authority of the Executive in military and national security affairs."[98] Thus, if the issue of press access to military operations ever reaches the Supreme Court, the military would probably win that battle.[99]

Conclusion

The media have no constitutional right of access to military operations. The decision on denying or granting access should be left to the battlefield commander, whose decision should be accorded extreme deference. Any later judicial challenge to his decision by the media is likely to be unsuccessful.

In so concluding, the constitutional considerations are resolved. From a policy perspective, however, the military has much to gain from working and improving relations with the press. Indeed, the most ironic aspect of the role of the media in the Grenada invasion has to be its role in shaping the public perception of the operation once it was concluded. As recounted by John Norton Moore, after the invasion had begun, congressional Democrats had scheduled hearings in the Senate Foreign Relations Committee to determine whether the president had acted in violation of the War Powers Resolution. They cancelled those hearings once American students, after being rescued from Grenada, were shown by the American media as kissing the tarmac after landing in the United States.[100] That media exposure helped significantly in developing popular support for the Grenada invasion.

The media can act as a two-edged sword. Recognition of that fact can help alleviate the military's concerns. For their part, the media can work with the military in providing specific types of coverage that they know will not affect the success of the military operations they are covering.

11
Afterword: The 1991
Middle East War

Loren B. Thompson

A ll of the chapters in this book were prepared before the outbreak of the most recent Middle East war in January 1991. Since that war was still underway as these words were written, I have found myself in the uncomfortable position of describing a conflict about which many readers will know more than I do as I write. In particular, they will know the final outcome of the war, while I do not. Nonetheless, as the war against Iraq entered its third week, it was already apparent that the dilemmas that arose in coverage of past conflicts would also be present in the reporting on Desert Storm. Some observations concerning the relationship between the military and the media during the first weeks of the war and the months leading up to the conflict seemed to be in order.

A recurrent theme in the public pronouncements of President Bush and other senior administration officials during the initial weeks of the 1991 war was that this conflict would not be "another Vietnam." The strong desire to avoid a repetition of that traumatic experience was especially evident in the administration's treatment of the press. In Vietnam journalists were allowed to travel freely throughout the war zone and report whatever they wished, so long as they observed some basic ground rules regarding nondisclosure of militarily sensitive information. The atmosphere was quite different in the 1991 war against Iraq. The 700 war correspondents and photographers accredited to the Desert Storm theater of operations by the military's Joint Information Bureau were kept on a very short leash. Journalists were not permitted to venture into the war zone except as part of designated media pools, which were under constant military supervision; all war dispatches, including taped video reports, were subject to "security review" (military censorship) prior to their transmission; and detailed ground rules were issued concerning what could and could not be reported, and journalists were required to adhere to the rules as a condition of accreditation.

Ironically, one of the ground rules was that reporters could not disclose the ground rules, a requirement ostensibly imposed so that the enemy would be less able to manipulate the media. However, the trade journal *Editor & Publisher* printed a list of the types of information journalists were forbidden to report; the list included details of war plans, information about troop movements, numbers of military personnel and weapons, photographs of deployment areas, rules of engagement, official assessments of the effectiveness of enemy tactics, descriptions of U.S. intelligence sources and methods, and reports of personnel losses in specific units. The list of restricted items appeared similar to lists created to manage coverage in World War II, the Korean War, and Vietnam. The Pentagon's original draft of ground rules for covering Desert Storm had also sought to limit impromptu interviews with senior officers, restrict coverage of wounded or traumatized soldiers, and require that all discussions with military personnel be on the record. These restrictions were eliminated because of complaints from the media.

There was considerable resentment among reporters about the way in which the ground rules were applied during the early days of the war. Malcolm Browne, a veteran war correspondent who had been one of the first to cover the buildup of U.S. forces in Vietnam, wrote in the *New York Times* on January 21, 1991, that "many news correspondents covering the war with Iraq are bridling under a system of conflicting rules and confusing censorship." Browne continued, "Seemingly haphazard application of censorship rules has blacked out or truncated the timely release of some important articles even after they survived the required military 'security review.' In other cases, information deemed dangerous to American troops by commanders in the field has been cleared by the Pentagon and published or broadcast."

Similar sentiments were expressed by other members of the media. *Newsweek*, noting that the pool system being used in the war zone was "widely viewed by the press as a disaster," alleged that a "fact gap" (a credibility gap) was developing because of military efforts to manage the news. These views, however, found little support among the public during the war's initial weeks. A nationwide poll conducted by *Time* magazine a week after the conflict began found 88 percent of the public supporting military censorship of war dispatches and only 9 percent opposed. The vast majority of those polled (79 percent) felt they were getting "enough information" about the war.

Predictably, television coverage of the war's early days became the main focus of both criticism and praise concerning the media's performance. David Martin's warning in chapter four that "there is no real protection when you are dealing with the short fuse of television and the inevitable confusion of combat" was certainly borne out. The networks repeatedly broadcast reports that were inaccurate or misleading because they lacked the information to get the story right and did not want to be scooped. There was concern that television news organizations were allowing themselves to be manipulated by the enemy, as in the case of Peter

Arnett, an experienced war correspondent with Cable News Network who was allowed by the Iraqis to continue live coverage from Baghdad after other journalists were expelled. Arnett's reports were constantly monitored by representatives of the Iraqi government, and he was frequently escorted to the sites of alleged American war crimes. Arnett struggled to maintain his objectivity under trying circumstances, but critics complained that Cable News Network was allowing itself to be used to further Iraqi war aims.

Whatever its drawbacks, though, the extensive television coverage that marked the early days of the war provided an immediacy and texture to war reporting that the print media could not hope to match. A number of major newspapers such as the *New York Times* and *Los Angeles Times* expended huge resources to provide thorough war coverage, but there is little question that most of the public depended on television for their first and most lasting impressions of how the war was progressing. For better or worse, television has become the dominant news medium of the modern era.

My own sense, as a participant in both the print and broadcast coverage (I was the designated on-air military expert at the local CBS affiliate in the nation's capital), was that the delays inherent in producing print coverage of the war tended to reduce the incidence of inaccurate reporting. War coverage in the nation's leading newspapers was consistently more accurate and thoughtful than that appearing on television. This had less to do with the people preparing the coverage than it did with the nature of the media. Television news coverage, particularly that of breaking events, stresses immediacy and visual impact. Print coverage, even at the most mediocre newspapers, emphasizes getting the story right. As a result, print coverage tends to be more reliable.

Whatever the differences between television and the print media, it appeared to me that the journalistic community did a generally competent and creditable job of covering Desert Storm. Fred Reed's criticisms of the media's shortcomings in chapter 7 notwithstanding, I was struck in my own encounters with the media by how much effort journalists were making to understand the subjects they were reporting. Reed's complaint that many journalists know little about the military certainly proved to be true, but most of the reporters I dealt with were aware of the gaps in their knowledge and were trying to fill them.

The Pentagon's provisions for media pools and security review of all war dispatches were necessary and desirable, despite the media's objections. In the conclusion to chapter 1, I stressed the virtues of voluntary restraint over formal censorship in managing the coverage of future wars. My views on that subject, however, were predicated on the assumption that most future conflicts would be limited wars fought for limited purposes. The 1991 Middle East war does not seem to me to have been a limited war in the sense in which I used that term. Rather, it was an intense conventional conflict that involved huge commitments of manpower and material. Over several months, the United States built up its forces in the Persian Gulf region to a level that took nearly a decade to achieve in Vietnam. Furthermore, the geopolitical stakes were such that the United States could not afford to lose. That was not the case in Vietnam.

In major conventional conflicts such as the 1991 Middle East war, some measure of military censorship is not only necessary but also in the interests of the media. Reporters who would prefer to operate under the kind of media ground rules prevailing in Vietnam tend to forget that the conflict in Southeast Asia was a low-intensity, fluid struggle in which front lines were seldom well defined and most engagements occurred at the company level or lower. Journalists could thus be permitted a measure of freedom that would have been dangerous, if not unthinkable, in World War II or the Korean conflict.

The immediacy with which television now reports news throughout the world, including to the capitals of enemy nations, underscores the need to exert some control over war coverage. Journalists were correct in asserting that the imposition of security review for all war dispatches during the 1991 Middle East conflict indicated that the military did not trust the media. But the truth of the matter is that most members of the journalistic community are not competent to determine what is militarily sensitive information, and therefore they should not be entrusted with the responsibility of self-censorship in conflicts where the stakes are very high, as in the war against Iraq. Voluntary restraint worked well in Vietnam, as it would in most other low-intensity conflicts, but the war against Iraq was a different kind of struggle and demanded a different approach to coverage.

None of this is intended to excuse the professional shortcomings and arbitrary behavior of some of the military officers charged with managing the press during Desert Storm. So many accounts of surliness and incompetence on the part of military press officers surfaced during the early days of the war that it was certain Desert Storm would produce a new round of recriminations between the military and the media. Perhaps Bernard Trainor was correct when he asserted in chapter 3 that the military "is the antithesis of a democracy and must be so if it is to be effective." Nonetheless, it is unsettling that the military has not learned to do a better job of dealing with the media. Surely even the most illiberal officers must be able to see the dangers of repeatedly and unnecessarily frustrating the media in their efforts to inform the public.

It would be premature for me to attempt to derive any long-term lessons from the 1991 Middle East war concerning military-media relations. The ground war has not even begun as I conclude this afterword.

However, it does seem that the thoughts with which I closed chapter 1 bear repeating here. The perennial friction between the military and the media is not only unavoidable, it is probably desirable. The two institutions are radically different in their makeup and customs, but they serve a common purpose in safeguarding democracy. One does not need to enjoy the constant bickering between them to recognize that the very existence of such frictions reflects the fact that each institution is doing its job and for the most part doing it well.

Notes

Chapter 1

1. Clinton Rossiter, ed., *The Federalist Papers* (New York: New American Library, 1961), p. 517.
2. Alexis de Tocqueville, *Democracy in America* (Garden City, N.Y.: Anchor Books, 1969), p. 186.
3. Ibid.
4. Ibid., p. 180.
5. Frank Luther Mott, *American Journalism, A History 1690–1960,* 3d ed. (New York: Macmillan, 1962), p. 339.
6. Joseph J. Mathews, *Reporting the Wars* (Minneapolis: University of Minnesota Press, 1957), p. 80.
7. Mott, *American Journalism,* pp. 95, 100.
8. Ibid., p. 101.
9. Frederic Hudson, *Journalism in the United States from 1690 to 1872* (1873; New York: Haskell House Publishers, 1968), p. 140.
10. Mott, *American Journalism,* p. 99.
11. Hudson, *Journalism in the United States,* p. 140.
12. Ibid., p. 476.
13. Quoted in ibid, p. 477.
14. Robert B. Sims, *The Pentagon Reporters* (Washington, D.C.: National Defense University Press, 1983), p. 3.
15. Phillip Knightley, *The First Casualty* (New York: Harcourt Brace Jovanovich, 1975), p. 14.
16. Mathews, *Reporting the Wars,* p. 79.
17. Hudson, *Journalism in the United States,* pp. 715–717.
18. Mott, *American Journalism,* pp. 329–330.
19. Ibid., p. 330; Knightley, *The First Casualty,* p. 20.
20. Knightley, *The First Casualty,* pp. 24–25.
21. Mathews, *Reporting the Wars,* p. 86.
22. Ibid., p. 85.
23. Hudson, *Journalism in the United States,* pp. 715–716.
24. Ibid., p. 716; Mathews, *Reporting the Wars,* p. 85.
25. Mathews, *Reporting the Wars,* pp. 84–85; Knightley, *The First Casualty,* p. 28.

26. Knightley, *The First Casualty,* p. 24.

27. Mott, *American Journalism,* pp. 88–89.

28. Mathews, *Reporting the Wars,* p. 82.

29. Knightley, *The First Casualty,* p. 29.

30. "The War Department," *New York Times,* July 9, 1861, p. 4.

31. The *Times* carried a detailed account of corruption during Cameron's tenure. See "Government Contracts: The Frauds of the Contractors," *New York Times,* February 6, 1862, p. 2.

32. Knightley, *The First Casualty,* p. 25.

33. Mathews, *Reporting the Wars,* p. 95.

34. Mott, *American Journalism,* p. 365.

35. Russell F. Weigley, *The American Way of War: A History of United States Military Strategy and Policy* (Bloomington: Indiana University Press, 1977), pp. 157–159.

36. *Historical Statistics of the United States,* pt. 2 (Washington, D.C.: U.S. Department of Commerce, 1976), p. 1114.

37. Knightley, *The First Casualty,* p. 46.

38. Weigley, *The American Way of War,* pp. 158–159.

39. "The Little Horn Massacre," *New York Times,* July 7, 1876, p. 1.

40. Quoted in W.A. Swanberg, *Citizen Hearst: A Biography of William Randolph Hearst* (New York: Charles Scribner's Sons, 1961), p. 108.

41. Ibid.

42. John Tebbel, *The Compact History of the American Newspaper,* rev. ed. (New York: Hawthorn Books, 1969), p. 199.

43. Swanberg, *Citizen Hearst,* pp. 110–111.

44. Ibid., p. 145.

45. Mott, *American Journalism,* p. 537.

46. Ibid., p. 637; Swanberg, *Citizen Hearst,* p. 138.

47. Knightley, *The First Casualty,* p. 43.

48. Mott, *American Journalism,* p. 536.

49. Garel A. Grunder and William E. Livezey, *The Philippines and the United States* (Norman: University of Oklahoma Press, 1951), pp. 28–33.

50. Thomas G. Paterson, J. Garry Clifford, and Kenneth J. Hagan, *American Foreign Policy: A History to 1914,* 2d ed. (Lexington, Mass.: Lexington Books, 1983), p. 208.

51. Brian McAllister Linn, *The U.S. Army and Counterinsurgency in the Philippine War, 1899–1902* (Chapel Hill: University of North Carolina Press, 1989), p. 27.

52. Robert D. Schulzinger, *American Diplomacy in the Twentieth Century* (New York: Oxford University Press, 1984), p. 24.

53. James A. LeRoy, *The Americans in the Philippines* (1914; New York: AMS Press, 1970), 2:56.

54. Ibid.

55. Ibid., p. 61.

56. Linn, *The U.S. Army and Counterinsurgency in the Philippine War,* p. 27.

57. J.M. Roberts, *The Pelican History of the World,* rev. ed. (New York: Viking Penguin, 1987), pp. 817–819.

58. William M. Hammond, *Public Affairs: The Military and the Media, 1962–1968* (Washington, D.C.: U.S. Army Center of Military History, 1988), p. 5.

59. Mott, *American Journalism*, pp. 615, 619.

60. Ibid., p. 623.

61. Ibid.

62. Knightley, *The First Casualty*, p. 124.

63. Ibid., p. 124; Hammond, *The Military and the Media*, p. 5.

64. Hammond, *The Military and the Media*, p. 5.

65. Knightley, *The First Casualty*, pp. 128, 130–131.

66. Meyer Berger, *The Story of the New York Times, 1851–1951* (New York: Simon and Schuster, 1961), p. 219.

67. Mott, *American Journalism*, pp. 622-623.

68. Knightley, *The First Casualty*, p. 129.

69. See, for example, "Goethals on War Supplies," *New York Times*, July 2, 1919.

70. Paterson, Clifford, and Hagan, *American Foreign Policy*, p. 329.

71. Ibid., p. 382.

72. "F.D.R.'s War Plans," *Chicago Tribune*, December 4, 1941, p. 1.

73. Mathews, *Reporting the Wars*, p. 195.

74. Robert W. Desmond, *Tides of War: World News Reporting, 1931–1945* (Iowa City: University of Iowa Press, 1984), pp. 448–449.

75. Knightley, *The First Casualty*, p. 315.

76. Ibid.

77. Mathews, *Reporting the Wars*, pp. 175, 192.

78. Knightley, *The First Casualty*, p. 315.

79. Lee G. Miller, *The Story of Ernie Pyle* (New York: Viking Press, 1950), pp. 223–232.

80. Mott, *American Journalism*, p. 761.

81. Desmond, *Tides of War*, p. 219.

82. Juergen Arthur Heise, *Minimum Disclosure: How the Pentagon Manipulates the News* (New York: W.W. Norton, 1979), p. 56.

83. Peter Braestrup, *Battle Lines: Report of the Twentieth Century Fund Task Force on the Military and the Media* (New York: Priority Press Publications, 1985), p. 29.

84. Lloyd Wendt, *Chicago Tribune: The Rise of a Great American Newspaper* (Chicago: Rand McNally, 1979), pp. 624–635.

85. Mott, *American Journalism*, pp. 761–763.

86. Berger, *Story of the New York Times*, pp. 510–523.

87. Braestrup, *Battle Lines*, pp. 29–30.

88. Knightley, *The First Casualty*, p. 322; Desmond, *Tides of War*, pp. 361–367.

89. Mott, *American Journalism*, p. 759.

90. A.M. Sperber, *Murrow: His Life and Times* (New York: Freundlich Books, 1986), p. 342.

91. Mott, *American Journalism*, pp. 852–853.

92. Sperber, *Murrow*, p. 346.

93. Ibid., p. 345.

94. Quoted in Mott, *American Journalism,* p. 854.

95. Braestrup, *Battle Lines,* pp. 56–57.

96. Hammond, *The Military and the Media,* pp. 6–7.

97. Mott, *American Journalism,* p. 854.

98. Ibid.; Braestrup, *Battle Lines,* p. 57.

99. Jerome H. Kahan, *Security in the Nuclear Age* (Washington, D.C.: Brookings, 1975), pp. 11–13.

100. James A. Nathan and James K. Oliver, *United States Foreign Policy and World Order,* 3d ed. (Boston: Little, Brown, 1985), p. 162.

101. George C. Herring, *America's Longest War: The United States and Vietnam, 1950–1975,* 2d ed. (New York: Alfred A. Knopf, 1986), pp. 73–107.

102. Knightley, *The First Casualty,* p. 374.

103. Hammond, *The Military and the Media,* p. 15.

104. Ibid., pp. 16–17, 21.

105. Derrik Mercer, Geoff Mungham, and Kevin Williams, *The Fog of War: The Media on the Battlefield* (London: Heinemann, 1987), p. 243.

106. Braestrup, *Battle Lines,* p. 64; Knightley, *The First Casualty,* p. 398.

107. Mercer, Mungham, and Williams, *The Fog of War,* p. 235.

108. Braestrup, *Battle Lines,* p. 64.

109. Hammond, *The Military and the Media,* pp. 134–138.

110. Ibid., pp. 144–145; Mercer, Mungham, and Williams, *The Fog of War,* pp. 250–251.

111. Braestrup, *Battle Lines,* p. 65.

112. Herring, *America's Longest War,* p. 160.

113. Hammond, *The Military and the Media,* pp. 332–349.

114. For a detailed examination of Tet coverage, see Peter Braestrup, *Big Story,* abr. ed. (New Haven: Yale University Press, 1977), esp. pp. 465–507.

115. Hammond, *The Military and the Media,* pp. 275–279.

116. Knightley, *The First Casualty,* pp. 390–397.

117. Mercer, Mungham, and Williams, *The Fog of War,* pp. 214, 223.

118. Ibid., p. 226.

119. Hammond, *The Military and the Media,* p. 387.

120. Douglas Kinnard, *The War Managers* (Hanover N.H.: University Press of New England, 1977), p. 175.

121. Knightley, *The First Casualty,* p. 298.

122. Herring, *America's Longest War,* pp. 264–267.

123. Hammond, *The Military and the Media* p. 338.

124. For a detailed discussion of low-intensity conflict, see Loren B. Thompson, *Low-Intensity Conflict: The Pattern of Warfare in the Modern World* (Lexington, Mass.: Lexington Books, 1989).

125. Braestrup, *Battle Lines,* pp. 19, 90.

126. Lt. Col. James O'Rourke, "The Media Pool: Is It the Solution?" *Military Media Review* (Summer 1989): 9.

127. Caspar W. Weinberger, *Fighting for Peace: Seven Critical Years in the Pentagon* (New York: Warner Books, 1990), p. 133.

128. Braestrup, *Battle Lines,* pp. 24, 101.

129. The full text of the Sidle commission final report is printed in ibid., p. 165.

130. O'Rourke, "The Media Pool," p. 11.

131. Ibid.

132. Fred S. Hoffman, *Review of Panama Pool Deployment, December 1989* (Washington, D.C.: Department of Defense, March 20, 1990), pp. 1–2; Steven Komarow, "Pooling Around in Panama," *Washington Journalism Review* (March 1990): 45.

133. Richard Harwood, "A Pool in Panama," *Washington Post,* January 14, 1990.

134. Hoffman, *Review of Panama Pool Deployment,* p. 1.

135. Ibid., p. 2.

136. Walter V. Robinson, "Journalists Constrained by Pentagon," *Boston Globe,* December 25, 1989, p. 3.

137. "The First Casualty," *Time,* September 10, 1990, p. 67; Debra Gersh, "General Fired for Talking to the Press," *Editor and Publisher,* September 22, 1990, p. 22.

138. Sperber, *Murrow,* pp. 346–347.

Chapter 2

1. Samuel Johnson, "Of the Duty of a Journalist", Payne's *Universal Chronicle* (1758) as reprinted in Donald Greene, editor, *Samuel Johnson: The Oxford Authors* (New York: Oxford University Press, 1984) pp. 544-546.

2. Edward Hallett Carr, *What Is History? The George Macauley Trevelyan Lectures* (New York: Vintage Books, 1961), p. 9.

3. Ignazio Silone, *Bread and Wine* (New York: New American Library, 1982), p. 154.

4. Stephen Hess, *The Washington Reporters* (Washington: The Brookings Institution, 1981), pp. 12-14.

5. Samuel Johnson, pp. 544-546.

6. *Ibid.*

7. Cornelius Tacitus, *The Histories* (Cambridge: Harvard University Press, 1939), p. 1.

8. Garry Wills, *Nixon Agonistes: The Crisis of the Self-Made Man* (Boston: Houghton Mifflin Co., 1970), p. 100.

9. Francesco Guiccardini, *Maxims and Reflections* (Philadelphia: University of Pennsylvania Press, 1965), p. 80.

10. "Senate Group Urges Pentagon Reorganization," *Aviation Week & Space Technology,* October 21, 1985, p. 29.

Chapter 5

1. Historically reporters have rarely let the absence of an eyewitness account limit their reports. The foibles of war correspondents, for instance, are told in both entertaining and scholarly detail in Phillip Knightley, *The First Casualty: From the Crimea to Vietnam—The War Correspondent as Hero, Propagandist and Mythmaker* (New York: Harvest Books, 1975).

2. There is much truth to the argument that "news," as it is defined by mainstream daily newspapers, essentially flavors official pronouncements over ideas that spring from outside the government. For a good discussion of the effects of that bias, see James Aronson, *The Press and the Cold War* (Boston: Beacon Press, 1970). A more forceful version of this argument contends that the press in the United States has become an apologist for the power elite and contributes to the perpetuation of an unjust social and economic system. It can be found in Noam Chomsky, *Necessary Illusions: Thought Control in Democratic Societies* (Boston: South End Press).

3. J.W. Fulbright, *The Pentagon Propaganda Machine* (New York: Liveright Books, 1970).

4. Ibid., p. 150.

Chapter 7

1. For example, in the July 18, 1989, *Washington Post*, Molly Moore, who for years has been a military reporter, wrote, "Because the Stealth Bomber is designed to elude radars at far greater distances than conventional aircraft. . ." Actually, it is designed to do so at far shorter distances. Robust incomprehension of this sort regularly provokes gales of laughter in military circles, but reporters do not move in military circles. The military in its own way is as badly behaved as the press, but that is another story.

2. Consistently poor on average. A few reporters, conspicuously Dick Halloran and Mick Trainor of the *New York Times*, are quite good. The *Wall Street Journal* on the whole is almost preternaturally competent. This chapter deals only with the print media.

3. Bright and egotistical people such as reporters tend to resent what they cannot understand, such as technology. I have wondered how much this resentment fuels the almost religious quest for stories about any real or imagined failure of technical equipment.

4. Stories sometimes grow wilder with age. Consider the story of Divad and the latrine fan. A test unit picked up stray signals that may have come from a ventilation fan. In the press, this soon became "locked on" to the fan, a very different thing. The next step was "pointed its guns at" and, finally, in the *New York Times*, "fired at" the latrine fan. Had the story run another week, Divad presumably would have been reported to have used nuclear weapons against a latrine fan.

5. When soldiers realize that a reporter knows their language and can talk

shop with them, they open up enormously. If journalists had any notion how stupid they seem as they stand around a tank peering in truculent unconscious puzzlement, asking foolish questions that make everyone else cringe, they would wear ski masks. Officers welcome reporters who know what they are talking about; they are terrified of those who do not.

6. A GAO report that got much attention charged that the military had cheated on testing major weapons. The report said that the air force, in testing a low-level night navigation device for fighters, had allowed the pilots to fly the test course by day to familiarize themselves with it, thus improving their nocturnal performance. The air force officials involved told me that other pilots had flown the course by day to make sure that no obstacles (high trees, power lines) existed. They also said they told GAO as much. Somebody is lying. No reporter even asked.

7. Editorial writers are particularly bad about using Nexis. Reporters at least specialize somewhat in a subject and have some contact with it. Editorial writers have to write opinions of subjects of which their knowledge is exceedingly limited. The results can be amusing. The *New York Times* has a fine military unit, but its military editorials are puerile gibberish. The editorial board of the *Times,* one can confidently bet, has no notion of its inadequacy.

8. For example, the reformers have asserted that the navy's proposed new submarine, the SSN-21, is a bad design because it is large and therefore an easier target for detection by sonar. It is a slightly better target for active sonar, which has a short range and is never used by submarines hunting submarines (the job of the SSN-21) because it reveals the location of the hunter. However, large size allows use of sound-deadening techniques that make the sub harder to detect by passive sonar—just listening—which has far longer range and is the real danger. Try explaining this to a reporter.

9. This is easy. As a hypothetical, but not unrealistic, example, suppose the army tests ten M-1s for engine reliability. One engine fails because a mechanic left a wrench in the turbine. Another fails because the transmission suddenly freezes— a transmission defect, not an engine defect. A third tank falls off a cliff, and the engine, as well as everything else, breaks. The engineers discount these examples because they have nothing to do with the engine's reliability. Cheating, say the reformers: the army is ignoring unpalatable evidence.

10. They also tend to pursue the stories that their colleagues pursue. If $400 hammers are currently in style, the entire Pentagon press corps will hunt hammers, ignoring all else. This in effect almost means that they amount to one reporter.

Chapter 8

1. Anthony Sampson, *The Changing Anatomy of Britain* (London: Hodder and Stoughten, 1982), pp. 246–247.

2. Peter Riddell, *The Thatcher Decade* (London: Blackwell, 1989), pp. 200–201.

3. *Defense White Paper* (London: Ministry of Defence, 1989).

4. Peter Riddell, *The Thatcher Government* (Oxford: Blackwell, 1983), pp. 220–221.

5. Interview with Max Hastings, editor, *Daily Telegraph,* 1989.

6. Brian Whitaker, *News Limited* (London: Minority Press Group, 1981), p. 67.

7. Ibid., pp. 72–73.

8. *Washington Post,* July 23, 1989.

9. Peter Kellner and Lord Crowther-Hunt, *The Civil Servants* (London: McDonald Futura, 1980), pp. 264–265.

10. Michael Cockerell, Peter Hennessy, and David Walker, *Sources Close to the Prime Minister* (London: Macmillan, 1984), p. 94.

11. Ibid., p. 112.

12. Riddell, *Thatcher Decade.*

13. Interview with British civil servant, 1989.

14. Leigh Linklater, *Not with Honour* (London: Observer Books, 1986), passim.

15. Donald Regan, *For the Record* (New York: Harcourt Brace Jovanovich, 1988), pp. 255–256.

Chapter 9

1. Caspar W. Weinberger, "A Free Press and National Security," *Defense* (October 1985): 2–3.

2. Chuck Henry, "Military-Media Relations," *Military Media Review* (January 1986): 2–3.

3. Ibid., p. 2.

4. Drew Middleton, *New York Times Magazine,* February 5, 1984, p. 37.

5. Ibid.

6. Henry, "Military-Media Relations," pp. 3–4.

7. Middleton, *New York Times*, p. 61.

8. Ibid.

9. Phillip Knightley, *The First Casualty* (New York: Harcourt Brace Jovanovich, 1975), p. 423.

10. Middleton, *New York Times*, p. 69.

11. Ibid., pp. 69, 92.

12. Jonathan Friendly, "Pentagon's Panel on Press Coverage to Meet," *New York Times,* February 5, 1984, p. A-8.

13. *Report of the Chairman of the Joint Chiefs of Staff Media-Military Relations Panel* [Sidle Panel Report] (Washington, D.C.: Department of Defense, 1984), p. 1.

14. Friendly, "Pentagon's Panel," p. A-8.

15. Clyde R. White, "The Sidle Commission," *Military Media Review* (April 1984): 18.

16. Ibid., pp. 18–19.

17. Jonathan Friendly, "War Zone Access by Press Affirmed," *New York Times,* February 7, 1984, A-12.

18. Sidle Panel Report, pp. 4–6.

19. Ibid., p. 17.

20. Fred Hiatt, "Pentagon Plans Media Pool to Cover Missions," *Washington Post,* August 24, 1984, p. A-18.

21. Charles Mohr, "The Pentagon: The Continuing Battle over Covering Wars," *New York Times,* September 14, 1984, p. 24.

22. Richard Halloran, "Pentagon Plans to Add Newspaper as Member of Its War Press Pool," *New York Times,* October 12, 1984, pp. A-1, A-9.

23. Richard Halloran, "Pentagon Is Proposing Rules for the Press at Battlefields," *New York Times,* October 13, 1984, p. A-5.

24. Barry Zorthian, "Now, How Will Unfettered Media Cover Combat?" *New York Times,* September 12, 1984, p. A-31.

25. Eleanor Randolph, "Defense News-Pool Test Described as Failure," *Washington Post,* April 27, 1985, p. A-10.

26. Walter Pincus, "Pentagon to Use 'Code Words' in Activating Media Pools," *Washington Post,* May 16, 1985, p. A-5.

27. "Pentagon Tests News System," *New York Times,* September 20, 1985, p. D-16.

28. Philip Shenon, "Press Units Frustrated on Libya, But Few Blame Pentagon," *New York Times,* March 27, 1986, p. A-10.

29. Eleanor Randolph, "The Networks' Libyan Fly-By," *Washington Post,* March 26, 1986, pp. D-1, D-3.

30. Barry E. Willey, "Military-Media Relations Come of Age," *Parameters, Journal of the U.S. Army War College* (March 1989): 76.

31. Ibid.

32. Donna Miles, "Media Pools and the Persian Gulf," *American Forces Press Service Press Pack,* September 28, 1987, p. 1.

33. Ibid., p. 2.

34. "National Security and the Press: Pentagon Press Pools, the Sidle Panel and the Gulf," *Defense Media Review,* August 7, 1987, pp. 6, 7.

35. Willey, "Military-Media Relations Come of Age," p. 77.

36. Ibid.

37. Ibid., p. 78.

38. Ibid., pp. 78–79.

39. Ibid., p. 79.

40. Ibid.

41. Ibid., p. 80.

42. Michael R. Gordon, "Pentagon Says It Will Act to Help Press in Combat," *New York Times,* March 21, 1990, p. 22.

43. Kevin Merida, "The Panama Press-Pool Fiasco," *Washington Post,* January 7, 1990, p. B-2.

44. Michael Spector, "Second-Hand News Coverage Blamed on Military," *Washington Post,* December 22, 1989, p. 29.

45. Walter V. Robinson, "Journalists Constrained by Pentagon," *Boston Globe,* December 25, 1989, p. 3.

46. Richard Harwood, "A Pool in Panama," *Washington Post,* January 14, 1990.

47. Alex S. Jones, "Editors Say Journalists Were Kept from Action," *New York Times,* December 22, 1989, p. 19.

48. Patrick E. Tyler, "Officially, Pentagon Takes Blame," *Washington Post,* March 21, 1990, p. 19.

49. Michael R. Gordon, "Pentagon Says It Will Act to Help Press in Combat," *New York Times,* March 21, 1990, p. 22.

50. Ibid., p. 81.

51. Gerald W. Sharpe, "A Look at the Media-Military Relationship," *Military Media Review* (July 1987): 21.

52. Gerald W. Sharpe, "A Look at the Media-Military Relationship," *Military Media Review* (April 1987): 5.

53. Richard Halloran, "Pentagon and the Press: The War Goes On," *New York Times,* January 29, 1986, p. A-20.

54. Alan Hooper, *The Military and the Media* (Aldershot, England: Gower Publishing Company, Limited, 1982), p. 158.

55. Sean Kelly, *Access Denied: The Politics of Press Censorship,* Washington Papers, No. 55 (Washington, D.C.: Center for Strategic and International Studies, Georgetown University, 1978), pp. 10–11.

56. Douglas H. Rogers, Richard Erickson, and James M. Winters, *The Military and the Media—A Need for Control* (Carlisle Barracks, Penn.: U.S. Army War College, 1983).

57. Knightley, *First Casualty.*

Chapter 10

1. See *New York Times,* Oct. 26 1983, at A-1, col. 5. The invasion force consisted of 1,200 U.S. Marines, 700 army rangers, and 300 troops from Barbados, Jamaica, Antigua, St. Vincent, St. Lucia, and Dominica. "Why the Surprise Move in Grenada—and What Next?" *U.S. News and World Report,* Nov. 7, 1983, at 33. For a detailed discussion of the legality of the invasion, see J. Moore, *Law and the Grenada Invasion* (1984).

2. For a history of the American media coverage of U.S. battles, see P. Knightley, *The First Casualty* (1975); Cross & Griffin, "A Right of Press Access to United States Military Operations," 21 *Suffolk L. Rev.* 989, 991–1007 (1987).

3. See Moore, *supra,* note 1; Gailey, "U.S. Bars Coverage of Grenada Action, News Groups Protest," *New York Times,* Oct. 27, 1983, at A-1, col. 6.

4. "Admiral Says It Was His Decision to Tether the Press," *New York Times,* Oct. 31, 1983, at A-12, col. 3. Secretary of Defense Caspar Weinberger said he did not want to interfere with that decision. Editorial, *New York Times,* Oct. 28, 1983, at A-26, col. 1.

5. General John W. Vessey, Jr., chairman of the Joint Chiefs of Staff, claimed that the success of the mission depended largely on the element of sur-

prise, thereby necessitating the exclusion of the press. See Editorial, *New York Times,* Oct. 28, 1983, at A-26, col. 1.

6. See *supra* note 4.

7. Secretary Weinberger stated that the invasion force was not large enough to ensure the safety of the press. See Editorial, *supra* note 4. Eventually the invasion force numbered over 5,000 troops. "The Battle for Grenada," *Newsweek,* Nov. 7, 1986, at 66.

8. By the third day of the invasion, the surviving Cuban fighters no longer posed a significant problem, and calm was restored to the island. Cody, "Information Out of Sync," *Washington Post,* Oct. 29, 1983, at A-1, col. 6. Two days later, on October 27, 1982, the U.S. military began taking small groups of correspondents on guided tours of the island. Weintraub, "U.S. Press Curbs: The Unanswered Questions," *New York Times,* Oct. 29, 1983, at 7, col. 5.

9. The American Society of Newspaper Editors (ASNE) "vehemently" protested the "deplorable" press exclusion in an October 27, 1983, telegram to President Reagan. The American Newspaper Publishers Association (ANPA) declared that it was "deeply concerned" about the "unprecedented and intolerable" Grenadian news blackout. ANPA, Press Release (Oct. 27, 1982).

10. See, *e.g.,* Editorial, *Washington Post,* Oct. 28, 1982, at 22, col. 1 (press exclusion was "inexcusable"); Editorial, *New York Times, supra* note 4 (ironic that U.S. government used Soviet ploy of denying press access to news to keep citizens uninformed).

11. "A Second Look at the Off-the-Record War," *Time,* Nov. 21, 1984, at 77.

12. The Sidle report recommended, and Secretary of Defense Weinberger adopted, proposals that the Department of Defense take several measures, including conducting concurrent public affairs and operational planning, using press pools in appropriate circumstances, considering whether a correspondent accreditation system should be developed, and encouraging voluntary media compliance with Pentagon Security guidelines. See Chairman of the Joint Chiefs of Staff Media—Military Relations Panel Sidle Report, reprinted in Office of Assistant Secretary of Defense (Public Affairs) News Release No. 450-84 (Aug. 23, 1984).

13. The *New York Times,* for example, editorialized that "for the most part [the Sidle report] provide[s] reasonable guidance of process and detail." "Commander, or Censor, in Chief?" *New York Times,* Sept. 17, 1984, at A-18, col. 1.

14. According to one account, attempts to establish dialogue between reporters and military personnel pursuant to recommendations of the Sidle report have not been very successful. See *New York Times,* Jan. 29, 1986, at A-20, col. 3.

15. Such injunctive relief was actually sought in the Grenada press exclusion. In *Flynt v. Weinberger,* 588 F. Supp. 57 (D.D.C. 1984), *aff'd but vacated on other grounds,* 762 F.2d 134 (D.C.Cir. 1985) *(per curiam),* a newspaper publisher challenged the press exclusion as being unconstitutional. Although the district court dismissed the suit as moot, it noted that even if the "press ban had violated plaintiffs' constitutional rights, which the Court doubts," the court "would exercise its equitable discretion and decline to enter an injunction restraining the government from restricting press access to future United States military opera-

tions" (588 F. Supp. at 60). On appeal, the U.S. Court of Appeals for the District of Columbia Circuit, while affirming the district court's holding on the mootness issue, found the district court's pronouncements on the merits to be improper and it vacated the district court's opinion. The circuit court ordered that the case be dismissed without prejudice (762 F.2d at 135–136).

16. Depending on the length of the conflict, the press would have to contend with significant time constraints in obtaining judicial resolution of the issue. This is especially true in short military engagements, such as the one in Grenada, where the most significant opposition was during the first two days when Cubans were actively fighting the invasion. In a longer campaign, in contrast, the courts could conceivably rule quickly enough to force the military to provide access to the press.

17. The First Amendment provides in pertinent part: "Congress shall make no law . . . abridging the freedom of speech, or of the press." U.S. Const. Amend. I.

18. See generally *Hirabayashi v. U.S.*, 320 U.S. 881, 93 (1943) (The Constitution gives the executive branch "wide scope for the exercise of judgement and discretion [in war] in determining the nature and extent of the threatened injury or danger and in the selecting of the means for resisting it").

19. See *Nebraska Press Ass'n. v. Stuart*, 427 U.S. 539, 559 (1976) ("Prior restraints [are] the most serious and least tolerable infringement on First Amendment rights"). The prior restraint doctrine, including the *Nebraska Press Ass'n* case, is discussed in "Symposium," 29 *Stan. L. Rev.* 383 (1977).

20. The one exception concerns matters of national security and is discussed *infra*.

21. Pincus, "Press Access to Military Operations: Grenada and the Need for a New Analytical Framework," 135 *U. Pa. L. Rev.* 813, 815 (1987).

22. See *infra* notes 27–30 and accompanying text.

23. See *Gannett Co. v. DePasquale*, 443 U.S. 368, 393 n. 25 (1979) ("The Court's decision in *Nebraska Press Ass'n v. Stuart* . . . is of no assistance to petitioner in this case. . . . The exclusion order in the present case did not prevent the petitioner from publishing any information in its possession. The proper inquiry, therefore, is whether the petitioner was denied any constitutional right of access."); *Pell v. Procunier*, 417 U.S. 817, 834 (1974) ("It is one thing to say . . . that government cannot restrain the publication of news emanating from certain sources. . . . It is quite another thing to suggest that the Constitution imposes upon government the affirmative duty to make available to journalists sources of information not available to members of the public generally.").

24. See ibid.

25. 283 U.S. 697 (1931).

26. Ibid. at 716.

27. 463 U.S. 713 (1971).

28. Brief for United States at 8, 15–16.

29. 463 U.S. at 714.

30. Ibid.

31. Ibid. at 726 (Brennan, J., concurring).

32. Ibid.

33. 53 U.S. 280 (1981).

34. Ibid. at 308.

35. Ibid. at 308–309.

36. Dunn and Bradstreet, *Ind. v. Greenmoss Builders,* 472 U.S. 749, 758 n. 5 (1985).

37. Note, "The First Amendment and National Security: The Constitutionality of Press Censorship and Access Denial in Military Operations," 17 *N.Y.U.J. Int'l L. & Pol.* 369, 380 (1985) (citations omitted).

38. Letter from James Madison to W.T. Barry, Aug. 4, 1822, in 9 *Writings of James Madison,* 103 (G. Hunt, ed., 1910). One commentator has noted that "Madison made this statement, however, not in the defense of first amendment freedoms; rather he made it in a letter applauding the liberal appropriations by Kentucky for a system of public education." O'Brien, "The First Amendment and the Public's 'Right to Know'," 7 *Hastings Const. L.Q.* 579, 587 (1980).

39. 408 U.S. 665 (1972).

40. Ibid. at 681.

41. Ibid. at 727 (Stewart, J., dissenting).

42. 417 U.S. 817 (1974).

43. 417 U.S. 843 (1974).

44. Pell, 417 U.S. at 834.

45. 438 U.S. 1 (1978).

46. Ibid. at 14 (Burger, C.J., joined by White, J. and Rehnquist, J.).

47. Ibid. at 32 (Stevens, J., joined by Brennan, J. and Powell, J., dissenting).

48. Ibid. at 16 (Stewart, J., concurring).

49. Ibid. at 17. Justices Blackmun and Marshall did not participate in this case.

50. 443 U.S. 368 (1979). In *Gannett,* a deeply divided Court rejected a newspaper's claim that it had a right of access to a pretrial suppression hearing. Ibid. at 381.

51. 448 U.S. 555 (1980).

52. Ibid. at 581 (plurality opinion).

53. Ibid. at 573.

54. Ibid.

55. Ibid. at 576 n. 11.

56. Ibid. at 582–583. (Stevens, J., concurring).

57. Ibid. at 599 (Stewart, J., concurring).

58. 457 U.S. 596 (1982).

59. Ibid. at 605.

60. Ibid. at 606.

61. Ibid. at 607.

62. Ibid. at 607–611.

63. 464 U.S. 501 (1984).

64. Ibid. at 510.

65. Ibid.

66. This position has been taken by W. Van Alstyne, *Interpretations of the First Amendment* 55 (1984).

67. Justice Brennan stated: "Because 'the stretch of this protection is theoretically endless,' it must be invoked with discrimination and temperance. For so far as the participating citizen's need for information is concerned, '[t]here are few

restrictions on action which could not be clothed by ingenious argument in the garb of decreased data flow.' " *Richmond Newspapers,* 448 U.S. at 588 (Brennan, J. concurring).

68. Ibid. at 576 (plurality opinion).

69. Ibid. at 554 (Stewart, J. concurring).

70. *Globe Newspaper,* 457 U.S. at 611 (O'Connor, J., concurring).

71. See *Richmond Newspapers,* 448 U.S. at 604–606 (Rehnquist, J. dissenting). It is not clear whether Justice Harry Blackmun would apply a right of access beyond the trial situation. In his opinion concurring in the judgment in *Richmond Newspapers,* Justice Blackmun, while relying primarily on the Sixth Amendment, also noted that "the First Amendment must provide some measure of protection for public access to the trial." Ibid. at 604 (Blackmun, J., concurring).

72. See, *e.g.,* Emerson, "The Affirmative Side of the First Amendment," 15 *Ga. L. Rev.* 795, 831 (1981) (contending that Justices Brennan, Marshall, and Stevens all support a broad right of access); but see *supra* note 67 (Justice Brennan's caution against overuse of right of access).

73. 455 U.S. 345 (1982).

74. Indeed, Exemption 3 of the Freedom of Information Act, 5 U.S.C. 552 (b)(3) allows the federal government to refuse to disclose information "specifically exempted from disclosure by statute." Under a broad right to access, such a provision would be unconstitutional in certain circumstances. Yet the Supreme Court has never so held.

75. 466 U.S. 463 (1984).

76. 466 U.S. 789 (1984).

77. 109 S. Ct. 1468 (1989).

78. Ibid. at 1473.

79. *Globe Newspaper,* 457 U.S. at 605.

80. Ibid. at 606.

81. Ibid. at 607.

82. This test is advocated by another commentator. See Cassell, "Restrictions on Press Coverage of Military Operations: The Right of Access, Grenada, and 'Off-the-Record Wars,' " 73 *Geo. L.J.* 931, 958–59 (1985).

83. See, *e.g.,* Cross & Griffin, "A Right of Press Access to United States Military Operations," 21 *Suffolk U.L. Rev.* 989, 1031–1043 (1987).

84. 109 S. Ct. at 1480.

85. See ibid., at 991–1004; Cassell, *supra* note 82, at 932–943.

86. See ibid.

87. 424 U.S. 828 (1976).

88. Ibid. at 838 (quoting *Cafeteria Workers v. McElroy,* 367 U.S. 886, 893 (1961)).

89. 367 U.S. 886 (1961).

90. Ibid. at 890.

91. See, *e.g.,* Cross & Griffin, *supra* note 83 at 383.

92. Some people have even claimed that the media "lost" the war in Vietnam. See generally G. MacDonald, *Report or Distort?* (1973); W. Westmoreland, *A Soldier Reports* 420 (1976).

93. See generally Mueller, "A Summary of Public Opinion and the Vietnam

War," in *Vietnam as History: Ten Years after the Paris Peace Accords* (P. Braes-trup, ed., 1984).

94. Landau, "Excluding the Press from the Grenada Invasion: A Violation of the Public's Constitutional Rights," *Editor & Publisher,* Dec. 10, 1983, at 10–11.

95. Both viewpoints were expressed on an ABC news program. Compare *ABC News Program Viewpoint 1984: Secrecy, Security and the Media* 5 (Jan. 19, 1984), (statement of Michael Burch, assistant secretary of defense for public affairs: "It was not a set battle plan such as journalists are used to covering with our forces. It was basically a commando-style operation where the first forces were to get to the students that were to be rescued, secure them and, basically, wait for rescue themselves. It was a relatively small force.") with ibid. at 6 (statement of Jack Nelson, Washington bureau chief of the *Los Angeles Times:* "I don't think anybody accepts it was strictly a commando-style operation. It was an invasion of almost traditional kind of planning.").

96. 462 U.S. 296 (1983).

97. Ibid. at 301 (quoting Orloff v. Willoughby, 345 U.S. 83, 93–94 (1953)).

98. *Department of Navy v. Egan,* 108 S. Ct. 818, 825 (1988).

99. As discussed in note 15 *supra,* the media did try to bring the issue of their exclusion in Grenada to the federal courts, but the matter was dismissed as moot. The district court's opinion was favorable to the military. See *supra* note 15.

100. Professor Moore, who was scheduled to testify at the hearings on behalf of the administration, notes that the hearings were abruptly cancelled after the episode of the students' kissing the tarmac and that he is still waiting to testify. Moore, "Do We Have an Imperial Congress?" 43 *U. Miami L. Rev.* 139, 150 (1988).

About the Contributors

Lionel Barber is a Washington correspondent of the *Financial Times of London*. In 1985 he was Lawrence Stern Fellow at the *Washington Post*, and in 1981 he received the British Press Award for Young Journalist of the Year.

Jeffrey J. Carnes is a U.S. Navy officer with extensive experience in surface warfare and operations analysis. At the time he wrote his chapter for this book, he was the plans, policy and operations officer for Southwest Asia and the Persian Gulf in the Office of the Chief of Naval Operations.

Melissa Healy is the Pentagon correspondent of the *Los Angeles Times*. She formerly was a reporter for *Defense Week*, a trade publication.

Paul Mann is the Washington bureau chief *of Aviation Week and Space Technology*. He has been a reporter and columnist on military affairs since 1976 and has covered the Departments of Defense and State, Congress, and the White House.

David C. Martin is Pentagon correspondent for CBS News. Prior to assuming that position, he covered defense issues for *Newsweek*.

Fred Reed is a nationally syndicated columnist and writer on military affairs. He formerly served as defense correspondent for the *Washington Times*.

Marshall Silverberg is the assistant U.S. attorney for Hawaii. At the time he wrote his contribution to this book, he was assistant general counsel at the Central Intelligence Agency.

Philip E. Soucy is manager of public relations at the British Aerospace Corporation in Washington, D.C. He formerly served as a major in the

U.S. Army, during which time he was a spokesman for the Department of the Army.

Bernard E. Trainor is director of national security programs and adjunct lecturer in public policy at Harvard University. A retired Marine Corps lieutenant general, he served as *New York Times* defense correspondent from 1985 to 1990.

About the Editor

Loren B. Thompson is deputy director of the National Security Studies Program and adjunct professor of strategy at Georgetown University.